THIS BOOK WAS PRESENTED TO

1892

....
Mr J Reid

By The Directors of

Shell International Marine Limited & Shell Tankers (U.K.) Limited

on the occasion of the

SHELL MARITIME CENTENARY

on 28th May 1992

1992

Sea Shell

Published by
Thomas Reed Publications Limited
Hazelbury Manor, Wadswick, Box,
Wiltshire, SN14 9HX, England

First Published in Great Britain, 1992

Design and Art Direction, Terry Anthony
Typeset by Shell Publicity Services
Portrait Illustrations Simon Williams, Map Illustrations Cato Studios
Printed in Great Britain by Bath Press Colour Books
A CIP catalogue record for this book is available from the British Library
ISBN 0 947637 32 X

Sea Shell

The Story of Shell's British Tanker Fleets 1892-1992

Stephen Howarth

THOMAS REED

PUBLICATIONS LTD

Nautical Publishers Since 1782

LONDON ☐ HAMBURG ☐ BOSTON

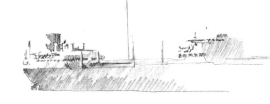

Contents

Foreword

by
Admiral Sir Julian Oswald, GCB, ADC
First Sea Lord

There is a story that one summer's day in 1899, a gentleman emerged from his office in London to find a stranger awaiting him in the street. Without preamble, the stranger said bluntly: 'Sir Marcus, I wish to meet you.'

It rings true, for the stranger was the then Vice Admiral Sir John Fisher – a forthright man if ever there was one. He later became Admiral of the Fleet Lord Fisher of Kilverstone, and, as First Sea Lord from 1904 to 1909 and again from 1914 to 1915, must be the most distinguished of my predecessors in this office. Fortunately, the gentleman whom he accosted – Sir Marcus Samuel, later Viscount Bearsted – shared his characteristics, and after that abrupt introduction, a life-long friendship began.

Both were men of extraordinary vision and dynamism. Fisher was the person primarily responsible for the Royal Navy's transformation from a moribund, overweight and unfit Victorian colossus into a thoroughly modern armed fleet. Similarly, Samuel – the son of a shell merchant – was responsible for the creation, from nothing, of an equally modern merchant fleet.

Their friendship is an appropriate symbol of the relationship between the Royal Navy and Great Britain's Merchant Navy. Although they are separate services, each proud of its own traditions, they are nonetheless closely (and usually amicably) linked by their common element, the sea; by their people, their seafaring traditions and by their common purpose – the protection and sustenance of this island.

In the century that has passed since the launch of SS *Murex*, Samuel's first ship, two World Wars and numerous other smaller conflicts have occurred. Throughout that period, whenever faced with war, the ships and people of Shell's British tanker fleets have served this country with the utmost bravery. In the turbulent peace of recent years, particularly in the Middle East, the Royal Navy has viewed their courage with continued respect, and has been glad to offer them support whenever necessary; after all, one of our first duties is to protect those who go about the seas on their lawful occasions. This is vividly demonstrated by the Navy's ongoing commitment to the ARMILLA Patrol.

On numerous occasions we have learned from Shell's sailors. Technical developments in Shell tankers have frequently found practical application in Her Majesty's Ships; so too have Shell's working practices, especially in the fields of personal and environmental safety.

Today I am happy to say that the relationship between the two fleets remains one of mutual respect and whether we sail under the White Ensign or the Red, we recognise the highest standards of professional seafaring. This book is a fitting tribute to all Shell sailors, past and present. I gladly salute them, and commend their story to you.

Prologue
The South China Sea
April 1991

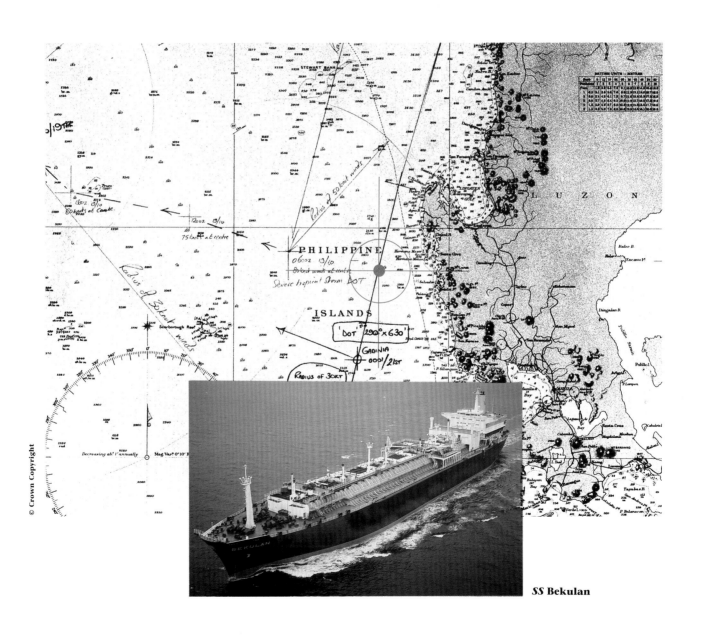

SS Bekulan

Photograph Stephen Howarth

Above: *Sunset, 3 April 1991.*
Mang Kwok Leung, whose sharp
eyes picked out the castaway alone
in the gathering darkness.
Above Right: *Captain David Hodson*
issues manoeuvring orders.

Illustration Steven Rudd

Only one ship was in sight, several miles away in a roughly westerly direction. Its course would take it past him, but by the time it was anywhere near, it would be a silhouette between him and the sunset, and he would be shrouded in the darkness already spreading from the east. The ship would steam serenely on, its people unconcerned, and he would be left alone again. It was obvious that if he was not seen now, then at some time in the night he would fall; or if he did not fall, some other vessel would come blindly along, swamp him, run him down, and pass onward, never knowing he had been there.

With his last remaining energy, balancing himself against the irregular motion of his sunken boat, the fisherman raised both his arms and waved in final desperation. Even two miles away, the ship looked huge; he himself could only be a distant, insignificant dot on an empty sea. It was no good: the ship would pass him by. But it was his only hope; he could not endure another night. He kept on waving – and at four minutes past seven pm, on board the Brunei Shell tanker SS *Bekulan* (Captain David Hodson), a sharp-eyed Chinese watchman named Mang Kwok Leung saw the tiny signal, and raised the alarm.

The 852-foot tanker and the castaway were then a mile and a half apart, in position 15° 51'N, 119° 24'E, Piedra Point lighthouse bearing approximately 217 degrees, 35 miles distant. The sighting was not a moment too soon, for exactly ten minutes later, at 7.14, the sun set. Nevertheless, before 8 pm, though suffering from exhaustion, shock and salt water exposure, the fisherman Camilo Arcelao was safe on board the giant tanker. While the pathetic remains of his boat slowly disappeared into the night, he was cared for by *Bekulan*'s crew. At the same time, radio contact was established with the Philippine coastguard. They requested a rendezvous in the approaches to Subic Bay.

No land was visible in any direction. Supported only by the submerged, waterlogged wreck of his canoe, the Filipino fisherman was standing with salt water covering his legs up to his knees. He had been like that for thirty-six hours. In all that time he had had nothing to eat or drink. He could not sit; he had nothing to hold on to. He was completely alone.

His name was Camilo Arcelao, and in a village called Lipay, on a shore so far distant he could not even make it out, he had a wife and seven children. He could not guess whether he would ever see them again. After drifting helplessly for so long, he was twenty-two miles from land. Now, slowly but steadily, he was being blown further off the coast of Luzon, his home island; the sun was within thirty minutes of setting; and he faced a second night of standing on the unstable wreckage.

He had no lights, not even a torch. There are more sharks than ships in the South China Sea, and the few vessels which had passed the fisherman in the preceding day and a half either had not seen him, or had chosen to ignore him. Physically exhausted, dizzy from thirst, hunger, heat and the lack of sleep, he could no longer remember how or why his little canoe had started to sink underneath him. All he knew, as the waves slopped around his thighs, was that it was more and more difficult to keep his balance, and that with nightfall he would be completely invisible. The chances that he would then live to see another dawn would be small.

Take a bow: business as usual for SS Bekulan, *still on time despite the delay*

Though this would require a diversion from his course, Captain Hodson agreed, and early the following morning (4 April 1991), the survivor was transferred to one of the coastguards' boats and taken ashore. *Bekulan* then proceeded on her way towards the Brunei port of Lumut, where she would pick up her latest LNG cargo – liquefied natural gas, chilled to minus 160 degrees Celsius; and despite the delay and diversion, the tanker arrived at her destination precisely on schedule.

Afterwards, Captain Hodson and his crew were modest about their effort, saying quite rightly that it was one life amongst many – literally thousands – which have been saved by Shell ships, and that any other Shell ship and any other Shell crew would have done exactly the same. Nevertheless, Camilo Arcelao, father of seven children, had been very close to being lost for ever. Through his brief and unexpected contact with *Bekulan*, the fisherman's life was saved, and his name found its way into this book: for this rescue of an obscure and humble individual touches many threads in the hundred-year history of Shell Tankers (U.K.) Ltd – the people, their training, their ships and their cargoes.

The geographical area of the rescue, the South China Sea, has an historic resonance for the company as well, echoing back to the very beginning of Shell's British tanker fleet.

Leaving the Philippine coasts behind, *Bekulan*'s voyage continued south-west past Palawan. The waters adjacent to that long, thin island cover a remarkable seabed of volcanic origin, where great depths may be suddenly interrupted by soaring underwater peaks. These plugs of rock (pinnacles would be a better word) may be isolated or in groups. If they could be seen, they would form a nightmarish, other-worldly landscape of abrupt, sharp fingers clawing upwards. As it is, although there might be very deep waters within a quarter of a mile, some of them are only just beneath the surface of the sea: not high enough to be visible, but fully high enough to be shoals which can tear the bottom from an unwary vessel. Not all of these dreadful hazards have been charted; not even the straight line of the Palawan Passage is entirely free of them; and in the early hours of 7 April 1991, *Bekulan* passed two of them, the Neritopsis shoal and the Murex shoal.

The names are significant. *Nerita* and *Murex* are the scientific Latin names for certain groups of molluscs, small shell-bearing animals. A *Nerita* is a gasteropod, like a snail; a *Murex* is a shell fish which produces a beautiful purple dye, highly prized in the ancient world. Among the many traditions of the sea, it is generally accepted that the captain who conducts the first accurate survey of a bay, or an inlet, or any other stretch of water, has the right and honour to give it a name. By the same tradition, if a ship runs aground on an uncharted shoal, reef, or rock, the obstacle is named after the ship. That kind of honour is understandably little sought after. However, these two shoals off the south-west tip of Palawan mark the grounding of two ships of the British Shell fleet: *Neritopsis*, wrecked in 1956, and *Murex* – the very first Shell tanker.

Bekulan's **complement, 3 April 1991**

Captain David J Hodson

Chief Officer Ian Foxwell
Second Officer Mark J Gooderham
Third Officer Keith Bland
Radio Officer John Cully
Chief Engineer John C Bindless
Second Engineer Raymond S Newell
Second Engineer (Cargo) Mike Johnson
Third Engineer Ryszard Szenher
Fourth Engineer Bernard Burns
Fifth Engineer Trevor A Martin
Deck Cadet Neil Jones
Chief Petty Officer Tsoi Chun
Petty Officer Chan Wai Kit
Petty Officer Kwok Loi Yau
G1S Mang Kwok Leung
G1S Man Sai
G1S Chan Fuk Chuen
G1S Chung Kam Kan
G1S Lai Chun Man
G1S Fung Kam Wang
G1S Leung Cheng Kan
G1S Mak Kin Chung
G1S Ng Ah Kan
G1S Lai Wan Lam
G1S Ng Yuk Ping
G1S Lam Hip Chi
Chief Steward Yu Yiu Ping
Assistant Steward Tang Tak Wing
Assistant Steward Chan Sau Pui
Assistant Steward Lau Wai Fun
Assistant Steward Li Shu Yung
Chief Cook Cheng Kee Kau
Second Cook Li Shu Sheung
Supernumerary Stephen Howarth

Illustration Simon Williams

Chapter One

Trinkets and Tankers
1853–1892

Left: *Text taken from the Northern Daily Mail, Saturday, 28th May 1892, describing the launch of SS Murex.*

LAUNCH AT WEST HARTLEPOOL

This morning, Messrs Wm. Gray and Co., Limited, West Hartlepool. launched the splendid steel screw-steamer Murex, the first of the three steamers they are building for Messrs Samuel and Co. of 31 Houndsditch, London, for the bulk petroleum trade to the East through the Suez Canal.

The vessel and machinery have been built under the superintendence of Messrs Flannery, Baggallay, and Johnson, of London. She will take Lloyd's highest class, and is built on the three-deck rule, with long poop and topgallant forecastle. Her dimensions are as follows: Length over-all, 349ft.; breadth extreme, 43ft.; depth, 28ft.; deadweight capacity, about 4,950 tons.

The engine and boiler rooms are in the after-part of the vessel, and underneath them there is a double bottom for water ballast in three compartments. The forward and after peaks are also fitted for water ballast for trimming purposes. Forward of the boiler-room there are nine strong transverse bulkheads, and there is also a very strong fore and after bulkhead from the keel to the main deck, forming ten separate oil tanks. These oil tanks are separated from the boiler-room and bunkers aft, and from the cargo hold forward by large coffer-dams, which are carried to the topmost deck in each case, and which can be filled with water when required, and they are under the control of special and separate pumps placed on deck.

Expansion trunks are carried up from the middle of each oil compartment to allow the oil to rise and fall with varying temperatures. These trunks, will be used for loading large hatchways, will be used for loading general cargoes. Two powerful pumps, by Messrs Hayward, Tyler, and Co., London,

are fitted in the pump room amidships for discharging the oil cargo. They are capable of pumping out the entire cargo of over 4,200 tons of oil in twelve hours, and will also pump water from the sea to fill the oil tanks when required for ballast, &c.

When the oil cargo has been discharged, the tanks will be cleansed and adapted to receive general cargo by means of steam led into each by pipes fitted for the purpose, then they will be flooded with water, and after this has been pumped out, the tanks will be dried and the portable ceiling laid ready for the cargo as in an ordinary vessel. A powerful fan will be fitted capable of exhausting the air from each tank in ten minutes in order to thoroughly ventilate the compartments when filled with general cargo, the exhaust air being delivered through a cowl a good way above the deck. The vessel will be fitted throughout with an electric light installation by Messrs Clarke, Chapman, and Co., of Gateshead-on-Tyne, the whole of the cabin, engine, and boiler-room, galley, chart and wheel-house, binnacle, and telegraph being included.

In addition she will have a 20in. project light and the necessary lighting for navigating the Suez Canal at night. In order that all parts of the ship may be thoroughly examined after cargo has been discharged, she will be provided with a number of portable lamps. The cabin and forecastle and petty officers' rooms will be all heated by steam, so as to avoid any risk of fire; in fact the only fire on board beyond the boiler fires will be in the galley, but this is at a great distance from the oil tanks.

The accommodation for captain, officers, and the saloon are under the poop deck. The engineers' rooms are in a large house on deck aft, and the crew in the forecastle. A

patent steam-steering gear will be fitted amidships, and screw gear aft. Patent steam windlass, two donkey boilers, patent stockless anchors, and in addition to all the necessary fittings and outfit for the oil trade, there will be a complete outfit for working general cargoes, including five steam winches.

Three masts will be fitted, and neatly rigged, and awnings all fore and aft for the Eastern climate. Great care has been taken to ensure strong and sound work. The riveting is closely spaced in shell-plating, decks, and bulkheads, and in order to reduce as far as possible the number of joints in way of the oil tanks most of the shell plates are nearly 30 feet long.

The vessel will be fitted with a very powerful set of triple expansion engines of the well-known type, manufactured at the Central Marine Engine Works of W. Gray and Co. Limited. The cylinders will be 25½, 40½in., and 67in. in diameter respectively, and of 45in. stroke. An extra large amount of boiler power also is provided in the shape of three large single-ended boilers working at a pressure of 160lbs. per square inch. Increased safety is ensured by placing two of the boilers with their backs towards the coffer-dam, removing the heat of the stoke-hold a considerable distance from the bulkheads.

The engines are capable of driving the ship a high rate of speed when loaded, and are furnished with all the latest improvements. The engine-room contains also one of Mudd's new patent feedwater evaporators, which is designed on a plan greatly facilitating cleaning and examination. The ceremony of naming the steamer Murex was gracefully performed by Mrs Samuel, wife of Alderman Samuel, of London.

THE DURHAM DEADLOCK.

TO-DAY'S SHIPPING.

TIME OF HIGH WATER THIS WEEK

DATE	H'TLEPOOL		SUNDLAND		SHIELDS		NEWCASTLE	
	Mor.	Eve.	Mor.	Eve.	Mor.	Eve.	Mor.	Eve.
Monday	8 30	8 56	0 25	0 15	8 16	8 41	9 35	1 3
Tuesday	1 33	1 46	1 17	1 43	1 8	1 33	1 28	1 57
Wednesday	2 12	2 38	2 7	2 33	1 57	2 23	2 17	2 48
Thursday	2 2	3 25	2 57	3 20	2 47	3 10	3 7	3 38
Friday	3 48	4 18	3 43	4 9	3 33	3 56	3 53	4 18
Saturday	4 34	4 57	4 29	4 52	4 19	4 42	4 39	5 2
Sunday	6 21	5 40	5 16	5 40	5 6	5 31	5 24	6 51

It is high water at Stockton, 27 minutes earlier than at Hartlepool. At Middlesborough, 31 minutes later; at Stockton, 1 hour 5 minutes later; and the Humber, at 2 hours later.

TO-DAYS WEATHER

OBSERVATIONS AT THE HEUGH LIGHTHOUSE, made at 8 a.m. from Instruments, 80ft above sea level.

	Barometer.		Ther. Max.	Ther. Max.	Deg of Dryness
	To-day	Yesterday.			
29.63	29.45	67	51	1	
Direction of Wind	Extr. Forces 1 to 11	Rain in Inches	Sea 1 to 9	Weather	
N.N.E.	2	8.50	0	M.O.R.	

Degrees of Dryness of air; Difference between wet and dry bulbs of hydrometer.

Extreme force of wind in 2¼ hours, 1 to 12 on Beauforts scale.

Sea crests of waves, 1 to 9 above sea level. Weather: B. blue sky; C. clouds detached; F. fog; H. hail; L. Lightning; M. misty; O. overcast; Q. Squally; R. rain; S. snow; T. thunder.

WEST HARTLEPOOL FOOTBALL CLUB.

ANNUAL MEETING

The annual meeting of the West Hartlepool Rugby Football Club was held last night at the head-quarters of the club, Victoria Hotel, West Hartlepool, Dr. Goarley, J. E., presiding. There were also present Messrs. Walker and Hurworth (captain and vice captain of the 1st team), Raymond Bradley (secretaries), F. W. Purvis, T. Braybrook, A. Barret, Battersby, Wason, Simpson, Passman, H. C. McBeath, and R. Martin – nearly 100 altogether, out of about 200 members of the club.

The CHAIRMAN said that in the absence of the president he had been asked to take the chair that evening. There was not much talking required, but there was a great deal of work to get through. With reference to the past seasons, although they had not done everything they had hoped to do, there was no doubt it had been a very successful season, and the public of West Hartlepool had been very much gratified at the play they had witnessed. A good deal of the success of next year would depend upon the play, but also a great deal on the committee that the members elected to conduct the business in a thoroughly business like way. It was absolutely necessary that they entrusted with carefully the business of the club for the ensuing year. (Hear hear.)

Headquarters of the club, Victoria Hotel, near Hartlepool, Dr. Goarley, J. E., presiding. There were also present Messrs. Walker and Hurworth (captain and vice captain of the 1st team), Raymond and Bradley (secretaries), F. W. Purvis, T. Braybrook, A. Barret, Battersby, Watson, Simpson, Passman, H.C. McBeath and R. Martin – nearly 100 altogether.

The minutes of the previous annual meeting having been adopted.

Mr. J. H. Bates (one of the secretaries) read the eighth annual report, in which the committee said they had great pleasure in congratulating the members upon the very successful season just terminated. The report continued, "The first team have played 34 matches, 23 of which were won, 5 drawn and 6 lost". It is gratifying to note that out of 30 matches played on the home ground, the team has only been defeated once, by Cleckhaston, by one point. Amongst the clubs defeated were the well-known combinations: Rockcliff, Percy Park, Checkheaten, York, Morley, Tottington, Normanton, Kirkstal, Tudhoe, Hartlepool and Rov

AN OWNER CENSURE THE MASTERS.

Mr T. W. Backhouse, of Sunderland, one of the owners of Newton Cap Colliery, in the Western part of the county, says in a letter enclosing a subscription to the workmen's relief fund:—I condemn strongly the action of both men and masters for refusing to submit their differences to arbitration." Newton Cap is one of the associated collieries.

LETTER FROM SIR H. HAVELOCK-ALLAN.

Sir Henry Havelock-Allan, M.P., has wired us fr..... ....ton asking us to insert the

Marcus Samuel and his Family. From left to right, Ida, Marcus, Walter, Gerald, Fanny, Nellie, c 1900.

15

According to one dictionary definition, a legend is 'an unauthentic story handed down by tradition and popularly regarded as historical.' For decades, company legend has said that the very first Shell oil tanker was launched on 27 May 1892; but it was not.

That date was a Friday. For Mrs Marcus Samuel and her elder daughter, nine-year-old Nellie, the day was taken up with a journey of over 200 miles from their home in London to the north-eastern port of West Hartlepool, where they joined Mr Samuel. He was 39 years old, an Alderman of the City of London, and partner (with his younger brother Sam) in a thriving family business established by their father. This had nothing directly to do with ships, and nothing at all to do with oil: the brothers'

main trade was in sea shells. Nevertheless, it was Alderman Samuel who had commissioned and now part-owned the ship which was destined to become Shell's first oil tanker. She would be launched next morning.

The weather on Saturday 28 May was typical for the place and time of year: misty, overcast and raining, with the temperature struggling to reach the mid-60s Fahrenheit. All the same, it was a good day for a launch, because the sea was flat calm and the wind (from the north-north-east) was negligible – a trifling Force 2 on the Beaufort scale. Catching the tide, and blessed by Mrs Samuel, the Alderman's first tanker slid off the ways and into the waters of West Hartlepool docks punctually at 4 am; and later that day, the *Northern Daily Mail* printed a detailed description of 'the splendid steel screw-steamer *Murex.*'

For the owners and builders of any new ship, its launch is a major event. Today, launches from British shipyards are, sadly, so rare that any one of them might well be reported in the national newspapers; but in 1892, they were such common events that (although the regional papers would report them) it was most unusual for national papers to note an individual one. Gray's yard alone launched 20 ships in 1892; and Gray's was only one of about four dozen busy yards in the Tyneside region of north-eastern England, which together typically supplied about 33% of Britain's annual ship production. In that particular year, the region collectively launched 251 vessels – five a week. At 5,010 deadweight tons *Murex* was only an average-size vessel for the time; from the outside there was little to show that she was anything remarkable; and with launches being practically a daily event, it might well be thought that as far as national newspapers were concerned, one more was nothing much to get excited about.

Despite appearances, however, she *was* remarkable – sufficiently so for her launch to be nationally reported. On 28 May, under the headline PETROLEUM STEAMERS FOR

Illustration Simon Williams

SS Murex

THE SUEZ CANAL, an article in *The Times* began:

The Murex, *the first of a fleet of steamers that is being built – for a syndicate of which Mr Alderman Samuel is the representative in this country – for the transportation of petroleum in bulk through the Suez Canal, was launched yesterday . . . .*

'Yesterday' was of course the 27th, so perhaps that article is where the old mistake about the launch date first occured; the shipyard's own records clearly show the correct date and time. But what was far more important than a few hours' discrepancy here and there was the nature of the ship herself, and the trade for which she was built – 'the transportation of petroleum [crude oil] in bulk through the Suez Canal'.

There was, then, no such trade. Since its opening in 1867, though many had tried, no one had ever been allowed to carry bulk petroleum through the Canal. It could be taken through in cases; but not in bulk. The *Northern Daily Mail* went into great detail, describing *Murex*'s ten separate oil tanks, built with as few joints as possible; the separation of the tanks from the after location of the boiler room; the expansion trunks, allowing the oil to swell and contract with changes in temperature; and even the steam cabin heating, reducing the risk of fire. Lloyd's of London, the newspaper stated confidently, would give *Murex* the highest and best classification.

Mr Alderman Samuel was just as remarkable as his new ship. He had never owned one before, yet inside two years – before the end of February 1894 – nine more would be launched for him. By then, both he and his brand-new fleet were known around the world: for with his ships Marcus Samuel successfully challenged

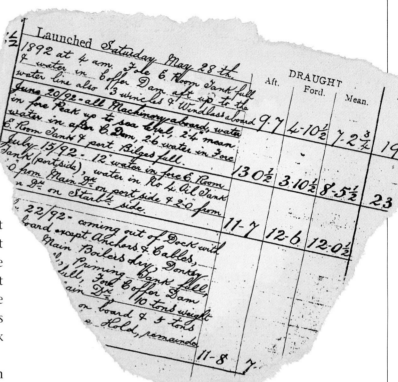

the worldwide oil monopoly of the American-based Standard Oil company, 'the Octopus'.

By itself, that would have been enough to make Samuel and his ships famous in their time; but there was more. The Samuel fleet revolutionised the carrying of oil at sea, and made it into an industry which, a hundred years on, remains central to the smooth running of our civilisation.

The detail about the real date of *Murex*'s launch only came to light during research for this book – but at least that legend was only one day wrong. Another company legend ('unauthentic... popularly regarded as historical') has it that *Murex* was a world first. This is a great deal further out: indeed, according to some authorities there were by that time as many as 80 fully-fledged oil tankers on transatlantic routes. Even so, to say that Samuel and *Murex* started a revolution *is* true; and to understand why, it is worth

Murex Shell

1880. Slvisjesdijk, Holland. Dockside oil storage installation.

taking the time to think about what oil is, and to glance back to the beginnings of the tanker trade. It is also worth trying to define a tanker, and that is not as easy as it sounds.

Chemically, unrefined or crude oil is a mix of hydrocarbons – molecules of hydrogen and carbon joined together in numerous different patterns and quantities – which requires physical or chemical processing to be turned into useable products. This processing separates molecules of different size, and alters the composition and patterns of some of them, thus determining what kind of end product is created. Crude oil contains varying proportions or fractions of the different hydrocarbons, and separating them out into useful products is what refining is all about. The densest fractions are almost solid unless heated, and have such high specific gravities that, unlike most oils, they will actually sink in water. Asphalt and tar are two of

these. Among the other lighter fractions, in descending order of specific gravity, are heating oils; diesel fuel; kerosene, or paraffin; naphtha; gasoline, or petrol; and at the lightest and most volatile end, petroleum gases, butane and propane. Finally, often found in association with crude oil, but not actually a product of it, there is the hugely important natural gas, methane.

One of the other noticeable features of crude oil is that it hardly ever seems to occur in the places where it is needed. 'God must be a shipowner', someone once said. 'Two-thirds of the planet is covered in water, with the most valuable resources located as far as possible from the centres of industry.' That, of course, is where the tankers come in.

Before reaching them, however, one should consider their predecessors, ancient and recent. Oil can hardly be called a new resource; it has been known since biblical days at least. The problems of transporting it at sea are almost as old: it was used in ships as a weapon ('Greek fire') as early as the 7th century AD. During the 18th century, the Chinese, Burmese, Persians and Russians were all recorded as transporting oil by water; but the quantities they carried at any one time were tiny (perhaps 7,000 gallons – the equivalent of about 170 barrels) and the markets were local, reached by river or short sea voyages.

Nevertheless, despite its antiquity in the East, oil did not become a valuable commodity as far as the Western world was concerned (and thus a globally valuable commodity) until well into the Industrial Revolution. First discovered in commercially viable quantities in 1859, in Pennsylvania, it soon found willing buyers. The parts which people wanted were the medium-density fractions: lubricating oils (which were much better than lard at keeping machinery running) and illuminating oils, particularly kerosene, the 'new light'. Except in a prolonged powercut, it is very hard today to imagine what a difference kerosene made to people's lives then; but instead of lard or

Marcus Samuel as a youth,
c 1871.

Sam Samuel as a youth,
c1871.

Oil well at Balachamy near Baku on the Caspian Sea in early 1890s.
Until the Samuels' own fields in the Indies came into commercial
production, Russian fields were the world's main source of kerosene
(paraffin).

One of the first oil wells in the Netherlands East Indies;
photograph undated – late 19th century.

tallow candles (which were expensive) or rags and reeds dipped in animal fat (which were smoky, smelly and dim), kerosene, provided it was handled properly, gave a generally safer, comparatively cheap and miraculously bright and steady light.

These were far and away the largest markets for refined oils. Most machinery, if not powered by muscle or wind, was powered either by water or coal – largely because most of the machines had been invented in Britain, which had plenty of both water and coal. These existing systems and strong vested interests meant there was scarcely any market for oil as a fuel; indeed, early oil producers generally threw away the heavier fractions of their crude and burned off the lightest, gaseous ones, because even though these together constituted 30 or 40% of the total, they were almost worthless.

But the lubricating and illuminating oils were immediately saleable on the east coast of America, and even more so in Europe. This obviously meant carrying them across the Atlantic, and the first such shipment was taken from Philadelphia to London in a sailing brig called *Elizabeth Watts*, in 1861.

Originally it was carried in wooden barrels, often as part of a mixed cargo. This was not satisfactory for very long: by their very shape, barrels were wasteful of cargo space, and being leaky, they were wasteful of cargo as well. Worse, the cargo itself was volatile and potentially explosive, and the quantity in a barrel (42 US gallons) was much more than many individual consumers wanted; so in answer to both problems the oil 'case' was invented. Instead of barrels, the oil was packed in rectangular tins, very like the 'downstream' container of lubricating oil one might buy in a Shell petrol station today. ('Upstream' operations are the actual exploration for and production of crude oil;

'downstream' involves the transportation, refining and selling of crude oil and its products.) These tins contained five US gallons each, and were generally packed in pairs in wooden cases. Compared to a barrel, they were much more handy and manageable for a small shop or individual household, and a much more economic shipment for a producer.

As the market gradually grew, though, it became evident that even case-oil had its limitations, not least the time spent in manhandling every single case into and out of a ship. Both in volume of cargo and in speed of loading and discharge, it would be more cost-effective to use large tanks, filling and emptying them with pumps. Such tanks (rectangular or cylindrical, vertical or horizontal) could be, and were, built into existing hulls; but they too wasted some space. From that point it was not a large step to imagining ships in which the hull itself would be the tank.

That, of course, is the primary characteristic of a modern bulk tanker. There is no record of the word 'tanker' before 1900, and even today the *Shorter Oxford English Dictionary* defines a tanker simply as 'a tank steamer', which is what they were called when Marcus began in 1892. Certainly the fact of having an engine, whether steam or motor, must be another characteristic, and on that basis the honour of being the world's first bulk tank steamer should go to a Belgian vessel, *Vaderland*, built in Jarrow in 1872. But *Vaderland* has to be disqualified for a rather simple reason: although built for the task, there is no evidence that she ever actually carried any bulk oil at all.

In seeking a fuller definition for such ships, another feature should be added: dedication of purpose and design. A bulk tanker carries only one cargo, whatever that might be, using the hull as the tank. (*Vaderland* would be discounted there too; her dual design enabled her to carry

Victorian oil lamp.

SS Glückauf; the first purpose-built, dedicated steam-driven, ocean-going oil tanker.

passengers as well.) Taking these criteria disposes of a number of developmental stages in the 1870s and 1880s: wooden general cargo ships with holds converted to oil carrying by being lined with felt or cement; ships of wood or metal with holds converted by having tanks built in; and ships which, like *Vaderland*, doubled as passenger vessels, or carried case-oil as a major part of their cargo in addition to oil in tanks.

Looking for a purpose-built, dedicated, steam-driven tanker, the Swedish-built *Zoroaster* (delivered in 1878 to Robert and Ludwig Nobel, brothers of Alfred, the inventor of dynamite) could have been an appropriately dynamic first to fit the bill. Certainly she was far ahead of her time in one respect: she not only carried oil, but burned fuel-oil too – something which would not be known in ocean trades until the 20th century. Yet even this forward-looking vessel

was first constructed with cylindrical tanks inside the hull; and she was not an *ocean* trader, but carried oil on the Caspian Sea.

By now, throwing in ocean trading as a qualification, it may sound as though the final definition of a tanker is being tailor-made for *Murex*. Not so: the real prototype of all modern tankers, the first purpose-built, dedicated, steam-driven, ocean-going oil tanker, was SS *Glückauf*, commissioned by a German firm, built and launched in Newcastle upon Tyne in 1886. Nor was Marcus Samuel the first Briton to commission a real tanker and to own an important fleet of them; that man was Alfred Suart, whose *Bakuin* was also launched in 1886, and who, a decade later, owned 19 tankers of various designs.

All that disposes pretty thoroughly of the company legend that *Murex* and her sisters were world firsts, or even

British firsts. Their historic importance lay in something else: the fact that Marcus Samuel had the money, the imagination and the nerve to commission the design (which was carried out in complete secrecy) and the building of not merely one tanker, but of a whole fleet, almost simultaneously.

· This *was* a first, in Britain or anywhere else. It was also a big risk for anyone, however well established in the shipping trade; and in 1892 it was an enormous risk for Samuel. He was still a young man; he had never owned a ship; and he faced the ruthless, virtually worldwide monopoly of the American giant, Standard Oil. One might well ask what in the world possessed him to do it. If his gamble succeeded, he could become very rich indeed; but if it failed, he could be ruined entirely.

In fact, the launch of *Murex* was the culmination of a very well laid plan. It was also the start of the 15 most exciting, most satisfying and most devastating years of his life.

His father, also called Marcus, had died in 1870, leaving the family business to be run by Joseph Samuel, the eldest son, then aged 31, 15 years older than Marcus junior, and 17 years older than the youngest son, Sam. With 11 children in all (of whom nine survived to adulthood), it was the typically large, hard-working family of Victorian Britain. What was less typical was that it was a Jewish family, at a time when Jews were only just becoming fully assimilated into British society. Even within the Jewish community, the Samuel family was not particularly distinguished; but it was these origins, and his own character, which gave Marcus junior his drive. He wanted distinction and respect, for himself, his family and his people; and just as importantly, he very much wanted to perform some sort of public service, for he was intensely patriotic. He knew perfectly well that in Poland, Romania and Russia, still a Tsarist autocracy, pogroms against Jews were frequent events, and he was proud and glad to be British.

A shell box, the basis of the elder Marcus's business.

Physically, he was a short, energetic, but ungainly man, plain but charming when young; stout, ugly and pompous in middle age. His British competitor, Alfred Suart, remarked that Marcus rode his horses as he conducted his businesses: 'He always looked as if he might roll off, but never quite did.' It was an apt description, for in several ways Marcus was not a very good businessman. He had little desire, and virtually no ability, to delegate; nor, on the other hand, did he have much grasp of detail. His character was basically straightforward, uncomplicated and honest. He was neither devious nor ruthless, and never suspected deviousness or ruthlessness in his business enemies; he was susceptible to charm in others; and when public office came his way, he revelled in the trappings of honour and, as we shall see, devoted himself to the associated work, to his company's serious detriment.

All these weaknesses (if that is what they were) sprang from one source: he did not regard money-making as an end in itself. The family business, M. Samuel & Co., was doing tolerably well when he and his brother Sam took it over. Over the years, their father had made connections in the Far East, establishing a network of agents to trade in rice and other grains, sugar, semi-precious stones and exotic sea shells. These last were particularly popular in Britain, and in London, Marcus senior employed about 40 girls in making shell-boxes – souvenir trinket boxes decorated all over with shells and embellished with genial mottoes such as 'A Gift from Brighton'. People liked them very much, both as mementoes of seaside holidays and as a means of feeling vaguely in touch with foreign lands which they would never see. The trade was reliable, modestly profitable and growing. The Samuels were not rich, but they were quite comfortably off: in 1878, when Marcus junior was 25, he and Sam each inherited £2,500 from their father's estate (a sum which in 1991 was worth £100,000), and if they had just wanted to make money in a safe and steady manner, they could have simply kept the firm going in the way it had been built up. The fact that they did not was because, some time in the middle of the 1880s, Marcus junior had An Idea.

He and his younger brother were the types often found at the root of a successful enterprise. Marcus was a great one for ideas, usually on a very large scale – indeed, the word most commonly used to describe him is 'visionary'. The problem with following a vision is that one might easily fall straight down an open man-hole. Luckily enough, young Sam was a more cautious individual, more or less able to keep a practical brake on Marcus's imagination. However, during the '80s, through the agency of Lane & MacAndrew (led by a shipbroker called Fred Lane), the Samuel brothers firstly added case-oil to their Far Eastern trade; and secondly, met a marine engineer with the splendid name of Fortescue Flannery. (Flannery was later made a baronet, and became a Member of Parliament.) Whether it blossomed suddenly or developed slowly, no one knows, but from these connections Marcus had his Idea: that with their Japanese firm, Samuel Samuel & Co., as operators, the brothers

Fred Lane, shipbroker, c 1890.

should get into the Far Eastern oil market on their own account – not merely chartering other people's ships to carry other people's tins of kerosene, but using their own ships to carry their own kerosene.

It was the most outlandish notion Marcus had ever had. The major risk was clear: as soon as Standard Oil got wind of it, 'the Octopus' would use its classic techniques to destroy or absorb the interlopers. With its monopoly, Standard could control oil prices in the United States, and use its profits there to undercut the competitor wherever else he dared to compete. Even more simply, it might just use the same threat to cut off the supply of oil from other dealers. Whatever the method, the result would be the same: takeover or ruin.

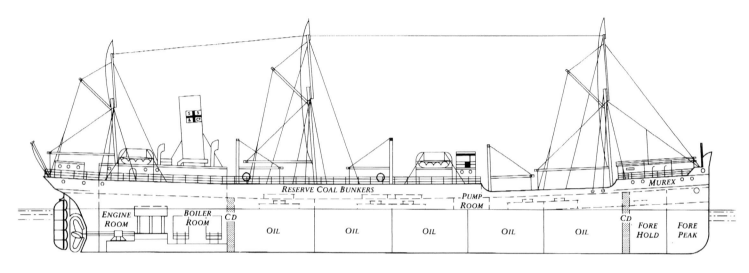

RESERVE COAL BUNKERS

PUMP ROOM

ENGINE ROOM | BOILER ROOM | C D | OIL | OIL | OIL | OIL | OIL | C D | FORE HOLD | FORE PEAK

MUREX

Section of SS Murex, showing arrangement of oil tanks and cofferdams (C D).

But if the risk was clear, and great, there was another side too. If kerosene were shipped *in bulk*, it would be cheaper than case-oil. If a guaranteed supply were found, independent of Standard Oil – from Russia, for example, the world's main source of oil outside America – it could not be cut off. If there were sufficient ships, not just one or two, to maintain the flow; if there were storage tanks at major ports to stock the oil; if there were inland depots for its distribution and sale; and if this were all done simultaneously and secretly, so that the whole system was ready to start operating at once – well: *then* the kerosene could be sold at a price which would always, or almost always, be lower than the Standard could contrive.

A great many if's; and there was one more. Hitherto, on grounds of safety, the Suez Canal authorities had permitted only the transport of case-oil through the

Canal; any bulk oil from Russia destined for the East had to be taken all the way round the Cape of Good Hope. But if a bulk carrier were designed to satisfy even the most stringent safety requirements, and thus gained passage through the Canal, its transport costs would be so much reduced that not even the Standard could compete.

That was the Idea; and that, in summary, was exactly what came about. The Samuels' network of Far Eastern contacts already existed. Credit for the new enterprise came from the Paris House of Rothschild. Marcus, Sam and Fred Lane sorted out a contract for oil from the Caspian Sea port of Baku, to be taken overland to the Black Sea port of Batum; Fortescue Flannery designed the ships to take it from Batum onwards; and (beginning in 1891) Mark Abrahams, a nephew of the Samuels, negotiated and oversaw the construction of storage tanks in Singapore (at Freshwater

Sir Fortescue Flannery, Bart. MP.

Island, now called Pulau Bukom), in Bangkok, Hong Kong, Djakarta (then called Batavia), Penang, Saigon, Shanghai and the Japanese port of Kobe.

Mark's job was not at all an easy one. Officials everywhere were frightened of the potential fire risks that seemed sure to accompany the bulk storage of oil, and in almost every place he went, he ran up against local laws restricting the use of tankers and construction of tanks. Other dealers, scenting rivalry, did all they could to hinder his plans; but perhaps worst were the constant niggling interferences he got from head office in London. The Samuel brothers did have an atlas in the office, but never seemed to grasp that an inch on the map might be 150 miles on the ground – or worse, on the sea; or worse still, in the jungle. Although the brothers Marcus and Sam were, respectively, only ten years and eight years older than their nephew Mark, and although they had chosen him for the job, they treated him as if he were an incompetent boy, peppering him with cables of complaint, changing lists of construction items he had ordered, and questioning every initiative he took. This was all the more odd because, whenever they were together at home, the three men got on well.

Fortescue Flannery was not harrassed by perpetual petty rebukes from his employers, but his job was a challenging one as well. Beginning in 1888 or '89, his problem was to try and divine the minds of the Canal authorities. They had often said that for going through the Canal, the designs of Standard's tankers were unacceptably out-dated, but they had never said what design would be acceptable.

Murex was Flannery's personal triumph. To counter the risk of grounding in the Canal, he gave her water ballast tanks, which could be deballasted to lighten her if necessary. To counter the risk of collision (which could rupture her five oil tanks) he placed these amidships, with a cofferdam, an empty space, at each end. This isolated the tanks from the boiler room and engine room aft, as well as from the fore hold and the empty fore peak. Coal bunkers were located on both sides of the boiler room, closest to where they would be needed, with reserve bunkers above the three aftermost tanks. To allow for the oil's inevitable expansion and contraction as the ambient temperature changed, there were trunks at the top of the tanks; and to reduce the oil's sideways movement, which could seriously endanger a ship's stability, an oil-tight bulkhead ran fore-and-aft through the centre of every tank. Loading and discharge were exclusively by pumps; lighting was exclusively by electricity; and last but not least, Flannery arranged a device to clean the tanks thoroughly after discharge, so that no residue (which, on mixing with air, would become explosive) was left.

By curious coincidence – in which some people suspected conspiracy – the Canal authorities issued new regulations for bulk oil tankers on 5 January 1892, stipulating requirements that were uncannily close to those of Flannery's design. They also demanded that such tankers must be rated 100.A.1 by Lloyd's of London. Lloyd's took a long careful look at *Murex*, liked what they saw, and rated the ship 100.A.1. The regulations would come into force on 1 July that year. As the *Northern Daily Mail*'s article on 28 May indicated, a good deal of work had to be done after the launch to complete the new ship. By 26 July it was all finished, and on that date, under Captain John R. Coundon, she sailed for Batum in the Black Sea. There she loaded her first cargo, destined for Thailand; and on 24 August, full of Russian kerosene, she passed through the Suez Canal – the first bulk oil tanker ever to do so. Shell ships were in business, and making history from the start.

Captain John R. Coundon,
*first Master of the oil tanker **Murex** and*
Shell's first Marine Superintendent.

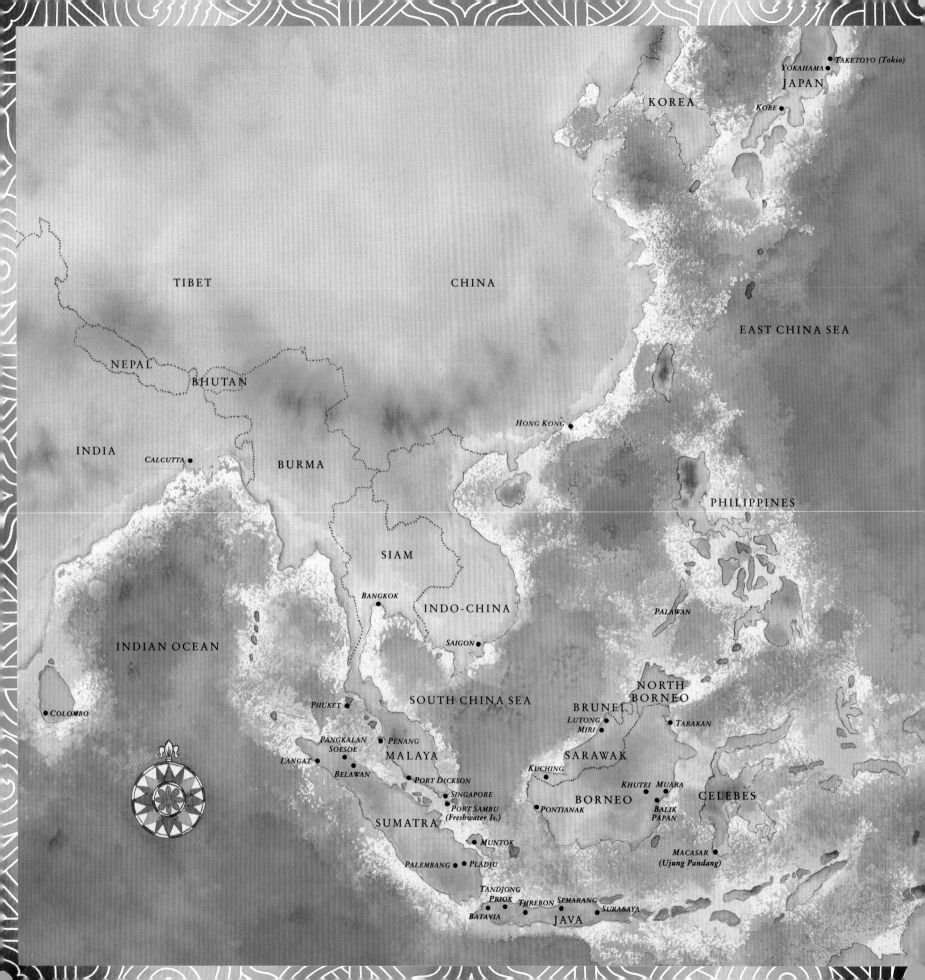

TAKETOYO *(Tokio)*

YOKAHAMA •

JAPAN

KOBE •

KOREA

TIBET

CHINA

EAST CHINA SEA

NEPAL

BHUTAN

HONG KONG •

INDIA

CALCUTTA •

BURMA

PHILIPPINES

SIAM

BANGKOK •

INDO-CHINA

PALAWAN

SAIGON •

INDIAN OCEAN

NORTH
BORNEO

COLOMBO •

SOUTH CHINA SEA

PHUKET •

BRUNEI

LUTONG •
MIRI •

TARAKAN •

Pangkalan
Soesoe •

Penang •

MALAYA

SARAWAK

KUCHING •

KHUTEI MUARA •

Langat •

BELAWAN •

Port Dickson •

BORNEO

PONTIANAK •

BALIK
PAPAN

CELEBES

SINGAPORE •

PORT SAMBU
(Freshwater Is.)

SUMATRA

MUNTOK •

MACASAR •
(Ujung Pandang)

PALEMBANG • • PLADJU

TANDJONG
PRIOK •

THREBON

SEMARANG •

SURABAYA •

BATAVIA •

JAVA

Chapter Two

Shaping the Shell
1893-1899

Built at West Hartlepool in 1892, the 5,000 dwt Conch was one of Shell's earliest tankers. She is seen above discharging cargo at Fiume, Italy.

Marcus Samuel

So far so good. Despite opposition – legal letters to the Prime Minister (believed to have been instigated by Standard Oil), questions in Parliament and baleful mutterings about 'Hebrew influence' – the Samuel family had secretly, successfully and sensationally entered the shipping market as major owners, rather than mere carriers. Their network of Far Eastern oil storage facilities was well into construction, their selling agents ready and eager; the Idea was taking shape beautifully. All that remained was to sell the kerosene and watch the proceeds start to flow.

But they did not. Instead, bewildered cables came in from the agents: no one wanted to buy the oil. It was as good as, and far cheaper than, Standard's product (called 'Devoes'), but not a fluid ounce could be sold, let alone thousands of tons. People actually seemed to prefer to spend more on Devoes, in its rusty blue cans, than to save money by bringing their own containers to be filled with the new stuff.

The reason (which nobody, not even the agents on the spot, had thought of beforehand) was that for ordinary people in the Far East, the expensive Devoes was actually more economical *because* of the blue cans. Even though they were rusty after being shipped from America, when empty they could be turned into all manner of practical utensils: anything from toys to tea strainers, bird cages to chamber-pots. Once this was understood, Marcus's response was immediate. If the consumers wanted cans, they could have them – and they would be made locally, near the eastern ports. It was a splendidly simple solution: without compromising the economic principle of bulk transport, employment was provided, creating good will towards the company; instead of being rusty, the cans were shiny and new; and even with the cost of making them added in, the bulk oil still undercut Devoes. Mark Abrahams, the Samuels'

much put-upon nephew, provided the imaginative finishing touch: the new cans were painted an instantly identifiable bright red. It worked like a charm. Within months, Oriental chamber-pots and tea strainers alike were changing from rusty blue to shiny red.

At the same time, however, Marcus himself fell ill and was diagnosed as suffering from cancer, with less than a year to live. The diagnosis was wrong (he lived until 1927) but it had an important effect on the firm of M. Samuel & Co. Its new shipping interest was, if not a hobby, very much a sideline, and had no formal basis at all; all agreements with agents were oral. If the Russian suppliers chose, there was nothing to stop them approaching the agents individually, or vice versa. Marcus realised that if he had died, his whole family business might have been put in jeopardy by these tenuous arrangements, so, in 1893, he established the Tank Syndicate, the precursor of today's company. In addition to the Samuel partners, it had seven members – the existing main agents, located in key ports of India, China, Asia and Malaysia. The ships themselves remained the property of M. Samuel & Co., but all transactions involving them were done on the Syndicate's joint account. Thus, each of the members shared the syndicate's overall profits and losses in proportion to his input; and each of them made his fortune.

By the end of 1893 ten ships had been launched for the Samuels. All were named after shells (in honour of the family's traditional business), all had coal-fired engines, and all had roughly similar physical dimensions – typically, 340 feet in length, 44 feet in beam. The first four (*Murex, Conch, Turbo* and *Clam*) were each of 5,010 deadweight tons; the other six (*Trocas, Spondilus, Elax, Volute, Bullmouth* and *Euplectela*) of 5,500. *Euplectela* was not completed until February 1894, but by then, all the others were trading steadily

Turbo at Gore Bay, Sydney Harbour, Australia. June 10th, 1901.

Shell oil tanker Trocas built at Sunderland in 1893 leaving the petroleum basin at Port Said, 1910.

Clam (1893-1926), probably the oldest Shell tanker photograph. (No picture of Murex has ever been traced.)

and profitably from the Black Sea to the Far East, and back to Europe. Most other tankers carried a paying cargo in only one direction, making their return voyage in ballast. This meant that profits from the oil had to cover the entire round trip. The reason the Samuels' ships were able to make profitable voyages both ways, when the oil was carried eastbound only, was because Marcus and Fortescue Flannery had had the foresight to incorporate sophist-icated steam-cleaning systems into the tank designs. After discharging a Russian cargo at Bombay, Kobe, Batavia or any one of their other eastern destinations, the tanks were thoroughly cleaned out, whitewashed inside, and filled with a dry cargo of tea, cereals or rice put together by the local agent.

This double profitable use of the fleet was an important factor in the Syndicate's early runaway success; but taking bulk oil through the Suez Canal, when hardly anyone else was equipped to do so, was at the heart of it. By the end of 1895, only 43 months after the launch of *Murex*, there had been a total of 69 such voyages, and 65 of them had been made by Samuel ships.

The traditional aspects of the family business were maintained in parallel, with an unexpected fillip in the

The Semantics of Tonnage

Maritime tonnage systems can be confusing, but they do not have to be; it is just that the same word is used to mean different things. The very word 'tonnage' was originally a merchant naval term, meaning the amount charged by the owner per ton of cargo carried, when the ship was hired out to someone else. In the 14th century, 'tunnage' was introduced, meaning a tax on each tun or barrel of wine imported into England. Today, in some systems tonnage is based on a calculation of cubic space, while in others it refers to an actual weight.

Since about 1870, warships have generally been measured by their displacement tonnage – that is, the weight of water displaced by the ship when all fuel, guns, ammunition, stores and water are on board. However, the most important measurements for merchant shipowners are *gross registered tonnage* (GRT), *net registered tonnage* (NRT) and *deadweight tonnage* (DWT). The first two of these are related to one another, and are calculations based on space: GRT is broadly, the capacity in cubic feet of the spaces within the hull, and of the enclosed spaces above the deck available for cargo, stores, fuel, passengers and crew, with certain exceptions, divided by 100. NRT is the GRT figure minus an allowance for accommodation, navigation and machinery spaces. To the merchant owner, the importance of these figures is that they usually form the basis for working out payments such as port and harbour dues, light and buoyage system dues, towage charges, and salvage assessments.

DWT in contrast expresses the ship's cargo-carrying ability measured in tons or, more usually today, in metric tonnes. In either case, dwt is the total actual weight of cargo, bunkers, stores and water that trims the vessel to her Plimsoll marks.

shape of the Sino-Japanese war of 1894-95: being neutral, the Syndicate's connections in both countries enabled it to trade with both belligerents. Overall, though, the new sideline of bulk oil shipping was making more money, and faster, than any of the others. Though Marcus had never been terribly poor, he was now becoming quite definitely rich; and since he always had a weakness for show and comfort, he indulged himself by acquiring the appropriate gentlemanly possessions – jewels for his wife; horses for himself, for riding in Hyde Park; ponies, and an Eton education, for his sons; a large house in London's Portland Place (from which he would travel to the office at 31, Houndsditch, in his own carriage); and, near Maidstone in Kent, a 500-acre estate with a lake and a great pile of a mansion, modestly called The Mote. It was scarcely the speck of dust its name would suggest, but a chap had to have a little place in the country.

Having embarked on this very agreeable way of life, he gave some thought to its continuance. The Russians were notoriously unreliable, and being dependent solely upon them for oil, the source of his new wealth, was clearly inadvisable; so he decided that M. Samuel & Co. should have its own oil, controlling the product at every stage, from pumping it out of the ground, through refining it and transporting it to selling it. Two of his nephews, Mark and Joe Abrahams, were accordingly instructed: Joe was to set up a storage and distribution system in India, Mark was to do the same in the Far East; and when that had been accomplished, Mark was to go and discover oil in Borneo.

Borneo was chosen firstly because, apart from the United States and Russia, the Dutch East Indies were the only other places in the world where oil was known to exist in commercially viable quantities; and secondly because Marcus had met an elderly Dutchman, Jacobus Menten, a buccaneering kind of man who had a drilling concession in a province of Borneo called Kutei. The concession covered 25,000 square miles or so – mostly thick jungle. After

Mark (standing) and Joe Abrahams c 1890

The Mote, near-Maidstone, Kent. From a painting by
George Shepherd in the Maidstone Museum.

several years spent prospecting there, Menten had not actually struck oil, but he had often seen oil from natural sources floating on rivers, and he had convinced himself it could be found in his concession in commercial quantities – even though a report from a Dutch geologist described the samples he provided as 'a thick brown mess, thicker than treacle in Holland in winter', quite unsuited for making kerosene. It was not the only possibility open to M. Samuel & Co. at the time (other regional groups needing support were some prospectors in Sumatra, and, operating in Borneo, an enterprise called Royal Dutch) but Menten managed to convince Marcus, who agreed to support the persuasive Dutchman.

Thus, backed by £1,200 of the Samuels' money, and with the promise of a further £2,400 plus royalties if oil were found, Menten returned jubilantly to Borneo at the end of 1895. There he recruited workers, cleared 18 acres of jungle, set up rudimentary accommodation, and decided to drill at a place called Sanga Sanga, 60 miles north of a beautiful untouched bay named Balik Papan. Mark – his movements watched and reported to their chiefs by agents of Standard Oil – joined Menten the following October, after finishing his tank installations, and after a two-week trip to the Russian oilfields. That fortnight was Mark's only tuition or experience in the production of oil. Neither he nor his uncles in London had any real idea about what was involved in searching for oil, especially in a tropical jungle. The physical problems of climate, disease, transport and communications were unlike anything Mark had ever encountered, and beyond anything his uncles could conceive. Their long-distance bickering by letter and cable began again, the uncles apparently imagining that Mark was idling away his time in a hammock under a palm tree. In fact he worked extremely hard against considerable difficulties (the very least being that of his three drillers, one was constantly drunk and had to be sacked, the second died of fever, and the third was convinced that they were

SS Volute. *Launched in 1893. One of the earliest Shell tankers.*

going to drill in the wrong place altogether) and on 5 February 1897 he succeeded: oil was found in sandstone at 150 feet.

He would have been very unlucky if he had found none. For years past, the native Dyaks had been mystified and a little frightened by a perpetual flame thereabouts, a leak of subterranean natural gas, and in the 'Black Spot', as they called it, oil was actually oozing to the surface of its own accord. News of the find reached the Tank Syndicate's partners in mid-February, prompting much mutual congratulation; it was timely information. On 6 March the previous year, the Samuels' fleet had suffered its first loss of a ship, when SS *Spondilus* (en route from Japan and China to the UK with a general cargo in her whitewashed tanks) had been stranded and completely wrecked on Cape Varela in Cochin China. Thus, apart from the promise of yet greater wealth, learning of Mark's discovery was a welcome off-set for what would otherwise have been a sombre anniversary.

It also helped justify the recent and continuing expansion of the fleet. During 1895, the ten original Samuel ships had been joined by three new and larger tankers, *Pectan*, *Nerite* and *Telena*, followed in January 1896 by *Cowrie*. As a minor aside, it is notable that two successive Shell ships have been given the name *Pectan*, with that spelling; it was not until 1927

that the third ship of the name was given the correct spelling, *Pecten*. But that was a detail. Much more important was the fact that in 1897, only four years after the launch of his first vessel, Marcus Samuel personally and his associates collectively were not only a significant force in the world of shipping, but also a coming force in the world of oil. At any rate, that was what they believed; and the belief prompted Marcus to make some important new moves, not all of which were good.

As usual, in between other business demands, he had been pondering the question of how to improve the Syndicate's defences against Standard's competition. Finding an independent source of oil was part of that, but one past decision now turned out to have been a considerable error of judgement. Marcus could have had an interest in the Sumatran concessions of an ailing company called Moeara Enim, but had turned it down, being persuaded that the Kutei concession in Borneo would be better. Within six months of his refusal, however, Moeara Enim had struck a gusher of light oil, ideal for refining into kerosene; whereas the stuff coming out of Kutei was thick and heavy. Nevertheless, Marcus remained confident, and went so far as to predict that in 1898, Kutei would yield 15-20 million cases of oil. This optimism betrayed him, both in the short and the long run: for had he not been quite

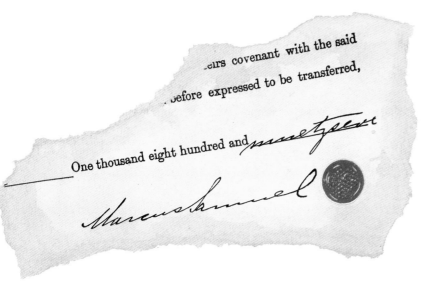

...eirs covenant with the said

...before expressed to be transferred,

One thousand eight hundred and *ninety seven*

Marcus Samuel

so sure of himself at that point, it is very probable that, early in 1897, he would have reached an historic agreement – an amalgamation with the third party in the East Indies, the Royal Dutch Petroleum Company. Today the date of the eventual amalgamation of the companies (1907) is so well known that people often overlook or forget the fact that a full ten years earlier, Marcus and his brother Sam on the one side, and Jean Baptiste Auguste Kessler (then Royal Dutch's managing director) on the other side, were contemplating just such a union. Even then, they were thinking not just of co-operation, but of actual amalgamation. The virtues were obvious: the Tank Syndicate had a good, established transport and marketing organization, and though its oil production was small, it had every intention of increasing that as much as possible; Royal Dutch, on the other hand, was already producing plenty of oil, but had no means of its own to distribute and sell the product.

Despite these manifest advantages, preliminary negotiations broke down in April 1897, in a sudden mood of mutual inflexibility. Though largely caused by the vast production figure Marcus foretold, this inflexibility was also partly because of reasons which are best left to the next chapter; but the net result was that as oil producers, M. Samuel & Co. still had only one well, producing oil of uncertain quantity and questionable quality.

In the context of his businesses overall, however, the termination of talks with Royal Dutch was not desperately important to Marcus, because his company's unusually good relations with Japan brought a sudden windfall: the right to float, on behalf of the Japanese Government, the

first sterling loan to Japan. This was handled so skilfully that other similar banking arrangements soon followed, providing funds which Marcus was able to pour into Kutei. Moving his head office from the cramped quarters of Houndsditch to a more spacious and prestigious building in Leadenhall Street, he also bought another seven ships – four general cargo vessels (*Ganges, Crathie, Elphinstone* and *Fleetwood*) which could carry case-oil, and three tankers (*Petriana, Robert Dickinson* and *Chigwell*) – and, perhaps most importantly in this busy year, he created 'the Shell'.

One of the oddities in the history of Shell Tankers (U.K.) Ltd is that one of its two parent companies, The "Shell" Transport and Trading Company plc (or, simply,

An example of the "Shell" Transport & Trading Co. Ltd. Stock Certificate. 1958

Shell Transport), is actually a younger concern. Shell Transport was born on 18 October 1897. Essentially, all that happened on that date was that ownership of the fleet changed, company names were changed, and the corporate structure was formalised. Having started as a sideline of ships belonging to M. Samuel & Co. and operated by S. Samuel & Co., the embryonic Shell Tankers had developed through the establishment of the Tank Syndicate (when the ships still belonged to the Samuels) to the point when Shell Transport was created, with the ships now belonging to the new company. But by then the fleet had already been trading with great success for over five years, so for all practical purposes the tanker company is actually older than its parent – the child really was father to the man.

As a measure of the tankers' profitability in those years, it is worth considering the sum that Marcus and Sam were able to put into the new company. In £100 shares, Shell Transport's original capital was £1.8 million, the equivalent in 1991 of £99 million. Its original shareholders were the members of the Syndicate, each receiving shares in proportion to his Syndicate input; and the Samuels' proportion was £1.2 million. This represented the value of the fleet (now, without any doubt, Shell tankers) and some Kutei assets; and in 1991 terms, the brothers' joint stake was worth no less than £66 million.

'The air is full of big talk here about bulk steamers which are being built for this Borneo trade – and refineries galore.' So wrote one C. F. Lufkin, an agent of Standard Oil, from Singapore in mid-1897. 'But', he added, '*a great big bluff* or an *awful mistake* is being perpetrated.' Standard's efficient intelligence-gathering system was usually right in its reports on competitors, and as 1897 closed and 1898 began, there was nothing to indicate any mistake in Lufkin's assessment. On New Year's Eve, 1897, Royal Dutch hit serious trouble: their wells began to produce not oil, but oil and water, a sure sign that the oil supply was running out. Within three months most of their wells were dry. At the same time, Shell's production in Kutei was no more than 15 barrels a day. At that rate, the concession's annual production would be no more than about 23,000 cases, a figure so woefully short of Marcus's grand forecast of 15-20 *million* cases a year that he found it very difficult to believe. Nephew Mark, he decided, must be doing something very badly wrong.

Unfortunately there was an almost complete absence of co-ordination between the London office and Mark's end of things in Borneo. The first two shipments of building and refinery materials, carried in *Elphinstone* and *Ganges*, arrived long before there was even a jetty to receive them; the cargoes could only be dumped on the beach, half in and half out of the water. Time after time, despite very clear requests, Mark was sent either the wrong tools or no tools at all; or pumps and other vital equipment were withheld; or, on arrival, workers (supposedly hand-picked by A. Syme & Co., Shell's agents in Singapore) were ill, crippled or blind. 'We are absolutely delayed on the refinery', Mark wrote in February, 'for want of masons, fitters, coolies, timber...' By then he had three separate sites (Sanga Sanga, Muara Djawa and Balik Papan) struggling towards operational status. On a map they did not look far apart, but the only practical way of getting from one to another was by water, with each journey taking at least 12 hours. Nevertheless, he could not persuade head office even to provide him with a suitable boat, and he had to depend on passing local vessels, or favours from the Dutch colonial administrators. Not surprisingly, his letters and cables became increasingly vexed in tone. At last, when a cable from London to Singapore enquired tersely 'Does Mr Abrahams drink?', he had had enough, and resigned.

'No one seems to know much,' reported John Fertig, another of Standard's intelligence-gatherers, 'and the business seems very poorly managed.' So it was. Promises of improvement induced Mark to stay on, and on 15 April his first well at Balik Papan struck oil at 725 feet. Sealing materials should have been on hand for just such a contingency – the Singapore agents had been asked often enough. The oil spurted out at 20 tons a day, multiplying daily production more than eight-fold to 130 barrels, or the equivalent over a year of 200,000 cases; but for week after week it was all lost, running away into the once clean, clear waters of the bay, because the agents had not got around to sending the sealing materials.

Meanwhile, talks between Shell and Royal Dutch reopened on a new basis. By prodigious effort, the Dutch company's Far Eastern marketing director, a very ambitious 30-year-old named Henri Deterding, now had a much improved sales system in action. In order to keep it supplied (indeed, to keep the business afloat, for they had not yet discovered any new fields of their own) his boss, J. B. A. Kessler, was buying kerosene wherever he could, principally from the Russians. Marcus, likewise, had begun to recognize that rather than trying to make his thick Kutei oil into kerosene, there was a better chance of selling it as fuel for ships and trains, and recent events gave him reason to hope he might corner the world's biggest single market for such a product. Accordingly, the two companies agreed not to undercut each other in the Orient, but to sell kerosene at the same price. Fertig was secretly complimentary: Standard's competitors, he declared, had 'the best talent' in their marketing departments – 'Their success in marketing testifies to their good judgement in this matter' – and he advised that Standard ought to buck up its own marketing ideas. But he did not guess at Marcus's new scheme.

What had happened was that on 15 February 1898, a British warship, HMS *Victorious*, ran hard aground at the entrance to the Suez Canal. Two other Royal Navy ships tried to get her off, and failed, as did the P&O line's *Sutlej* and Canal Company tugs. Loud European complaints, and suspicions that the whole thing had been done on purpose to block the strategic canal, brought the Admiralty close to deciding to blow up the unlucky vessel, despite the large financial loss this would mean for the British Government;

© Illustrated London News

HMS Victorious *stranded at Port Said on her way to China.*

then Marcus ordered his new big tanker, SS *Pectan* (Captain N. Hocken), to go and help.

As far as anyone could be in 1898, Hocken was a veteran tanker captain. He had first heard rumour of the Samuels' new venture while *Murex* was still under construction. At the time, he was over 2,000 miles away from home, in the Black Sea oil port of Batum, working for the Prince Line; but, when he returned to Britain, he was given a letter of introduction by Fred Lane's partner Mr Macandrew, met Marcus – 'Alderman Samuel' – and was offered a job as Chief Officer in *Murex*. He told Marcus straight 'that, having been accustomed to being at the top of the ladder, I did not take kindly to the idea of a position on one of the lower rungs', but when Marcus promised him a Master's salary from the start, and a new command of his own in the very near future, Hocken accepted.

Thus, he accompanied Coundon in *Murex*'s first historic voyage through Suez; met Mark Abrahams in the Far East, and Mark's brother Joe, who was building up the storage and distribution system in India; and with a good deal of ceremony, helped to 'christen' many ports with their first deliveries of bulk oil, always 'a novel and

SS Cowrie of 1896 at Port Tewfik, Egypt.

wonderful experience'. Before long, as Marcus had promised, he had his own command again – first *Spondilus*, then *Pectan*.

Pectan's design was well suited to the job. The engines of most steamships were positioned centrally, but in order to minimize the risk of fire, Fortescue Flannery had arranged *Murex* and the others differently, with the engines aft, entirely separated from the cargo spaces. As Marcus recalled many years later, when it came to hauling a grounded ship off, this arrangement had the unexpected bonus of providing 'a great weight where it was wanted'.

Back in the Canal, while other attempts continued, *Pectan* stood by for 3 days; then when everyone else had given up, she began to tow. The operation took 21 hours, but it worked: the warship was refloated, 'the first case of its kind', Hocken was told, 'of a merchant ship towing off a man of war.' Ten minutes later, to everyone's surprise, another British warship turned up, HMS *Venice*, from Malta. She had brought with her 'all necessary towing tackle,' Hocken noted, before remarking complacently: 'But of course her services were not required.'

It turned out to be a very profitable day's work. Accepting the principle of salvage, the Admiralty duly offered £500 to be divided between *Pectan*'s crew. (In 1991,

that would have been equivalent to nearly £28,000.) The same was offered to her Master, and £5,000 to her owners, which in practical terms meant Marcus personally: his shares outweighed anyone else's. The crew and Captain Hocken accepted with alacrity; Marcus did not. Their Lordships may well have expected a larger counter-claim from him; they certainly did not expect him to refuse outright. But to their confusion he did just that, explaining that he regarded the rescue simply as a patriotic duty, and adding that the Royal Navy could call on the services of Shell ships whenever necessary.

He meant what he said; he was not trying to negotiate, and would have been happy to leave it at that. Instead, he was offered a knighthood, which delighted him. The ceremony took place at Osborne, Queen Victoria's house in the Isle of Wight, on Saturday 6 August 1898 – a proud occasion which made the loss of the valiant *Pectan*, only nine days later, all the more sad. Under another Master, while on passage from Calcutta to Hamburg, she was hit on 20 August by a steamer belonging to another company and sank off the coast of north Africa.

But Sir Marcus now had a goal which, if achieved, would make the loss of a ship a small misfortune. Armed with his new distinction and connections, he began his campaign to persuade the Admiralty that the entire Royal Navy should change from coal-fired to oil-fired ships. Oil was a much cheaper fuel for any ship, producing 50% more heat per unit of cost and weight, and requiring far fewer men. He hoped the Admiralty would jump at it, for if Shell could gain the contract to supply the whole Royal Navy, what a market that would be; and to add to his campaign, he was becoming much more certain that the Borneo concession was going to work.

On 20 September, John Fertig, Standard's agent in the Far East, wrote to his employers: 'The most astounding operations in the whole Netherlands Indies thus far we consider to be those of the Samuels at Kutei. They have a pay-roll of no less than 48 Europeans, besides a small army

Illustration Simon Williams

of imported native workmen, and four steamers plying to and fro, and yet from the best and most exclusive evidence they have not one gallon of real crude oil!!!'

For once – despite his exclamations – the agent was mistaken. The 'steamers plying to and fro' were busy carrying crude to Singapore, both for sale as fuel-oil and for the fleet's own use: the latest additions, *Haliotis* and *Trigonia* (both completed in August 1898) were designed by Fortescue Flannery to run on either coal or oil, while *Clam* was converted in 1899 to run exclusively on oil. The Kutei wells were beginning to flow in earnest, with Sanga Sanga providing 400 tons of crude oil a day. By 21 February 1899, Fertig had changed his mind: 'They have demonstrated', he said gloomily, 'that a considerable body of oil, suitable for fuel, exists in that territory.' Nor was it only fuel. Looking towards October 1900, when his contract with the Russian suppliers would expire, Marcus gained an agreement with Moeara Enim for the supply of a minimum 50,000 tons of kerosene a year, to begin on 1 January 1901; and on 27 February 1899, Shell's twelfth well at Sanga Sanga struck real light oil, perfect for kerosene, at 850 feet.

To celebrate, Mark gave a champagne supper for government and company officials. Life looked good all round, except for the still acerbic relationship between Mark in the field and his uncles in the office. Old Jacobus Menten was writing so unpleasantly about Mark's management of the concession that in February, Sam Samuel left London to go and see Kutei for himself. What he saw soon persuaded him that Mark had been right all along, and still was; ships would arrive full of unmarked crates of equipment, or even without manifests, and under the circumstances Sam felt there was little to criticize in the local running of the business. So much the better, one might suppose. But Sam was away from London for a long time – nine whole months – and during that time, Marcus was obliged to face, on his own, certain momentous decisions.

One of the early drilling rigs in action at Sanga Sanga.

Late 19th century rigs in the Dutch East Indies – believed to be Well No.1 Kutei.

A percussion bit used in the Caucasian oilfields c. 1900.

Chapter Three

The Beautiful Bubble
1899-1902

The beach at Balik Papan, 1896. Crathie is close into the shore, the first service steamer in the Company in Borneo, on which the staff lived during river and marine surveys. On the right is Elphinstone, which brought out the refinery. On the left is the sailing barque Fleetwood, which carried the cement and firebricks.

Mark Abrahams as British Vice-Consul in Borneo c. 1898

On 15 March 1899, just after Sam had left for Borneo, Marcus delivered a paper to the Royal Society of Arts on the subject of liquid fuels. This led to a meeting, and an immediate life-long friendship, with Vice Admiral Sir John (later Admiral of the Fleet Lord) Fisher, a man whose vision and energy matched Marcus's, and who would soon be notorious throughout the Navy as the greatest iconoclast it had ever known.

From the first, Fisher was completely in favour of oil: the strategic and tactical advantages it would confer upon the armed fleet were to him self-evident. Marcus had already seen the economies of weight, space and personnel, but only in commercial terms. To Fisher, they raised the possibility of putting larger guns in the same size hull, while oil, generating less tell-tale smoke than coal, would allow a fleet to approach an enemy closer before detection. Marcus had not thought of it in quite *those* terms before, but he quickly understood that these arguments must strengthen his case with the Admiralty. At the same time, Fisher's worldwide vision awakened Marcus to a concept which had not struck him before: that Shell tankers could become not only an Eastern interest, but a global one. So began a theme which would occupy him for more than a decade.

Another new possibility was the product known variously as gasoline, benzine, or petrol. In London, on 17 June 1899, the Automobile Association organized a trial rally of motor cars, which Marcus attended. He personally did not like the machines at all, but he had decided they were the coming thing; and at the rally he noticed that all their fuel was supplied in the familiar yet unwelcome blue cans of Standard Oil. There were not many British oilmen, but he was one of their leaders, and here on his very doorstep was a potentially good market which he had done nothing to supply – which instead was being supplied by a foreign firm. Both as a businessman and as a patriot, the

The company began to include petrol in its business.

sight of the blue cans irritated him, and he decided he must refine petrol out of his Kutei oil. It could certainly be done, and no doubt the product could be brought back to the UK at a very good rate through the Suez Canal, in the same way as his kerosene was taken out east.

As he was cogitating these new horizons, Standard (for reasons of its own) suddenly launched a price war against its allies in Germany, the Nobels. The Nobels retaliated by negotiating with the Rothschilds and independent Russian producers. Standard found itself unexpectedly short of oil in Europe, began buying Russian oil, and approached the Nobels, Rothschilds and Russian independents with the suggestion that they should all join forces. This kind of shifting, breaking and remaking of alliances went on all the time in the oil trade; but in the summer of 1899, Marcus Samuel decided that unless he could gain control of vast stocks of oil, the potential monopoly, which did not include him, could break him and Shell.

His response was correspondingly aggressive: he expanded his company's interests enormously. The instruction to begin refining petrol was sent to Mark in Balik Papan. An option was bought to drill for oil in Kutei Lama, a adjacent concession. In Newcastle, the North-

Eastern Marine Engineering Company was building two new tankers for him, to be named *Strombus* and *Cardium*. Fitted throughout with electric light, each was of 8,500 deadweight tons, with an overall length of 426 feet and a beam of 52 feet. Their boilers (three apiece) each had four furnaces capable of burning either coal or oil, with triple expansion engines of 2,200 horsepower producing nine knots, and their entire cargo – oil eastwards, grain, sugar or rice westwards – could be discharged in twelve hours. Altogether, they were going to be among the largest and most modern tankers in the world; and now Marcus ordered a third to be laid down and a fourth to be designed. In the Far East, he increased his oil storage capacity and (though its price was steadily rising) bought all the oil he could, from any available source. When his own fleet proved insufficient, he chartered other vessels: at one time he had 16 tankers simultaneously in the Suez Canal, either hurrying out to the Far East or hastening back – empty, for there was no time to take in dry cargoes – to Russia. He was spending huge amounts of money, but the market was still rising without any sign of a slowdown, and he was sure Borneo would be the trump card. During October, his tanker *Nerite* gained the company another world first when, dressed overall with celebrational flags, she discharged a cargo of fuel-oil at Suez. It seemed an emblem for the future.

On 12 December 1899 the habitually cautious Sam returned from Borneo, learned of his brother's strategy, and was appalled at the colossally expensive stockpiles which had been accumulated. He and Marcus had a ferocious argument, Sam asserting Marcus was going mad, and Marcus retorting icily that Sam was never satisfied. For better or worse, though, it was done, and at first all seemed well. Through the spring of 1900 there were problems in Kutei – an outbreak of smallpox in *Petriana*, a fire in which two men died, a dropping of the quality of the oil, and tankers queueing to be filled – but soon the refineries there

were producing first-class petrol, and, on 21 June, Marcus reported to the AGM that in the first quarter of the year, 10,000 tons of liquid fuel had been exported from Kutei. Nor was he simply selling it: the economic benefits of actually using it – the reductions in fuel cost and manpower – were so clear that, in a pointed example to the Admiralty, over

A Suez Canal hopper bought for Mark Abrahams.

*One of the twenty-four vessels in the original Shell fleet, the SS **Nerite** (6,200 dwt) discharging the first cargo of liquid fuel at Suez in October 1899.*

1,100 tons had been used in Shell tankers. (*Strombus* had been completed in January, and her sister *Cardium* in May, while the third of the type, *Bulysses*, was due in August. All could burn coal or oil, and *Volute* had been converted to burn oil only.) *Bulysses* would bring the company's deepsea tanker fleet to 15, and a dozen 300dwt sandhoppers had been bought for conversion into small coastal tankers, which Mark Abrahams could use in the Far East.

Marcus also predicted that the company's annual profits from Kutei would soon exceed a million pounds. Already the value of their shares had tripled from its base price of £100, which meant, though he did not mention it, that his and Sam's joint stake had also tripled in value, to £3.6 million. (In 1991 terms it would have been worth £198 million.) He also announced that the company's capital had been increased to £2 million; that £100,000 from the past year's profits were being put into reserve; and that £40,000 was being carried forward. He did not mention that these large sums altogether roughly equalled the value of oils held in stock, which included 60,000 tons of kerosene in China alone; but that was the measure of the risk he was running through his policy of purchasing whatever the price. Nor did he mention to shareholders that the purpose of the expenditure was to impress, to give the outside world the picture of a vastly prosperous Shell, and thereby to secure a renewal of the Russian kerosene contract.

It worked, in one way. On 11 October 1900, the new contract was gained. But almost immediately afterwards, the price of kerosene began to slide, and slide, and slide. There had been a bad harvest in Russia, followed by a famine. To earn foreign currency, Russian kerosene production was increased many times over. It was nothing to do with Marcus; but suddenly Shell found itself with stocks of kerosene, the value of which was dropping steadily to below the price paid for it. Simultaneously the Boxer rebellion in China damaged Shell's large interests

there, physically and financially; in India the Burmah Oil Company took practical control of the kerosene market, negating Shell's investment in the subcontinent; and in the UK, though Marcus did not realize it at once, Standard stole a very considerable march by wrapping up the majority of petrol outlets with exclusive supply contracts.

All this was precisely what Sam had feared: Marcus's gamble had failed. To make matters worse, the Boer war was by then in full swing, prompting nationalism in Holland. There, it was decided that Borneo should become part of the customs union of the Dutch East Indies, which meant that ships trading there would in future have to fly the Dutch flag. Shell ships, trading under the Red Ensign, would be cut out. On 8 December 1900, Marcus personally launched his next tanker, *Pinna*, a vessel similar to but somewhat larger than even *Bulysses*. (These four sisters were so modern that, 11 years later, *Pinna*, being marginally the biggest, was mentioned with admiration in the *Encyclopaedia Britannica*.) At the launch, however, Marcus took the opportunity to make a speech, seconded by Fortescue Flannery, bitterly denouncing the Dutch move. Coming as it did hot on the heels of horrible conditions in southern Africa, where the British had established concentration camps, the speech caused grave damage to Shell's relations with the Dutch; and on 14 December, Royal Dutch's managing director Jean Kessler died. In his way he had been a good friend to Marcus. His successor was the company's former Far Eastern marketing director, Henri Deterding, now 34 years old and just as ambitious as ever. It remained to be seen how he and Marcus would relate.

'For Shell in Borneo,' Deterding wrote a few months later, 'all is not quite so *couleur de rose* as Sir Marcus has been making out...' During the company's first AGM, in August 1899, Marcus had told shareholders that £350,000 had been spent in Kutei to that date, then added: 'Fortunately this company are largely dependent upon

SS Cardium (1900-1925) Note her characteristic bridge, open to all weathers – only fragile canvas screens protected those on watch from the wind and waves.

their trade as carriers rather than as oil merchants for their earning powers...' Since then the situation had altered radically. By the beginning of 1901, overstocked with overpriced oil, Shell's carrying trade had slumped too. The drilling in Kutei Lama had come to a halt at the end of 1900. Nothing had been found, largely because Marcus disagreed with the notion of using geologists to prospect for oil. Now Deterding was beginning to suspect that Shell was much weaker than it appeared.

He was right. Since Marcus's price gamble had failed and the slump had begun, Shell as a carrier had come perilously close to collapse, and was now merely hanging on. With a facade of strength, but without enough to support it, the company had really resorted to bluff, hoping to find some new source of oil to transport before its bluff was perceived.

Deterding, as a producer, was also eager to find a new source of oil. Through the first half of 1901 he bought more East Indian concessions, steadily strengthening Royal Dutch, and wondering how best he could use Shell. In the same period, tension at Shell's head office was acute: for on 10 January there *had* been a new find, a vast, spectacular new find in a place called Spindletop in Texas, where the state laws discouraged Standard from operating. For Shell to gain a carrying contract there would introduce the problems of working in another hemisphere; but if Shell

failed to gain a contract, there would soon be no more Shell.

A substantial part of the new field was owned by a Colonel James McClurg Guffey. From the moment he read of the Spindletop gushers, Marcus bombarded Guffey with urgent offers by cable and letter, eventually sending his brother-in-law Henry Benjamin over to negotiate in person. The first six months of 1901 passed in an agony of suspense, but at the AGM on 18 June Marcus triumphantly announced that a contract would be signed in ten days' time. For the following 21 years, Shell tankers would carry half of Guffey's production, at a fixed rate of $1.75 a ton, with a minimum annual delivery of 100,000 tons.

In July, *Pinna* carried the first Guffey cargo from Port Arthur in Texas to Europe, and made three more such voyages that year. *Cardium* also made four, and *Strombus* one, all using much less fuel in the form of oil than they would ever have done with coal. The big ships could look forward to a steady, profitable job.

Once again all seemed well; but if Marcus had been superstitious, he might have taken valuable note of another event that year. *Murex,* Shell's very first tanker, hit an unmarked shoal off the south-west tip of Palawan. She survived, but only just; and that was a much more accurate portent of things to come.

Standard now began to woo Shell in a most flattering way. Simultaneously, Marcus's old friend and colleague, Fred Lane, re-entered negotiations with Royal Dutch, and, on 1 November, presented Marcus with a draft agreement between the two companies. Marcus swiftly rejected it, proposing instead that Royal Dutch and he together should create a new distributing company, which would charter Shell tankers at seven shillings a ton freight. This was a high figure (seven shillings then was equivalent to £18.75 in 1991) and he only demanded it because he believed that a Shell-Standard union was imminent: that Standard had offered him both a very large amount of money, and continued independence. The fact that

Helcion *and* Pinna *at Pulau Bukom (Singapore).*

Standard had never dealt that way did not arise in his mind; he was confident that his position between the Dutch and the American enterprises had become of pivotal importance to both.

Now it was Henri Deterding's turn to agonize over the politics of business. If he accepted, it could be a ruinously expensive commitment; if he refused, and Shell and Standard joined forces, they could gobble up Royal Dutch whenever they chose. At last, on 27 December 1901, he consented, and signed an agreement with Marcus based on their companies' comparative capital investments. Just about the same time, Standard came back to Marcus to clarify their earlier discussions. They did indeed offer him a huge amount of money – even more than he had expected. In fact, it was $40 million, which in 1991 would have been about $500 million, or £300 million. But for this fantastic sum, Standard also made it clear that the price, for him, was complete absorption. He would still have a high status within the business, but all major decisions would be taken centrally in New York.

This was (in both senses) Standard procedure, yet with Royal Dutch now alongside, Marcus turned it down; despite the fabulous wealth within his reach, he decided he did not want Shell to become an American concern. His

ships would earn well enough from their charters with Deterding and Guffey, and he had never had any desire to be a part of the Standard machine. Entering the New Year, 1902, he was happy in his choices; and a remarkable event at the start of the year only emphasised his pleasure. On 31 January, the Anglo-Japanese Alliance was signed, the first full alliance Britain had made with any other nation for a whole century. Looking back from today, this marked the end of Britain's 'splendid isolation', while its very necessity was a milestone in the decline of Britain's maritime power; but looking at it then, with his excellent Japanese connections, Marcus saw only another wonderful door of business opportunity opening before him.

In sharp contrast, Henri Deterding found that he had hitched Royal Dutch to an unnecessarily costly agreement. During February 1902, overstretched by his efforts to work out some way of replacing it, the unhappy man suffered a nervous breakdown, and had to go to hospital for a month; but that was minor compared to the events which 1902 held for Marcus and Shell. By the end of the year, he and his shipping business had been through the wildest roller-coaster he could have imagined.

There were many more lows than highs. In March, *Bulysses* ran aground in the Suez Canal's Great Bitter Lake. Coming to her aid, *Nerite* took off too much of the bigger ship's kerosene. Her own tanks overflowed, flooded the stokehold, caught fire, and blazed until all the oil was gone and *Nerite* a sunken wreck.

Bad as it was, the accident had a worse and completely unexpected outcome. As part of the scheme to oust those blue Standard petrol cans from the UK, Shell had been negotiating for permission to carry bulk petrol through the Canal. Now, probably because of *Nerite*'s terrible fire, the Canal authorities simply and adamantly said no to petrol. The heat in Suez must, they believed, make such an intrinsically risky cargo perilous in the extreme. Marcus had always assumed he would be allowed to use the short

HMS Hannibal *of the Channel Fleet, one of the first warships fitted to burn fuel-oil. From a drawing in* The Illustrated London News *which carried the comment '. . . . The experiment has been successful as far as locomotion is concerned, but has the drawback that the ships using oil emit enormous volumes of dense black smoke – very picturesque, but by no means convenient or pleasant.'*

offered the Admiralty seats on the board of Shell. By now he was thoroughly convinced of the value of fuel-oil for ships, and had become the acknowledged prophet of that cause, but Their Lordships remained firmly unconverted. They had three reasons for this. The first was that if oil replaced coal in the Royal Navy, a worldwide network of supply bases would have to be established to meet the fleet's needs. This was true, though Marcus asserted that Shell ships could be available to meet and work with the Navy anywhere at any time. The second reason was that Shell was (they said) a foreign company dependent on foreign sources of supply, which could not be guaranteed in wartime. This was far from the real truth, but contained a large enough element of truth to make it difficult for Marcus to persuade them otherwise. The third reason was that (again, in the Admiralty's view) fuel-oil had not been sufficiently tested. That was claptrap. So, having offered them his ships for trials, having passed on all the information he possessed on fuel-oil, and having taken Royal Navy engineer officers in his ships, in exasperation Marcus now offered them a voice in the company itself.

Oddly enough, he seems to have imagined they would accept. They did not; but they did agree to test Shell's smokeless (or almost smokeless) liquid fuel in one of their own ships, HMS *Hannibal*.

The day before the trial was set aside for Shell's 1902 AGM. It was not a happy meeting. Profits in 1901 had declined from £376,000 to £254,000, a result made all the more gloomy when contrasted with the bright hopes Marcus had always held out for Kutei. Oil prices were still falling; freight rates were still falling; £100,000 had been laid out in Australia, without any result; past competition with Royal Dutch had been damaging, and the financial benefits of Spindletop would not be visible for another

cut. Instead, when carrying petrol from Kutei to the UK, his tankers had to travel all the way around the Cape of Good Hope, increasing both the time and the cost of their voyages.

Nevertheless, the scheme had to go ahead. Under a Master named Scott, *Murex* was the first of his ships to bring bulk petrol to Great Britain (and indeed the world's first tanker to ship bulk petrol over such a long distance). It was said that during the voyage, Captain Scott's hair turned white with worry, but the long passage was made without incident; it was only when she discharged her cargo that Marcus discovered, too late, that Standard had already stitched up most of the fuel's possible retail outlets.

It was also in March 1902 that Marcus made a very surprising suggestion: he

year. The best notes, indeed the only good ones, were the forthcoming co-operation with Royal Dutch, and the imminent trial with the Royal Navy.

If Marcus had been able to use one of his own ships in the trial, it would probably have worked. If he had been able to inspect the burners in *Hannibal*, he would probably have cancelled it. But neither was the case, and on 26 July the well-publicised trial was an absolute fiasco. *Hannibal* steamed out of Portsmouth, trailing a cloud of light smoke from her Welsh coal. At a given signal, her engineers switched to Shell's liquid fuel; and in moments the entire ship was engulfed in a dense black cloud.

Apparently *Hannibal*'s furnaces were fitted with out-dated (and notoriously smoky) vapourising burners, instead of modern (and virtually smoke-free) atomising burners. Whatever the reason, Marcus was humiliated. The Admiralty officials were probably not very much surprised; they had always been sceptical, and the disastrous experiment confirmed their beliefs.

On 27 June, back in London and nursing wounded pride, Marcus signed his new agreement with Royal Dutch. Henri Deterding, on recovering his health, had managed to replace the original agreement of the previous December with another. This allocated the same high freight rates, seven shillings a ton, to chartered Shell tankers, and also led to the creation of a brand new company, Asiatic Petroleum, in which Shell, Royal Dutch and the Rothschilds were equal partners. It is not quite certain why Marcus accepted this arrangement; perhaps he was too despondent, after the *Hannibal* affair, to argue. But almost as soon as the signature was written, Deterding began to charter cheaper vessels from other companies, and to play games with the Rothschilds, the Nobels and the independent Russians. His target was to get them all into a pan-European anti-Standard monopoly, with the sweetener (to use a modern term) of buying large cargoes of case-oil from them – cargoes which could only further depress the already low price of oil in the East, and which by their nature competed with Shell's bulk oil carriers. And then, in August, Spindletop ran dry.

Perhaps it could have been foretold. Marcus had taken no legal or geological advice in the matter, but had relied solely upon what he heard and read. Now, though, he found his still large stocks of kerosene could be sold only at a loss; his dream of supplying the Royal Navy with fuel-oil had been dashed, perhaps permanently; without any breaking of the agreement with Royal Dutch, the anticipated Far Eastern employment of his ships was being undercut by his own associates; and the ships' transatlantic employment had vanished.

Throughout his life, in addition to his businesses, Marcus Samuel had always felt the need to perform public service. Since 1891 he had been an Alderman of the City of London, and for one year, beginning in 1894, its Sheriff. That placed him in line to become Lord Mayor, an honour which came his way on 29 September 1902. His year of office was crammed with civic duties, which he carried out extremely conscientiously. This was partly because he enjoyed the fuss and flim-flam; partly because of his need to serve society; and partly because he viewed the mayoralty as a fine reflection on the Jewish community. (At the beginning of his year, he directed the Lord Mayor's Parade – which Henri Deterding, his guest, derisively likened to a circus – to go through the East End area of his birth, a place no Lord Mayor had officially visited before.) Amongst it all, he probably also found some respite from the travail of managing Shell. Even before the Parade, his latest tanker – the second *Pectan* – had been laid up, idle for lack of work, and from the date of his inauguration, 9½ weeks passed before he entered his offices in Leadenhall Street again. During those weeks, the nearest he came to Shell and its tankers was at the end of November, in Newcastle. There, on the 28th, he and Lady Samuel saw

Marcus Samuel in civic robes.

two new Shell ships, *Silverlip* and *Goldmouth*, and on the 29th the Lady Mayoress launched *Silverlip*. It was not until 4 December that (in Marcus's own words) he was able to 'put in an hour at the office', and it was literally only an hour. After that he was away from Leadenhall Street for another fortnight, returning on 17 December to learn that Shell's earnings that year could only warrant a 2½ per cent dividend. This was disappointing, but nothing could be done about it just then, so he went off for his Christmas holidays at The Mote, and did not go back to the office until 27 December.

He returned to find a long letter from Fred Lane awaiting him. The letter was systematic but emotional, as well it might be. Lane and Marcus had been friends for close on 20 years, yet now Lane was delivering a blistering critique of Marcus and all his business methods. London management, said Lane, gained nothing by experience but was reckless and blundering. When Shell had been established, it had not been given its own carefully selected staff, fit to run the business, but had been contracted to M.

Samuel & Co. This was natural enough 'under the peculiar circumstances', said Lane, but a great mistake: the people in charge (first and foremost Marcus) were 'either too busy to devote their mind and time to it, or too incompetent.' The word 'reckless' came up repeatedly in this long letter, and much more: the culpable squandering of hundreds of thousands of pounds; the 'most absolute ignorance' of distributing bulk oil; haphazard, shameful expenditure; the refusal carefully to calculate results – instead, there was only 'a happy-go-lucky frame of mind' that Lane had never encountered in business before. The company, if treated on its merits, 'would undoubtedly have to be written off as a failure.... It is a business, I clearly see, that has no head or tail to its management. There seems only one idea: sink capital, create a great bluster, and trust to providence.'

'It is easy enough', Lane continued, 'to have a quick perception of opportunities, and sound ideas of business in general; but when a business is based on the continual sinking of vast capital, a profound study is necessary before entering upon it; and steady and continued devotion of the time, as well as the brains of the leader; and an organised and competent staff are necessary to see that the Capital expenditure is warranted, and will be permanently remunerative. Business like this cannot be conducted by an occasional glance in one's spare time, or by some brilliant *coup* from time to time. It is steady, treadmill work; and unless one is prepared for this, better let it alone altogether.'

That was exactly what he himself was proposing to do. 'I see no hope for the Shell Co. conducted on such lines as I have indicated. A great splash has been made, and the situation capitalised; but it cannot last, and the bubble will burst...' By carrying through the Asiatic, he felt he might be able 'to stave off the evil day for some time', yet this would not be enough 'unless, as I said, some very radical change is made.' However, he did not believe such a change would come; and so he was resigning from the board of Shell.

Above left: *The aviator, Mr Claude Grahame-White, who flew 113 miles across England.*

Above: *Alcock and Brown*

Left: *Taking aboard supplies for the second part of the flight: filling the petrol-tank of Mr Grahame-White's biplane.*

Chapter Four

Dutch Courage
1903-1914

© Illustrated London News

© Illustrated London News

*The Peking to Paris motor ride – Coolies
drawing one of the cars by means of ropes
after one of the many adventure
incidents to the remarkable journey.*

*Henry Farman's record-breaking flight of
112 miles in 1909.*

At an international oil conference in Berlin towards the end of the 19th century, one of the chief delegates asked Fred Lane the identity of a surprisingly 'young fellow' whom he had noticed at the conference table. 'A Dutchman named Deterding,' Lane answered. 'You don't know him yet, but you soon will. He is the coming man!'

Born in 1866, Henri Deterding – managing director of Royal Dutch from 1901 to 1936 – was 13 years younger than Marcus Samuel. Deterding's father, a sea captain, died when Henri was young, and the boy received little formal education. Nevertheless, he had an innate brilliance, bordering on genius, with book-keeping and accountancy. It was this which prompted Jean Kessler to take him on in 1895, and make him Royal Dutch's marketing director in 1896, at the age of 30. Deterding was not an easy colleague; but from the point of view of Royal Dutch, his appointment was the best decision Kessler ever made. Without his influence, Royal Dutch would almost certainly have become, early on, a subordinate part of Marcus's rambling, rather amateurish empire. In 1896-97, when Kessler was discussing a possible amalgamation with Marcus and Sam Samuel, it was Deterding who (at long distance, by cable and letter) argued vehemently against the suggestion. He was not opposed to amalgamation as such, but to the timing. Likewise, in 1898, when Royal Dutch was struggling to survive the drying-up of its oilwells, it was Deterding who established its Far Eastern distribution and sales network, and who maintained passionately that the company must remain independent. In 1901, Deterding's appointment as managing director in succession to Kessler was confirmed. He was still only 35 years old, and he remained in office for a further 35 years – always active, never a figurehead, and consistently utterly dominant.

Physically short, with unnervingly piercing eyes, he was a person of restless disposition, very different from the middle-aged Englishman. He was single-minded, ruthless when necessary (which was often), with a powerful ability to concentrate, and an almost complete lack of tolerance. Somewhat paradoxically (though it often happens with such people), Deterding also had great personal charm – when he chose to use it – and could be extremely likeable.

This was the man against whom Marcus was competing while he was Lord Mayor in 1902-03. They had a link, in the shape of the marketing organization of the Asiatic Petroleum Company (from 2 July 1903 Marcus was its chairman and Deterding its managing director), yet in every other way they remained competitors. Marcus seems scarcely to have realized this. *Turbo,* the third of the original Samuel tankers, carried Asiatic's first consignment of oil, sailing from Singapore to Mauritius and arriving there on 6 August; Deterding, however, did not hesitate to charter cheaper tankers for Asiatic from companies other than Shell. Whenever this happened, Marcus protested, but to no effect; there was nothing in their revised agreement to prevent Deterding doing just that. Nor was Marcus's protest very strong: throughout his year as Lord Mayor he gave very little time indeed to business, chiefly because of the incessant demands of his civic office – but also because he was gaining far more satisfaction there than from his troubled commercial life.

It was nevertheless a crucial year for Shell. Had he been able or willing to take a close, critical and creative look at its affairs, he would have seen that the company was sliding through confusion towards destruction, and he would have done something about it. But he let at least one key opportunity – a proposed marketing alliance with the Nobels and Rothschilds, excluding Royal Dutch – go by, simply

Sir Henri Deterding,
1866 - 1939

because his Lord Mayor's diary was too full for him to see their representatives, though they waited for six days. Another of his decisions in this period, morally sound but commercially disastrous, was to absolve the Guffey Oil Company from its contracted responsibilities. An American legal adviser, taken on to see what could be done about Guffey's inability to deliver, read through the original contract and pronounced it 'incredibly neglectful', containing practically no hope of a successful comeback in law against Guffey in America. If a lawsuit could be served in England, he said, it would be a different matter; yet when the banker Andrew Mellon, Guffey's chairman, personally visited Marcus at The Mote – and thereby ran the serious risk of having a legal summons flung at him – the two men agreed within a few days to cancel the existing contract altogether. Rich as the Mellon family was, enforcement of the contract under English law might have ruined them, and it appears that Marcus had no particular desire to do that. He was not a vindictive man; recognizing that the contract had been made in good faith, he held no personal rancour and did not wish to crush the Mellons. Instead he accepted a new, far smaller contract, for the annual delivery over the next five years of no more than 55,000 tons of various oils; but not even that was fulfilled. Guffey only provided one more cargo of oil to Shell, and that was all.

All this meant that his fleet was severely under-employed, with as many as half its ships laid up. Late in 1903, *Petriana* – one of the comparatively few in use – was wrecked while on passage from Sydney to Melbourne with petroleum. The reef she hit, then known as the Corsair reef, was renamed the Petriana reef: another unwelcome distinction. Meanwhile, the four biggest and newest tankers, purpose-built to carry Guffey's non-existent product, had to be converted by Fortescue Flannery into cattleboats. Carrying beef on the hoof from Texas to Europe, instead of oil, was imaginative and better than nothing; but it was

21 Biliter Street (in the old Marine Exchange Building), offices of the Asiatic Petroleum Company, acquired 1902-1903.

also a humiliating occupation for such ships, whose masters were beginning to see themselves as agents of the highest technology.

In short, Asiatic (which began functioning under Henri Deterding in May 1902, long before its legal structure was complete) should have been an eastern lifeline; Guffey should have been a western one. Now the former proved to be doubtful, and the latter broken. The glass of the future had never been darker.

Shell's AGM of June 1903 had to be postponed for lack of firm figures concerning the Asiatic; all that could be said for sure was that over the preceding 18 months, Shell dividends had averaged less than 1%. Shareholders and the

Early example of a
Royal Dutch Share Certificate.

press were understandably dissatisfied and 'pessimistic rumours' rife; but out of respect for Marcus's role as Lord Mayor, little actual criticism emerged. Once his term of office was over, that changed. The overdue report for 1902 was at last published in mid-December 1903, still with only provisional figures for Asiatic: 'Very unsatisfactory', said the *Daily Mail*. 'Not exactly a report of which Sir Marcus Samuel and his co-directors need feel proud.'

The Financier echoed and enlarged on this, noting that the summer report ('bad') and this winter one ('a great deal worse') had both come out when public holidays were in full swing and few shareholders available to attend the meetings. 'However the directors may try to excuse themselves,' it said, 'they cannot escape the reproach of exceedingly poor management.'

Still worse was to come. At the end of 1904, professional journals were full of acid remarks. The accounts were 'as usual belated...their shareholders are sick of excuses...' 'For all the value the Shell accounts are, the Directors might have saved the money spent in printing them. The Board of the concern would be all the better for a little drill in business principles – from their shareholders.' 'Needless to say, there is no dividend on the Ordinary shares.... We have no faith in the future of the Shell...'

Meanwhile Royal Dutch shareholders were cheerfully receiving a hefty 50% dividend; and by 3 September 1905 the *New York Herald* stated that Standard Oil had 'wellnigh driven the Shell Company to the wall'. Marcus sued the paper, and won, but its report was painfully near the truth. Through a complicated series of manoeuvres involving Standard, the Deutsche Bank, and a European oil marketing organization called PPAG in which both Shell and the bank held shares, Marcus found himself in an inescapable financial dilemma that brought him personally and Shell as a company face to face with ruin. Someone suggested Shell should sell its way out: the Deutsche Bank could buy its PPAG shareholding. The bank agreed – provided it could

buy Shell's PPAG shares at par, and that Shell also sold it its six best tankers at their written-down value after depreciation. To Marcus, this was insupportable, and not only financially. Today, in the Royal Dutch/Shell Group, German-flag vessels follow the British- and Dutch-flag fleets in quantity, value and size of operation, yet in 1906 Marcus was adamant: he did not want to sell his tankers, but if he had to, he certainly did not want them flying the German flag. There was only one course left – Henri Deterding. Royal Dutch and Shell must amalgamate.

Of course it was not a new idea; but in the years since it was first discussed, things had changed – not least the fact that Shell's survival was now at stake, while Royal Dutch was prospering. Marcus decided the best he could pitch for was a 50:50 division, 'neither party' (in a phrase Deterding had often used when negotiating the Asiatic contract) 'to have any advantage over the other'. Deterding dismissed the suggestion immediately. Shell's shares, he pointed out caustically, had slumped from their high of £3 to 23

*Romany, 1908-1918. Built by Armstrong Whitworth, Newcastle, 1902. Bought by Anglo-Saxon 1908. Torpedoed and sunk by **U48** while on passage from Marseille to Port Said in ballast, 27 April 1918.*

shillings (£1.15), and Shell's dividends had only just scraped a piffling 5%; for the same year, Royal Dutch's dividends were expected to be 73%. He would accept a 60:40 division in favour of Royal Dutch, but nothing less.

Early in April 1906, Marcus agreed. There was no other real choice open to him; but it hurt. He had long since sold the traditional family business of making shell-boxes to a relative; now the fleet, named after that business, was going out of his control. With what must have been considerable understatement, he admitted to the press that he was 'a disappointed man'. On 1 January 1907, Shell's shareholders approved the terms of the amalgamation. Two new companies were formed, one (the Bataafsche Petroleum Maatschappij, known as Bataafsche) to handle production, manufacture and refining, and the other, Anglo-Saxon Petroleum, to handle transport and storage. In future the ships would belong to Anglo-Saxon. Asiatic handled the marketing of their cargoes, while Royal Dutch and Shell Transport became holding companies, with 60% and 40% respectively of the two new companies' shares.

Exactly four months later, on 1 May, *Silverlip* (launched by Lady Samuel during that proud, hectic and commercially

calamitous Lord Mayoral year) was lost at sea while on passage from Singapore to the UK with a cargo of petrol. Under Captain Hocken's command, she was in the Bay of Biscay when (as Hocken related) 'a terrific explosion' shook her No 4 tank. The Second Officer, a Mr Pearson, had charge of the deck at the time; Hocken was below. Hurrying at once to the deck, he found that 'in an instant the amidship portion of the great vessel was enveloped in flames.'

There was a rush of fire which leapt to the bridge, the tongues of fire rapidly licking up and consuming all the woodwork and canvas fittings....Then quickly followed the sound of rending and tearing as the decks of the vessel and her side plates were split apart. To reach the bridge I had to make my way through a living wall of flame....so dense was the smoke, and so overpowering the fumes from the burning oil, that I was almost overcome. As it was, I encountered the horrible spectacle of the already charred remains of one of the crew, so disfigured and burnt in that short space of time as to be unrecognizable. A glance around the ship convinced me that there was not the slightest semblance of hope of saving the vessel...

Silverlip had seven tanks separated by bulkheads, with each being divided into two compartments. With her cargo, she had been worth about a quarter of a million pounds; but one after another, the tanks exploded.

> *The flames attained a height of 70 to 80 feet, and, when there was an explosion, must have shot up over 100 feet....There was never any chance of subduing it.*

Ordering his men to abandon ship, Hocken had to rush through the fire again to join his crew at the three steel lifeboats, located aft; his clothes were smouldering from the heat, and his large beard, once neat and trim, caught fire and was burned from his face. Fortunately another steamer was only ten miles away, and, seeing what was happening, reached *Silverlip* in about an hour, and took in survivors. But of the crew of 53, five had died, including the Chief Engineer, a Mr Bell; and of course the ship and her cargo were a total loss.

No shipowner could ever wish to hear or impart such news; yet barely three months later, at Shell's AGM on 29 July, Marcus had to tell shareholders not only about the *Silverlip* tragedy, but also about the definite trade figures which had just come from the Asiatic. To him personally, these were just as painful, twisting the knife of amalgamation further; for they showed that Shell's profits during the preceding year had been a good deal better than imagined – to the extent that had they been known earlier, the amalgamation on Deterding's terms might not have been essential. It was noted that providing these accounts had been Deterding's responsibility. Strangely, for someone so gifted with figures, he had consistently failed to provide them; yet had they been given, they could have proved crucial to deciding the proportion of shares held in the new Group by the two parent companies: it could have been not 60:40 in favour of Royal Dutch, but 50:50 – 'neither party to have any advantage over the other'. Had Deterding pulled a fast one? If so, Marcus did not record any such thought, though his unhappiness was plain; and anyway, for better or worse, the amalgamation was done.

However, Marcus was certain – and said so in his chairman's address – that in Britain's national terms, the amalgamation was for the worse; and he blamed the Admiralty. Having consistently refused his proposals for a safe supply of fuel-oil to the Navy, they, he asserted, were guilty of 'the folly, nay, I will say the crime, of compelling a British company to part with property [Shell's East Indian oil-bearing territories] of vital import for the future of naval warfare'. This, he was sure, would be 'bitterly regretted'. He was right.

On quaysides and jetties in the Far East, the Middle East, Africa, Europe and Britain, sharp-eyed observers could see evidence of the change, because the livery of the tankers – their house flags and funnel patterns – had been altered. For their first five years, as ships belonging to the Samuel brothers personally, their flags had been white, quartered by a blue vertical cross, with a red circle in the centre and 'S. S. & Co.' (the initials of the brothers' Japanese company) in the cantons. The funnels at that time had been yellow with a black band around the top, displaying the flag design – minus the initials – on the side (see page 28). For the following ten years (the period of Shell Transport's independent existence), the flag remained the same, but the funnels were slightly different: the black band was removed, so that they were now bright yellow from top to bottom, with the flag design replicated fully, including the initials S. S. & Co., on the side. In 1907, though, the flag changed subtly but definitely. Still with

The case-oil ship **Havre, 1912-1942. Built by W. Gray & Co., 1905. Bought by Anglo-Saxon 1912. Torpedoed by U-431 off Tobruk, 10 June 1942.**

its white background and red central circle, the blue quartering cross was now diagonal, from corner to corner, instead of vertical, and the initials had gone altogether. As for the funnels, they remained yellow; the black band around the top was restored, and the flag design on the side was removed completely.

This new livery remained in use for 38 years, until the end of World War Two. There was a degree of lucky coincidence in its creation, because prior to the amalgamation, Royal Dutch's own smaller tanker fleet had sported yellow funnels with their red-white-blue house flag on the side. But coincidental or not, the new livery was well thought out – different, yet not too different;

new, yet not completely unfamiliar. Strictly speaking, the ships – whether originally Dutch or originally British – were now Anglo-Saxon tankers, owned by a company which was part of the new Royal Dutch/Shell Group. (The term 'the Group', still in constant worldwide use, began very soon after the amalgamation.) From the customers' point of view, however, the important thing was – and is – not merely the ownership or shore management of the vessels, but their speed, punctuality, reliability and economy as carriers; so to anyone who saw it in 1907, the new livery signalled continuation rather than transformation, and helped maintain confidence in the tankers' trusted service.

Shoreside, however, there *was* a transformation, and even Marcus was soon happy to acknowledge that it was actually all to the company's benefit. Following the amalgamation, he had gone into retirement, defeated, disappointed and disgruntled, only to find to his surprise that his influence was undiminished. Managing the business from London, Henri Deterding was scrupulous in providing Marcus with regular briefings and in consulting him on any strategic decisions. There was more to this than courtesy, or the kindness of keeping an ex-rival happy: Deterding knew perfectly well that Marcus's good will was vital to the company's smooth and successful running, that his name still carried considerable sway in commercial circles, and that his connections were invaluable. But even if those factors had not been present, Deterding would probably have done the same anyway; neither he nor Marcus had ever been inclined towards destructive monopoly, or to grinding a defeated opponent into the dust. Indeed, their attitude was very much the contrary, as Deterding himself spelled out a few years later. Referring to Standard Oil, he said: 'Their system is to crush competition....'

Because of this, many producers are at a standstill, many refineries are ruined, while subsidiary industries cannot make progress. Everywhere where we come we bring our experience, our work and our capital, and we are happy when we are received as sincere and faithful allies, who succeed in finding a satisfactory profit for ourselves, as well as assuring prosperity and progress for our neighbours, thanks to the natural riches of the country, the work of the population side by side with us, and a community of interests and reciprocal good feeling.

Originally no more than a shared characteristic of the two leaders, this inclina-tion towards mutually beneficial co-operation may sound Utopian; nevertheless, today it is still stated Group policy. No doubt it does not always work out perfectly, but generally, it does work well. After all, trading is much more likely to succeed in a harmonious atmosphere of mutual benefit – and is much more enjoyable as well.

Such was the situation that Marcus found a few months after the amalgamation: business life was once again profitable and fun. Within a year, Shell's share price had recovered from its low of 23 shillings (£1.15) to 43 shillings and ninepence (£2.19), and at the 1908 AGM Marcus paid his new partners a warm tribute. Reminding shareholders that their original directors were now a minority, he described Deterding as 'a gentleman who is nothing less than a genius', and added:

It is due to our Dutch colleagues that we have never had any difference with them, that the greatest weight is given to our views, and I have absolute faith that the future of the business is in safe hands.

He also found many enjoyable, spectacular opportunities to publicize what was rapidly becoming the tankers' most famous and widely used cargo, petrol. The Shell brand was used in the Peking to Paris car race of 1907; by Henry Farman in his record-breaking flight of 112 miles in 1909; by Claude Grahame-White in a flight from London to Manchester in 1910, and by Captain Scott in the Antarctic expedition that same year; in cross-Channel flights, and flights from London to Paris; and, in 1919, by Alcock and Brown in the first non-stop trans-atlantic flight.

Once again the fleet began to grow, as increased demand (prompted largely by the burgeoning motor-car industry) overtook available tanker tonnage. In 1908, *Romany*

Captain Robert Falcon Scott, C.V.O., R.N.

SS Fuh Wo: *built 1879, Shanghai; speed 7.5 knots; gross tonnage 608; deadweight 380.*

was bought, and *Patella* and the second *Conch* (both of 7,700 dwt) were ordered. *Romany* soon became the first Shell tanker to deliver petrol from the Dutch East Indies to California. (Before the outbreak of the First World War, Group companies had sold ten million gallons of the product there.) Between 1910 and 1914, Anglo Saxon bought no fewer than ten dry cargo ships (*Anamba, Fuh Wo, Nord, Castor, Unda, Min, Siam, Havre, Cyrena* and *Physa*) for carrying case-oil. These – the first such purchases since 1899 – demonstrated that in ports without bulk handling facilities, the market for case-oil was still very much alive; but they were all quite small vessels, averaging

The Growth of Diesel Power

Marcus's enthusiasm for the diesel engine was matched by his impatience. He genuinely wanted Shell to provide a service of national value to the Royal Navy; he also naturally hoped to win a contract as supplier of liquid fuel to the Navy; and he was rightly convinced of the diesel engine's potential value. However, it was still, then, more a potential than a real value. The Admiralty needed 6,000 or more horsepower per shaft to propel their heavy capital ships, but the diesels of the day could manage only 250-300 HP per cylinder. Nine or ten cylinders were (and still are) normal, with a maximum of 12 – but providing the power to meet the Admiralty's requirements would have meant a minimum of 20 cylinders per shaft, and even a small warship would have needed an unmanageably large array of diesel engine cylinders. During the First World War, submarines – despite their modest size and surface speed – still required up to 900 HP per shaft; it was their operators who knew the dubious joys of nursing the diesel engine through infancy.

It was 1957-58 before development produced the 1,000-horsepower cylinder. With this, manageable engines could be built for ships of 20,000 dwt with a service speed of 15 knots. Not until 1965 was the 2,000-horsepower cylinder achieved, and the new hull sizes and service speeds then being contracted for crude carriers required engine powers at the top limit of, or above, what was obtainable from the engine makers. This remained true through to the mid-1970s. For Shell's product carriers since the H-Class, with engine powers between 9,000 and 15,000 HP, diesel engines have been the rule.

The continued development of the large diesel since the mid-1960s has been truly impressive. The engines of the time could manage 2,000 HP per cylinder, provided a propellor speed not less than about 90 rpm was acceptable. Higher levels of cylinder pressure charging and further improvement in fuel injection technique have taken the 'per cylinder' power beyond 3,000 HP at the sedate 60 rpm propeller speed desirable in large tankers and bulkers for good propulsion efficiency. (A similar engine turning a fast container ship propellor at 90 rpm would be producing above 4,000 HP per cylinder.) In terms of torque, therefore – a true yardstick of engine muscle – output from the large slow-revving marine diesel has more than doubled in the two decades since the 1970s.

about 1,745 grt each. (The largest, *Physa*, was 3,899 grt, and the smallest, *Min* – perhaps an apt name – only 540.) But just as Marcus had seen back in the days before 1892, it was the bulk ships which carried the big business.

In 1912 Anglo-Saxon's shopping list included seven new deep-sea tankers – *Arca*, *Donax*, *Eburna*, *Mitra*, *Natica*, the second *Turbo* and *Ranella* – which averaged 7,048 dwt or 6,230 grt each. (Every one of these came from yards in Jarrow, Wallsend or Sunderland; indeed, so many of the fleet's early ships came from the same area that Anglo-Saxon was unofficially known as the Anglo-Geordie Paraffin Oil Company.) All were powered by oil-fired steam reciprocating engines, and, being British-registered ships, they all naturally flew the Red Ensign. More than a year before, however, at the end of 1910, a Group ship named *Vulcanus* had established another global first: the use of diesel motors in an ocean-going vessel.

With Grahame-White's French flight and Captain Scott's Antarctic expedition taking place in 1910 as well, it was a proud time for Shell ships; today in Shell Tankers (U.K.) Ltd, the pioneering *Vulcanus* is fondly recalled as another historic milestone for the company. But like the company legend concerning *Murex*, this is not quite right. Certainly she was a Shell ship, but a quirk of legal necessity meant that she flew not the British but the Dutch national flag. Even so, precisely because of her flag, and her motors as well, she is important in the history of Shell's British tanker fleet. Both relate directly to Marcus's unremitting battle with the Admiralty, and to the fundamental reason for the existence, post-amalgamation, of Shell's British fleet; so it will soon be worth spending a moment with each of these. First, though, a jump back in time, to the year 1903.

Despite the farcical outcome of the *Hannibal* trial in 1902, and despite every official discouragement, Marcus did not cease to offer the Admiralty new ideas. In 1903 (four years before the amalgamation) a new analysis of his

MS Vulcanus: *built 1910, 1,194dwt, speed 7 knots, the world's first ocean-going motor vessel.*

Kutei oil had revealed that it was exceptionally high in toluene content, bearing as much as 10% of the chemical, essential to the manufacture of tri-nitro-toluene – the high explosive, TNT. Immediately, he wrote to the Admiralty to let them know of this exceedingly valuable military resource, emphasizing that it lay in territory controlled by a British company. The Admiralty replied almost as quickly. For reasons essentially the same as those for resisting a change to oil-powered ships, they did not want the toluene. Never mind that the German arms firm, Krupps, did want it, and soon began buying it; never mind that the French army and navy followed suit. Except for Admiral Fisher, no one in Britain seriously thought that there would be a major war inside the next 15 years or so, and for the time being, Britain's own small but secure production of toluene from coal tar was quite enough for foreseeable needs, with the added benefit of supporting the domestic coal industry.

Admiralty officials had always been sceptical of

statistics showed that for any given voyage, she needed to carry, by weight, only one-fifth of the fuel that a coal-fired steamship of similar size would require. Likewise, instead of the 16 engine-room staff that the owner of an equivalent coal-fired ship would have to employ, *Vulcanus* needed only five. Assuming such ships could run without too many technical problems, a motor vessel's economic advantages for a commercial company were obvious, and (as Marcus learned from Admiral Lord Fisher – he was made a peer in 1909) other constructional and strategic advantages would apply if the Royal Navy had such ships.

As for *Vulcanus*'s Dutch flag, that too became part of Marcus's armoury in his fight with the Admiralty. Describing the amalgamation of Shell and Royal Dutch, Marcus told Their Lordships:

Our Dutch friends show extreme broadmindedness insofar that it was on my suggestion that the whole of the fleet of tank steamers and the whole of the installations are run by a British company. ...It would have been a deep grief to me if I had not succeeded in arranging with our Dutch friends that the fleet should be under the British flag. The Dutch company very kindly and very wisely consented.

Marcus's claims; in 1903, no doubt the still recent memory of *Hannibal* strengthened their prejudice. But prejudice it was. In Marcus's position, many other people would have thrown up their hands in dismay and disgust, and resolved never again to have anything to do with those officials. Yet in 1912, with *Vulcanus* firmly in commission, there he was again: as ever, firm in his views; as ever, insistent that they should be heard, for the good of the country; and in the hearing – as ever, unsuccessful.

Here we return to *Vulcanus*, her diesel engine, and her Dutch flag. To begin with her engine: as far as ships were concerned, the key point of the diesel internal combustion engine (compared to a steam engine) was and is its much greater efficiency, and therefore economy. *Vulcanus* (even for the time, a small ship – 1,194 dwt) was built in Amsterdam by the Netherland Shipbuilding Company, with a six-cylinder Werkspoor engine fitted aft. Her bridge was amidships, and she had a 25-foot forecastle and a 48-foot poop deck – an early model of the 'three-island' superstructure which would become the norm for tankers. She proved capable of undertaking voyages as long as 88 days without refuelling; and no less importantly, typical

So they had; yet though there was certainly wisdom, it was not a matter of gracious broadmindedness or kindness on the part of the Dutch: it was pure commercial common sense. Though the Imperial German Navy was growing rapidly, with the United States Navy not far behind, the British Royal Navy was still far and away the most powerful armed fleet in the world. Likewise, the British merchant shipping register was the world's largest, and every ship in it could be assured of two things which no foreign registered ship could take for granted: undisputed access to any port in the entire British Empire, and the Royal Navy's protection in time of trouble.

He had already told the Institute of Naval Architects that he was convinced 'engines of the diesel type are going to take the place of steam', that 'anyone who goes on building steam engines with the knowledge now afforded will only court disaster', and that Shell would positively 'never build another steamer'. With the Admiralty he was just as emphatic. On 19 November 1912 he sat on one side of a 'big round table' facing members of the Royal Commission on Fuel and Engines, and threw almost all commercial caution to the wind. In the course of a long, robust interview, there were a few business secrets he did not impart, but only a few; what came to the fore was Sir Marcus Samuel as a dedicated British patriot, urgently desiring that his knowledge, experience, enthusiasm, drive, connections and capabilities should be exploited to the full for the national benefit.

Together, the commissioners and he reviewed virtually the whole of the relationship between himself and the Admiralty. They analysed every aspect, pondered every prospect. By the end of an arduous day Marcus had told the commissioners why they should use diesel engines, why they should have oil, how much they should have, how they should store it, where they should buy it from, and how they should deliver it to their ships. This did not necessarily mean Shell every time, either as supplier or carrier: he explained how a government purchaser could sometimes find a better buy, and how government ships could sometimes offer better terms of carriage. Commercially, such advice was against his own interests, and those of Shell; yet he gave it nonetheless, and forcefully, because when it came to naval matters, he had only one concern – Britain's best national interest.

He might as well have saved himself the effort. His old friend Fisher was chairman of the board – it was he who arranged for Marcus to be present – and skilfully directed the questioning down avenues both he and Marcus knew were important. But Fisher's friendship could be a mixed blessing. 'I trust you will *rub it in*', he had written privately to Marcus, 'that for the first time in Sea History the British Admiralty is not leading the way but following the Germans in the most momentous advance of modern times in Internal Combustion Propulsion and the exclusive use of fuel oil! *The present Admiralty officials are simply damned fools!* Timid as rabbits and silly as ostriches! I told Winston this.'

Winston Churchill was then First Lord of the Admiralty, the Royal Navy's civilian head. Before long he took a distinct dislike to Marcus. In the years between the *Hannibal* trial and the *Vulcanus* launch (specifically, from October 1904 to January 1910), Fisher had been First Sea Lord – the Admiralty's most senior active officer. Those five years had been the most turbulent the Royal Navy had known for a century, because Fisher, given his chance, had put into effect many of the iconoclastic reforms which he (against enormous opposition) had long favoured. Nothing was sacrosanct to him if it prevented the Royal Navy from being anything less than the most efficient fighting force on any ocean in the world. Under his rule, ships were scrapped wholesale; ancient social and professional distinctions within the Navy, revered because of their very age, were thrown out. Without consideration for personal feelings, disciplines were ditched, manoeuvres remoulded, though they had been in force for four generations; and in that great age of naval reform – most of it essential, and all of it contentious – some said hooray, and many others, with their careers and status cracked and tarnished, bayed in revengeful defiance. To be known as his friend could therefore be as much a drawback as an advantage; and it can hardly be a coincidence that when the

Winston Churchill as First Lord of the Admiralty.

Anamba: *typical of the company's Far East case-oil ships. Served Shell safely, reliably and profitably for 21 years.*

First Lord, Churchill, was asked questions in the House of Commons about oil and the Royal Navy, one of the opening questioners was Admiral Lord Charles Beresford, MP, whose personal loathing of Fisher was second to none.

Despite Marcus's efforts (and those of Deterding, who testified to the commission as well), Shell had not been asked for a single ton of fuel oil by the Admiralty between 1907 and 1911. In 1912, the company supplied 14% of the Navy's oil needs, and in 1913, though Admiralty demand increased by 150%, the proportion of purchases from Shell dropped to 12% of the whole. The Group's successful explorations for oil had expanded worldwide in those years: from Romania in 1907 to Russia and British Borneo in 1910; on, under the direction of Mark Abrahams, to Egypt in 1911, a country then ruled by a British governor general; onward again to Oklahoma in 1912; onward further to Mexico, Trinidad and California in 1913; and onward further still to Venezuela in 1914. From one source or another, therefore, Marcus Samuel and Henri Deterding could (and did) guarantee to supply all British naval oil in peace or war. The Egyptian fields, Gemsah and Hurghada, were of special strategic and commercial interest. Located respectively 180 and 210 miles south of Suez, close to the Red Sea, they were firmly within the British sphere of influence. Egypt became a British protectorate in 1914; freight costs from there to Britain were comparatively low; and the route was well guarded by the Royal Navy. These were almost exactly the criteria Churchill had laid down in

1913, when he said that a safe oil supply should come 'from sources under British control or British influence and along those sea routes which the Navy can most easily protect'. Hurghada was particularly productive (by 1914, 80,000 tons of oil were flowing from it annually) and offered a natural dovetail for the company and the government; yet Churchill remained unconvinced. Equally mistrustful both of the Group's foreign connections and of what he believed to be its potential stranglehold on prices, he judged that the government should have its own oil company; and in May 1914, the government bought 2,000,000 shares in the Anglo-Persian Oil Company (now BP), gaining two seats on its board.

The Times was baffled, observing that this simply did not conform to Churchill's own criteria of 1913, and Marcus was exasperated. In a long letter published in the *Daily Telegraph* on 9 June 1914, he pointed out that the government would now have to get into the whole business of refining oil, and selling those fractions it did not need. Worse: for British naval needs, the Persian (now Iranian) fields were 'very badly situated geographically'. Freight costs would inevitably be higher than from Egypt or even Trinidad, 'and', Marcus warned, 'we may well see the state of things that whilst the British Government is drawing its supplies from fields under this disadvantage, the German, French and Italian Navies will obtain their supplies from British Possessions!' Barely two months later, the First World War began.

Delphinula: *built 1908 by Armstrong Whitworth, Newcastle . . .*

. . . torpedoed 24 August 1918 by U63 in the Mediterranean while on passage from Naples . . .

. . . and later beached in Suda Bay.

Chapter Five
Those In Peril
1914-1919

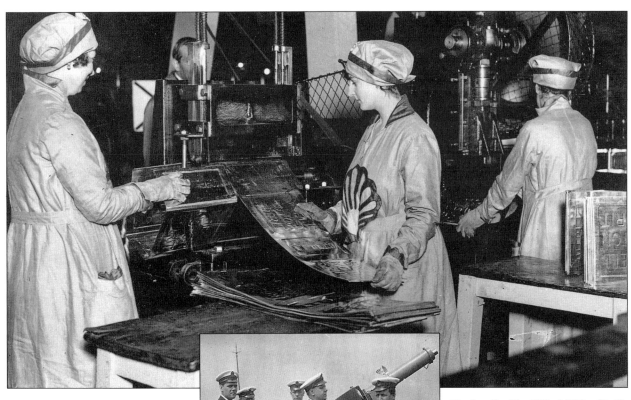

St Helen's Court, London.
A gun-crew on the roof at
Shell's offices, during the
First World War.

During the First World War Shell
organised the supply of petrol for
the fighting services. In 1916,
when the U-boat offensive was at
its height, a petrol distribution
plant was moved to Rouen in
France, and special petrol-can
factories built at Calais and
Rouen staffed by French women
trained at the main Shell
can-making factory at Fulham.

If nothing else, Marcus Samuel now had the opportunity to prove the truth of what he had been saying for years past: that in time of national emergency, Shell and its ships should be regarded as an adjunct of government, available for whatever purpose they were best suited, in whatever place they were most urgently needed. During the 1914 AGM, when the wounds of his latest rejection by the Admiralty were still open, he made this readiness clear to the shareholders. Acknowledging that their company had many grievances against individuals in government, he affirmed that 'under no circumstances whatever' would these grievances be remembered 'to the injury of the British Empire'.

'In spite of what has occurred,' he continued, 'such service, advice, or assistance as we can possibly render to the Admiralty will be freely, willingly, disinterestedly, and always at their disposal...' Then he added drily: 'if they choose to avail themselves of it.'

On the day that war was declared (4 August 1914), Marcus stated at once that Shell would not profiteer from the hostilities. This seemed such a ridiculous thing to say that hardly anyone outside the company believed him, and newspapers made a good many sarcastic comments. Over the war years, these seemed justified: at the same 1914 AGM, Shell shareholders had received a record 35% dividend, and thereafter profits remained high. Attempts were made to extend the capital base and so reduce the percentage of profit – in 1917, a million shares were issued at par; in 1918, £3 million of the reserve fund was capitalized with a bonus issue to shareholders of three shares for every five held – but the 35% dividend continued. Marcus found himself in the position (odd for the chairman of a successful business) of feeling obliged to apologize for and explain the profits, most of which came from outside the British Empire altogether, and were often simply the result of altered exchange rates.

St. Helen's Court Bulletin.

No. 1.—Vol. I.   LONDON, 21st NOVEMBER, 1914.   Price ONE PENNY.

Editorial.

A FOREWORD.

IN submitting to our readers the first number of the St. Helen's Court Bulletin we think it advisable to explain that the inception of this unpretentious enterprise is primarily due to a desire to enable the staffs of the combined Companies to obtain news from time to time regarding their colleagues who have joined the colours.

No less than 249 St. Helen's Court employés have taken ... in defence of their country. This is in itself a splendid ... Directors are legitimately proud. ... force stay behind. But one and ... their more favoured brethren, ... columns, with the liveliest

musketry, etc. On returning I was posted to another company. This was a training company, which means that it will be the next to go to the front and reinforce the line battalions. This meant very hard work, especially as two days after the Major in command of the company fell ill, and for the past three weeks I have been in command with only three subalterns to help me instead of four. We are on parade at 7 o'clock and go on then until 8 p.m. without a break, doing route marches of anything from 15 to 20 miles, attacks, entrenching, bayonet fighting, fire control, etc. Then on three nights a week we are out from 6 p.m. to 9 p.m. or even later on night operations. The gap between 8 o'clock and 6 o'clock is well filled with my work as O.C. of the company. The men are all awfully keen to get on, and, of course, that helps one a great deal. We have been under canvas until the end of last week, and found it extremely cold and wet. We are now in huts in this battery on detachment duty. I hope to be out within the next two weeks. Everyone has, of course, been inoculated against enteric, and has also been vaccinated. It is all very painful too, as there is no time to go on light duty for two or three days to give it a chance. The men are all very cheerful and will be fine chaps to have ... one when it comes to a scrap. I am afraid this ... rather a rambling letter, but it is close on midnight, ... day's work, so you must excuse me. I will ... soon. if of interest to you.

But there is, anyway, a big difference between making profits and profiteering, and from the outset Shell voluntarily accepted loss-making arrangements as well: first and foremost, in the tanker fleet. Freight charges began to rise rapidly as soon as the war started. Nevertheless, almost all Shell tankers were immediately chartered to the government at Blue Book rates – fixed pre-war rates which varied only according to the tonnage, design and age of the ship concerned. Any company which did this was guaranteed to sustain a loss on the deal, because to replace the charters to government with other shipping for its own needs meant chartering neutrals, at rates which were soon four times higher than the Blue Book. Because of this, most shipowners naturally preferred to wait until their vessels were requisitioned before footing such potentially ruinous bills themselves; and Shell was the only oil company to put its tanker fleet forward without compulsion.

The company positively encouraged its employees of military age to join the armed forces, and many of them did so, knowing that if they survived the war, a post in Shell would be kept or created for them. Some joined the Royal Navy, the Royal Naval Reserve (which put them just as actively at sea as their RN counterparts) or the nascent Royal Naval Air Service; but by no means everyone went to sea. Names of Shell personnel occur in an astonishing variety of Rolls of Honour: those of the Royal Flying Corps and its successor, the Royal Air Force; the American, the New Zealand and the Australian Expeditionary Forces; and no fewer than 69 different regiments or battalions of the British Army. (Two of Marcus's children, Gerald and Walter, joined the Army. Walter, who won the Military Cross, eventually succeeded his father as chairman of the company and as Viscount Bearsted; Gerald was killed in action in 1916. Similarly, Henri Deterding had efficiently and thoroughly Anglicized himself, and his son fought in the British Army.) Wherever Shell people went to serve, their colleagues in the London offices (by then based in St Helen's Court in the City of London) remembered them

and worked for their support. Every month each man was sent a parcel of food, clothing and little luxuries collected by those too young or too old to fight; and to keep them in touch with each other, and with company developments, they were also sent the *St Helen's Court Bulletin*, an in-house magazine created for the purpose. These small echoes of normality were disproportionately important in maintaining their morale – 'I find it difficult', wrote one, 'adequately to express my appreciation of the kind interest you take in us fellows'. 'It is particularly pleasant,' agreed another, 'when with all our new pals, to have so many remembrances of old friends and times as the *Bulletin* always contains. Very kindest regards to you and all friends at St Helen's Court...'

Those who joined the Navy fully anticipated that sooner or later there would be a second Trafalgar; that the Germans would be beaten at sea as thoroughly as Nelson had beaten the French and Spanish in 1805; and that if they personally were lucky, they would take part in 'a glorious victory'. Day after day they looked forward to it with complete confidence; yet it never came. Instead, to their dismay, they found that practically all the fighting was taking place on land, and in the *St Helen's Court Bulletin* they read with jealousy and embarrassment of the deeds of their colleagues, enduring the unspeakable conflicts ashore. But over the end of May and beginning of June 1916, some of them finally had their chance; and on 8 June, an exhausted but elated Sub-Lieutenant named P. S. Robinson wrote:

> *On return to our base the only mail for me was a copy of the Bulletin, and for the first time since I joined the R.N.R. I read through the correspondence from friends serving in the Army without feeling a certain amount of envy....Now I feel at last that I have assisted to do something in the war more than sentry duty.*

A view of Shell's head office in St Helen's Court.

Though the name of his ship was struck out by the censor, the anonymous vessel was part of the Grand Fleet based in Scapa Flow, and had just taken part in the Battle of Jutland. 'Difficult to describe', said Robinson apologetically, then invoked 'the well known phrase of Lord Fisher's... "Short, but Hell while it lasts."

To anyone familiar with the history of that inconclusive conflict – an important strategic victory for the British, but a notable tactical victory for the Germans – Robinson's brief account is a remarkably accurate reflection both of the constraints of battle and the misapprehensions within the Grand Fleet. The first news of contact with the enemy, by distant British cruisers and battlecruisers, had reached his ship about 3 pm on 31 May. For nearly three hours thereafter, 'the whole British battle fleet was moving towards the "fighting district" at full tear. It really was a sight that will impress me for a lifetime.' About 4.15, still far away, 'we saw through the haze the flashes of guns, and began to make out the outlines of our own battlecruisers. We sounded off action at 5.45...'

For the next quarter of an hour he was still able to look outside, so he 'saw the first shots from the German guns pitched first short of us and then just between us and the ship ahead... It must have been fully ten minutes after I left the deck that we fired our first shot, and that was the worst suspense of the whole lot.'

After that, though, he was so involved with his work that he could not see anything outside at all; and that, perhaps surprisingly, was far and away the most common experience – for even in a battleship with some thousands of men on board, there were very few indeed (maybe three dozen at most) whose action stations put them in a position to see anything of what was going on beyond their own particular steel box.

Even those who should have been able to see out very often could not, because of gunsmoke, and, as happened at Jutland, mist and the onset of night. Nevertheless, in the British fleet everyone was perfectly sure that the Germans were using submarines, and Robinson's ship (so he reported) had to manoeuvre at least once to avoid an attack from one. He also described 'most of the British losses' to mines; yet there were no submarines on either side at Jutland, and the major British losses were caused by hits leading to internal explosions due to faulty design. Robinson was certainly right, though, when he added: 'How we [his own ship] managed to pull through without damage or a single casualty is a marvel.'

At least two other Shell men were present in this, the German Navy's only fleet action, and the last such action ever fought by the Royal Navy. Their names were J. H. Young and A. Kell. Young, who in peace used to serve in SS *Donax*, was fighting in one of the fast battleships supporting the battlecruisers, and was killed in the opening part of the battle. His body was taken back to Scapa and buried there. Kell (who had come from *Euplectela*, one of the Samuels' original ships) was in a destroyer, among those which continued the fighting after nightfall. He survived Jutland – he and Robinson met on shore – and 'is writing to you as soon as he has the chance.' But he never did have the chance. Somewhere, somehow, he was killed too, and with J. H. Young, his name became one of the 109 on Shell's Roll of Honour.

As the war proceeded, there was no doubt in the collective mind of the Allies (particularly of the French) of the vital need for oil. Marshal Ferdinand Foch halted the German advance at the Marne in 1914, fought at Ypres in 1915 and the Somme in 1916, was Chief of the French General Staff in 1917 and commander of the unified French, British and American armies in 1918. Not only a man who knew what he was talking about, he could also turn a memorable phrase, declaring on one occasion: 'My centre is giving way, my right is falling back. Situation excellent. I attack.'

Just as succinctly, though less cheerfully, it was also he who said, 'We must have oil, or we shall lose the war'; and it was Georges Clemenceau, Premier of France from 1917, who said, 'Oil is as necessary as blood.'

The same recognition remained after the war: 'The Allies', remarked Lord Curzon, 'floated to victory on a wave of oil.' Moreover, when Foch, Clemenceau and Curzon spoke of 'oil', they meant not just fuel-oil, but all the other derivatives of crude petroleum as well; and there, Shell's record as a supplier was unequalled.

Writing about Marcus Samuel, Admiral Fisher said, 'Where would we have been in this War but for this Prime Mover?' In 1921, the Group published an account of its war record, proudly entitled *The Shell That Hit Germany Hardest*. Naturally enough, this included an enormous amount of self-congratulation, with many statistics of vast production and delivery, often printed in double size bold type, with a generous sprinkling of exclamation marks. What is perhaps more surprising is that the passing of time has not altered this judgement, except perhaps to strengthen it. In dispassionate assessment of Shell's contribution, a historian of the oil industry as a whole has said simply:

> ...the company became integral to the Allies' war effort; in effect, Shell acted as the quartermaster general for oil, acquiring and organizing supplies around the world for the British forces and the entire war effort and ensuring the delivery of the required products from Borneo, Sumatra and the United States to the railheads and airfields in France. Shell, thus, was central to Britain's prosecution of the war.

This is true. Henri Bérenger, the French Commissioner General for Petroleum, may have been overstating the case when he declared publicly that without Shell, 'the war could not possibly have been won by the Allies'; but if it

An example of an early Shell advertisement (c. 1912).

was an overstatement, it was not a gross one. Elaborating on 'the magnificent efforts made by the Shell Company', Lord Montagu remarked:

> The Germans were keener on sinking vessels conveying oil than on any other ships that sailed the ocean. They realized at the very beginning of the War that the liquid fuel supply was vital to our sea supremacy then, and to our air supremacy later. Without liquid fuel you cannot fly, you cannot use submarines (at least until very lately), and you cannot run the mechanical transport of your Army on land.

Shell was the principal supplier of petrol to the British Expeditionary Force, and until the middle of 1917 the sole supplier of aviation spirit to the Royal Flying Corps. (A pleasant incidental note is that all such fuel had to be supplied in uniform grey cans, so that the user, soldier or airman, could not tell from which company it had come. Shell dutifully supplied both its petrol and its aviation spirit in just such cans; but it is said that until the cans of aviation spirit were repainted with the familiar Shell red, the pilots refused to use them.) Nor was Shell's contribution limited to the fuel derivatives of crude oil. Not for the first time, Marcus put his money where his mouth was, and, since the Admiralty had ignored him, set Shell to distilling toluene in a big way.

Mark Abrahams said later that it had been his idea originally, from a similar action he had had to carry out once in Japan. Henri Deterding agreed to it, of course; it would not have happened otherwise. Certainly it was a shared responsibility and decision, and it gave rise to a quite extraordinary episode: the dismantling in one night (30 January 1915) of an entire refinery, built in Rotterdam by Shell before the war; the transport of all the individually numbered pieces across the Channel the following night; their further transport 150 miles by rail from London to a new site at Portishead in Somerset; and the re-erection of the factory so that, within nine weeks of leaving Rotterdam, the plant was refining toluene from Kutei crude oil. This was passed on to a brand-new factory built by Shell in Oldbury-on-Severn, 12 miles north-east, where it was nitrated into tri-nitro-toluene – 1,300 tons a month.

The overnight dismantling of the Rotterdam refinery, conducted in as much secrecy as possible, involved connivance from the Bataafsche (part of Shell's Dutch arm), and from the Dutch government, both officially neutral. Their status meant that sailings from Rotterdam were still normally announced beforehand, in the peacetime way. But it was suspected that SS *Laertes* (the chartered ship carrying the refinery components) would be attacked by a U-boat, and so her departure time was published as being 24 hours later than was really the case. It was a simple but effective deception: with her valuable cargo, *Laertes* left port a day ahead of her promulgated time, beginning a safe passage to London. Twenty-four hours later, though, at the announced time of her departure, another vessel (named *Moordrecht*, and co-incidentally similar in appearance) left Rotterdam, and was torpedoed at the mouth of the harbour. Today we should perhaps spare a thought for those unintended victims.

During 1915, the Portishead distillery produced about 80% of Britain's total output of toluene. Later in that same year a duplicate pair of factories for refining and nitrating

Dazzle Painting

Often the simplest ideas are the best. Early in the First World War, the British marine artist Norman Wilkinson (then a lieutenant commander in the Royal Naval Volunteer Reserve) came up with an ingenious method of disguising ships at sea: an idea which was so simple that unless you saw it for yourself, it was hard to believe it would work – but it did. He called it dazzle painting.

It involved painting a ship's hull with an apparently random, but actually scientifically worked out, set of stripes, patches, blobs and silhouettes. These muddled the ship's real perspective, so that an onlooker found it very hard even to tell which way the vessel was heading. A single ship could be made to look like two separate ships, one slightly ahead of the other; three real ships in line ahead could be made to look as if they were all going in different directions. On 27 September 1917, when 'the weather was light and visibility good', the officer of the watch in HMS *Martin* wrote a rueful note showing how well the system worked:

were built further north. Between them, in the course of the war, the two sets of plants produced more than 30,000 tons of toluene, which in turn yielded about 60,000 tons of TNT, supplied to British and French alike. Nowadays, some may decry the fact that Shell's crude oil was ever put to such a use; but that comes from a new and quite different context of life, with the grace of nearly 50 years of peace in Europe behind us. Just after the war, when creating Henri Deterding an Officer of the Legion of Honour, Henri Bérenger said that the Anglicized Dutchman was 'known and loved in France' just as much for his supplies of toluene (which 'saved Verdun') as for his charitable endowments 'in our departments devastated by German barbarism'. The Gallic emotions may sound overblown, but the gratitude of the French in particular was deep and genuine; and though the product, high explosive, may be horrible, we too should surely be grateful that through the joint initiative of Marcus Samuel, Mark Abrahams and Henri Deterding, it was made available in a time of such desperate need.

'Sighted *Clam*' – Marcus Samuel's fourth ship – 'about 9 miles distant, 4 points on starboard bow, and for some time could make nothing of her. When about 5 miles distant I decided it was a tug towing a lighter with a short drift of tow rope. The lighter, towing badly and working up to the windward, appeared to be steering on the opposite course. It was not until she was within a mile that I could make out she was one ship, steering a course at right angles, crossing from [our] starboard to port. The dark painted stripes on her after part made her stern appear her bow, and a broad band of green paint amidships looked like a patch of water.'

As if to show he was not the only one to be fooled, the officer added: 'A lightship reported of the same vessel that from 2 to 3 miles distant, the *Clam* appeared as a wreck on her beam ends.'

Example of a dazzle-painted ship. Unfortunately she cannot be identified – but that was the intention.

At the same time as the war was beginning in Europe, the Panama Canal was opened for navigation (15 August 1914), and once again a Shell ship scored a world first, when *Eburna*, travelling from the Caribbean to the Pacific, became the first tanker to pass through the Canal. That, however, was on the peaceful side of the ocean. In European and Middle Eastern waters, whether acting as suppliers in vessels chartered by the company, or as carriers in vessels chartered to the government (and therefore under naval direction), Shell men and Shell tankers faced dreadful risks in their wartime voyages. Aerial warfare at sea was still mercifully in its infancy, but in this motorized, technological war, the tankers were always and everywhere at threat from mines and submarines. Submarines would often attack on the surface rather than from underwater, but until the attack, they, like mines, were invisible, and their very invisibility created a ghastly tension in every voyage. Shipping lanes were well defined, almost inevitably beginning or ending in bottlenecks such as the entrance to a harbour. Such places were easy to sow with mines, and if the mines did not get you, the submarines could – and with its valuable cargo, its weak or non-existent defences and its readily identifiable silhouette, a tanker made a highly attractive target.

Indeed, it is notable that of all the British Shell tankers lost to enemy action, only one, *Eburna*, was mined. (Exactly where and when is not known: Shell's surviving records merely list the event, without date or place. However, she was certainly not sunk by the explosion – she was scrapped in 1931, having been with the company all her 28 working years; so perhaps the damage was not very great.) It is notable, too, that in the first 20 months of the war, there were no recorded attacks on the company's ships. That period ended in the Mediterranean on 3 March 1916, when *Turbo* came under fire from a U-boat. Fortunately, she was one merchant ship which had been given a gun, and she actually managed to fight off her assailant. But in the 32 further months which elapsed before the Armistice, tankers owned or managed by Anglo-Saxon were attacked on 27 separate occasions, in places as far apart as the Orkneys and the Red Sea; and 11 of the ships, totalling 54,947 grt, were sunk.

There were four losses in 1916: *Goldmouth*, 31 March; *Elax*, 10 October; *Murex*'s sistership *Conch*, 7-8 December, with the loss of 28 lives; and the original *Murex* herself, mother of the fleet, on 21 December. Four more followed in 1917: *Turritella*, 27 February; *Telena*, 21 April; *Bullmouth*, 28 April; and *Bulysses*, 20 August. Another three followed in 1918: *Trocas*, 19 January, with 24 dead; *Romany*, 27 April; and *Arca*, 2 October. *Arca* was particularly unlucky: she had already survived an earlier attack, having been torpedoed in the Channel on 6 January 1918. The fatal attack against her took place just five weeks before the Armistice, north-west of Ireland, and her entire crew was killed – 52 officers and men.

In contrast, perhaps the luckiest of all the ships attacked was *Mitra*. On 6 June 1917 she was torpedoed in the Mediterranean, but did not sink. The damage was kept under control, and she managed to reach port under her own steam, only to be torpedoed again nine months later, on 8 March 1918. Yet on that occasion, too, she got back to port, without the loss of a single life either time.

Eleven other ships, owned or managed by Anglo-Saxon, lived through torpedo attacks. Chronologically, these were *Melania*, 2 October 1916; *Ranella*, 14 March 1917; *Fornebo*, 17 June; *Cowrie*, 4 July; *Natica*, 14 August; *Echunga*, 5 September; the second *Silverlip*, 21 October; *Crenella*, 26 November; *Clam*, 5 April 1918; *Strombus*, 4 June; and *Delphinula*, 24 August 1918. But merely listing names and dates conveys nothing of the experience. One has to remember that each of those ships was an individual creation, the result of many months of patient effort in design and building; that each had her own trading pattern and working history, and, like a person, her own character, faults, quirks and virtues; and that each was worked by a crew of about 50 men. Most of those men, too, are now only names on lists; but they all once lived and breathed,

people just as worried and apprehensive as we would be – and often, when it came to a fight, astonishingly brave. Perhaps the story of one of them, who lived through the company's first loss, may stand for all the others.

Ironically, his name was Peace: Davie Peace, 29 years old in 1916. Born in Orkney, he had joined Anglo-Saxon in 1912, and was soon Chief Officer on board the 10,000dwt *Goldmouth*, which at the time of her launch in 1903 was the largest vessel in the fleet. Having taken in a cargo of fuel-oil in Borneo, they were returning to the UK in March 1916, and by the last day of the month had reached a point 60 miles WNW of Ushant, the westerly entrance to the Channel. Only 60 or 70 miles remained to their destination, Falmouth, and as Peace remembered later, 31 March 1916 was 'a lovely, calm spring day'. Slightly ahead of them and on their starboard side was a neutral Norwegian vessel. 'As we passed the Norwegian,' said Peace, 'we had our glasses on her, and we saw two men with a great big white flag, deliberately waving it over the side. We thought nothing of it. It seemed a senseless thing to do.'

*Crenella, 5,478grt (1897) Palmers S.B. & Iron Co. Ltd., Jarrow.
Built as a cargo ship and converted to a tanker: torpedoed by U-101
26 November 1917, but survived. Sold 1920, eventually scrapped
1952.*

In fact the Norwegian sailors, decent souls that they were, were trying to give *Goldmouth* a discreet warning, for on their own starboard side there was a German submarine, *U-44*, lying in wait.

Faster than the Norwegian, *Goldmouth* overtook her shortly; and as she passed, a shell from the surfaced U-boat whistled overhead, signalling the tanker to stop. But *Goldmouth*'s captain, R. L. Allinson, had no intention of doing so until he was absolutely forced; his ship had been given a gun, and though he must have known there was very little hope of success, he decided to fight back. So began an extraordinary two-and-a-half hour battle.

Sending the Chinese crew to relative safety below decks, Allinson ordered the Third Mate to take the wheel and the Second Mate to man the gun, while Davie Peace and he remained on the bridge. A wireless message for help was broadcast, but the nearest friendly warship was 170 miles away, and (as was usual with merchant ships, which could only be given minimal armament from the Royal Navy) *Goldmouth*'s single gun was a three-pounder, a small, old, short-ranged piece, placed there more for morale than as a serious weapon of self-defence. Nevertheless, the Second Mate used it effectively enough to keep the U-boat at a distance – but not a great enough distance. 'He lay outside our range', said Peace ruefully, 'and knocked the stuffing out of us.'

One salvo hit *Goldmouth*'s bunkers and pumps. Another penetrated the wireless room and tore off the leg of R. C. Older, the Wireless Officer. A fragment from another one ripped off the seat of Davie Peace's trousers, an unusually lucky escape; and at last the Chief Engineer telephoned from down below and warned Captain Allinson that if they did not stop, the engines would explode.

When it comes to engines, Chief Engineers are not given to joking or exaggeration. Allinson could either fight to the death or surrender, which was not much of a choice. He ordered the flag to be hauled down, and the ship, Shell's first and largest loss in the war, was captured, torpedoed, and sunk.

Despite the loss of the ship and the various wounds sustained by individuals, at least no lives were lost; and there is an epilogue, part amusing, part well-deserved and honourable. After the ship had been sunk, the crew members were rescued from their lifeboats by a pair of British trawlers, transferred to a frigate, and landed at Penzance. From there the key personnel headed to London as fast as they could, to report to the company's head office. Such was their haste that Davie Peace literally did not have time to change his trousers, and he entered the head office wearing a raincoat. The manager who met him told him to take it off. 'Sir,' said Peace, 'I dare not', and explained why. 'Oh, we can't have that,' the astonished manager exclaimed, and sent him away to buy a new pair of trousers on the firm's account.

A little later came the more public rewards: Chief Officer Peace and Wireless Officer Older were both mentioned in despatches, and Captain Allinson was awarded the DSC – three among nearly 50 wartime distinctions won by Shell personnel.

Goldmouth was not the only Anglo-Saxon tanker to be captured before being sunk. A similar thing happened, twice, to *Turritella*, managed by the company on behalf of the British government. Built in Germany as a dry cargo ship and completed in 1906, this vessel originally belonged to the Hansa Line of Hamburg, when she was known as *Gutenfels*. At the outbreak of war she happened to be in Port Said, where she was promptly taken over by the British authorities, added to their own national register, and given a new name, *Polavon*. In 1916 she was converted for carrying oil by having cylindrical tanks installed inside her holds, and, with the official designation RN Oiler No. 147, was handed over to Anglo-Saxon management. *Turritella* then became her third name. Whether or not it was the bad luck which traditionally is said to follow a change of name without a change of ownership, it was on her maiden voyage as a tanker (Captain T. G. Meadows), from Tarakan and Singapore to the UK, that she was recaptured by the Germans, in the shape of the surface raider *Wolf* (Captain Nerger). Knowing a useful vessel when he saw one, Nerger did not sink *Turritella*, but decided to use her instead as a minelayer. He also decided to rename her. It was as *Iltis*, therefore, that she mined the approaches to Aden, and under the German flag that, only a week later, she was intercepted by HMS *Odin* (Lt Cdr E. N. Palmer, RN), and sunk.

So much for the fortunes, or misfortunes, of war. Apart from her chequered history, though, *Turritella* (or *Gutenfels*, *Polavon* or *Iltis*) was important in the history of Shell tankers because, in her conversion from a dry cargo ship to a tanker, she exemplified further strands in the company's contribution to the Allied victory in the First World War.

The depredations of the U-boats against all British shipping were so terrible that, despite every effort, there was by no means enough fuel-oil coming into Great Britain. As members of a major shipping line, Shell personnel had greater knowledge and understanding of merchant ships' losses than did most civilians, and in the summer of 1915 the company produced another constructive suggestion for the Admiralty: extra oil could be brought into the country using dry cargo merchant vessels' 'double bottoms' – the space between their holds and their hulls, which was normally either empty, or else filled with water ballast.

Shell ships had often used the same technique in the past, as a commonsense method of using space which would otherwise be wasted. But no one had considered its wartime application, and in that context, it was one of those ideas which, once expressed, was blindingly obvious. The originator was Shell's Marine Superintendent, a Dutchman named Cornelis Zulver. Sir Marcus swiftly wrote to the Admiralty describing the system and proposing that, since it would involve shipowners in some expense, it should be adopted as official rather than voluntary policy. While awaiting a reply, he did his best to persuade other owners to follow Shell's lead. Some did, others refused; so, after several weeks, having not heard at all from the Admiralty, he went personally to their offices to find out what was going on. The short answer was, nothing, because the Fourth Sea Lord's secretary had let the letter slip down behind his desk, and had forgotten all about it.

Their Lordships' embarrassment brought immediate approval in principle. In practice, however, the system was not instituted officially until 1917. In April of that year the United States entered the war. Allied shipping losses were climbing to catastrophic levels.

'On the deck of a German U-boat', *by Clause Bergen, (1885-1964), 1918.*
A portent of the future war at sea came in 1914 with the sinking of three armoured cruisers by one U-boat. By 1917 the U-boats were so successful against merchant shipping that in the middle of that year stocks of grain in Britain were down to just six weeks supply. Disaster was only averted by the re-introduction of convoys.

MS Dolphin Shell: (1897-1931) W. Hamilton & Co., Port Glasgow; built as a sailing ship and converted to a tanker, fitted with an oil engine (1918). . .

... and under sail.

During the month, 395 Allied merchantmen totalling 881,027 grt were sunk. Of that total, more than 545,000 grt were British, and all but 4% were sunk by submarines. There was only six weeks' supply of corn left in the country, and Admiral Sir John Jellicoe (who had been First Sea Lord since November 1916) informed the American Rear Admiral William S. Sims that it would soon be impossible for Britain to continue the war. By June the Royal Navy had only ten weeks' supply of oil remaining, and the manoeuvres and exercises of its Grand Fleet had to be restricted.

Jellicoe's gloom had become utter despondency: on 20 June he told the British General Sir Douglas (later Field Marshal Earl) Haig, 'There is no good

Admiral Lord Jellicoe.

discussing plans for next Spring – we cannot go on.'

The following day, 21 June, the double-bottom scheme was put into full operation. It would be an absurd exaggeration to suggest it defeated the U-boats: that was done largely by the introduction, grotesquely belated, of the convoy system, beginning in May 1917. But it is no exaggeration to say that the double-bottom scheme worked tremendously well. Over the remainder of the war, 1,280 ordinary cargo vessels were converted to carry liquid fuel in their double bottoms. Their added capacity was reckoned to be the equivalent of a fleet of at least 100 new tankers, and by the time the Armistice was signed 17 months later, a grand total of 1,014,570 extra tons of liquid fuel had been brought into Britain by that means.

The ingenuity of Shell's Marine Superintendent, Mr Zulver, did not stop there. Searching for other means to bring oil into the country, he also initiated a successful programme (of which *Turritella* was a not very successful part) to convert cargo ships into tankers by putting cylindrical tanks into their holds. These conveyed about 700,000 more tons of oil to Britain in the remainder of the war; and with a third programme, Zulver created one of the most imaginative uses of available resources that one could hope to see.

There were still, in those days, a fair number of wooden or iron sailing ships trading here and there around the world. (One, indeed, had the unnerving experience of finding herself becalmed in the very middle of the Battle of Jutland, with gigantic shells from both the British Grand Fleet and the German *Hochseekriegsflotte* shrieking overhead from one side to the other.) Zulver reasoned that these ships could provide useful hulls; their major drawback was that they were sailers, not steam or motor vessels. Then on 3 March 1918, the new revolutionary government in Russia signed

Scala Shell *(1902-1931), A. McMillan & Sons Ltd., Dumbarton, 1918, converted to a tanker.*

the treaty of Brest-Litovsk, an independent peace treaty with Germany. Earlier on, the Tsarist navy had contracted with the British firm of Vickers for a supply of submarine engines. The treaty left Vickers with these engines on their hands, and Zulver bought some. These were put into a total of eight iron sailing ships bought for the purpose (*Gaper Shell*, *Circe Shell*, *Fiona Shell*, *Horn Shell*, *Ortina Shell*, *Dolphin Shell*, *Myr Shell* and *Scala Shell*). They were small vessels, of course; they averaged just over 2,400 grt, and the largest was 3283 grt. But they all traded successfully both during the war and after it – the longest-lived, *Ortina Shell*, remained in Group use until she was scrapped in 1946. Though in one sense they were a backward step, nevertheless

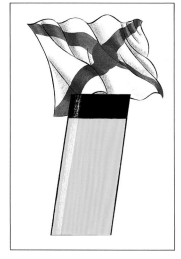

there was something strangely satisfying about them. Being part of their structure, their masts and rigging were often retained, and sometimes their sails as well, for auxiliary use. In the case of *Scala Shell*, only the hull was kept in the conversion: her masts and rigging were entirely removed, with a new superstructure and bridge being placed amidships and her engine and funnel aft; but even she kept her beautiful clipper bow.

Thus, hybrid though they were, these craft all somehow retained the graceful appearance of an earlier maritime age; and at the same time, they used submarine engines to help Great Britain survive the submarines, the most modern and most deadly of all naval weapons.

'A merchant navy fireman at work', *by Henry Marvell Carr (b 1894).*
A fireman – or stoker as he was known in the Royal Navy – would feed around five tons of coal into the furnaces a day. SS Aquitania of 1914 had 184 firemen in her engineering staff of 339. Of the rest, 100 were trimmers – the men who brought the coal from the bunkers.

Chapter Six

Ensuring Shell
1919-1939

Above: *The second Murex, built HM Dockyard, Portsmouth, 1922, 8,887dwt; served the company without incident until scrapping in 1936.*

The vanished insignia of the Eagle Oil Transport Company.

The second *Silverlip*, one of the survivors in Anglo-Saxon's war books, deserves a second mention. She was not owned but managed by Anglo-Saxon; her original owners were the Mexican Eagle Oil Company, founded by Weetman Pearson in 1908. Though he was something of a latecomer to the oil industry, Pearson was one of the first to invest heavily in Mexico; he won his first large contract there (to build the so called 'Grand Canal', draining the marshes around Mexico City) in 1889, when he was only 33 years old. By training and experience he was a civil engineer, but in 1901 he entered the world of oil, buying drilling options on land around San Cristobal, on the Tehuantapec isthmus. In 1909 he bought three coastal tank steamers, but by 1912 these were far too small for his company's needs: as Lord Cowdray (he was ennobled in 1910), he owned 1.6 million Mexican acres producing 20,000 barrels of oil a day, with production only limited by the amount of company-owned shipping available. In 1912, therefore, Cowdray founded the Eagle Oil Transport Company, and ordered for it no fewer than 19 big new ocean-going tankers, nine of 9,000 dwt each and ten of 15-16,000 dwt. All the ships were built in British yards, with the first two (*San Dunstano* and *San Eduardo*) being delivered before 1912 was over.

Every ship in the Eagle fleet was named after a Mexican saint, so they all had the prefix *San*, or, if the saint was female, *Santa*. Looking at the black eagle displayed on their funnels, they were also known unofficially, and much less reverently, as 'the Shite-Hawk ships'; but whatever their appellation, Cowdray's own decisiveness, and the astonishing production speeds of which British yards were capable, meant that by 1914 they formed a notable part of the world deep-sea tanker fleet, and a significant rival to any other tanker company.

One of that first batch was *San Isidoro*, 15,355 dwt, delivered on 18 March 1914. At the outbreak of war, she was sold to the French government and renamed *Dordogne*, then in June 1915 lent to the British Admiralty. It was they who passed her on to be managed by Anglo-Saxon, and Anglo-Saxon (presumably preferring not to use a French name) called her *Silverlip*. Having survived the 1917 submarine attack against her, outside Scapa Flow, she was returned (as *Dordogne*) to the French after the war, and continued in peaceful service until 1940, when she was scuttled in Brest harbour.

She was also the first link (indirect though it was) between Anglo-Saxon and Eagle Oil, a link which developed into a close alliance, and eventually (on 1 January 1960) into the complete union of the fleets.

During the First World War, Eagle, with a smaller fleet than Anglo-Saxon, had suffered a proportionately greater shipping loss, with a total of about 56,000grt sunk. By 1916 Eagle's managers, optimistic about eventual victory, were already planning new construction. At the end of the war, a boom began in trade of every sort, as enormous production resources which had been tied up for years were suddenly released into the marketplace; and in 1919 Eagle started a five-year ship-building programme. This would more than replace its war losses: 25 new ships were to be constructed, doubling the size of the 1914 fleet. The new vessels were to include six tankers of 18-19,000 dwt, which would be among the largest in the world.

At the same time and for the same reasons, Shell embarked on a similar programme of replacement and expansion; but rather than wait for building, they bought existing ships, on a massive scale. The great majority of their purchases were from the government, many of the ships

Lord Cowdray

SS San Dunstano (1912) 9,100dwt.

being ones they had managed during the war; and though none of them was even close to the size that Eagle was projecting for its biggest new vessels, it was still an amazing shopping spree, for in 1919 the company bought no fewer than 23 ships, totalling 134,346 grt, and in 1920 a further nine totalling 44,465 grt. Many were ex-RN oilers, built for the Admiralty or the government's wartime Shipping Controller, and fairly well suited for Shell's peacetime needs. Most of the others were former dry cargo ships with cylindrical tanks built into their holds – at best an inefficient method of carrying oil, but a swift way to increase capacity without waiting for the luxury of building from the keel up. With these purchases, it was rather a matter of taking what you could get; and two of them had very odd histories.

No one could have called *Leonard* a beautiful craft: she was a train ferry, built in Birkenhead in 1913-14 for use on the St. Lawrence river in Canada. At 313 feet length overall, she was a short ship (most Shell tankers then averaged around 400 feet in length overall), and with a disproportionately wide beam of 65 feet. When working on the tidal St. Lawrence, she looked rather as if she was still being built, for above a very low freeboard she carried a network of what seemed to be permanent scaffolding. Inside this were the tracks on which the trains sat while on

passage; and depending on the state of the tide, the whole lot could be lifted or lowered vertically by as much as 20 feet, so that the ship-board tracks married up with those on shore.

In 1920, when the St. Lawrence railway bridge made her redundant, all that superstructure went in her conversion, as did her name; she became *Limax*, and because of her wide beam and shallow draft was sent out for river and short sea work in the Far East. But she did not steer well, she pitched tremendously, and, since she did not have an oil-tight central bulkhead, in any seaway she would roll horribly too. A bit of a mistake, perhaps, but she lasted 11 years until (probably to her sailors' relief) she was scrapped in 1931.

Radix was completed as a dry cargo liner in October 1919 by a Sunderland builder, W. Doxford & Sons, for the Newcastle firm of Chapman & Willan. In November 1919 she was driven ashore on the beach at South Shields, broke in two, and was abandoned as a total loss. Only five months later, though, in April 1920, the bow section was refloated; in May the stern section followed; and with a sharp eye for a bargain, Anglo-Saxon bought the two parts, had them towed to Rotterdam, and joined them back together. Reborn as a 6,698grt tanker of perfectly respectable looks and efficiency, she too served the

MS Elax – 10,708dwt, 7,403 gross tonnage – built in 1927 by the Nederlandsche Scheepsmaats, Amsterdam.

company until 1931, and worked under other names with other owners for a further 13 years as well.

'Newbuilding' (to use one of the industry's portmanteau words) recommenced in 1920, with eight new Anglo-Saxon ships being completed in 1921 and nine, including a new *Murex*, in 1922. The first of this new post-war construction was the 5,767grt (8,400dwt) *Acardo*, a ship remarkable for only one thing. In the 28 years since the first *Murex* was launched, the list of British Shell ships had grown to 103, of which 64 had been bought second-hand. Obviously the company had no control over where those ships were built; but of the other 39 (totalling over 182,000 grt) built to the company's order, each and every one had been built in British yards,

providing employment for thousands of workers, mostly in the north-east. Newcastle, Wallsend, West Hartlepool and Jarrow had all been favoured locations, and would continue to be whenever possible; but with *Acardo*, for the first time the company had to place a building order abroad. Her builders were the Union Construction Company of Oakland, California; and of the 17 new-buildings of 1921-22, four came from this yard, four from the Hong Kong & Whampoa Dockyard Co. Ltd., and one from W. S. Bailey & Co., also of Hong Kong. In other words, a majority of the orders had been placed overseas – a portentous note for British builders.

A tenth acquisition in 1922 (the second-hand *Purpura*) meant that in the four years since the Armistice, a full 50

MS Goldmouth, 10,479 dwt, 7,402 gross tonnage built 1927.

extra vessels had joined Shell's British-owned fleet; and that was not all. Approaching his 63rd birthday, Lord Cowdray decided to retire, and, in April 1919, agreed to transfer management of all his Mexican interests, including the Eagle fleet, built and building, to Shell. Marcus Samuel (himself already 66) was naturally delighted, declaring to shareholders at Shell's 1919 AGM:

> *This company's position for the supply of liquid fuel is quite unique. Your Directors had long foreseen its advent, and by joining forces with the Mexican Eagle Oil Company...have placed themselves in the position of being able to give security of contracts to their customers throughout the world in a manner which is not possible to any other petroleum company.*

Most of the benefits of oil-fired ships, as opposed to coal-fired ones, showed up clearly and simply in the accounts books as lower costs, in fuel and manpower within the ship, and in faster turn-rounds in port. There was, however, one benefit which would have been very difficult to calculate financially, but which certainly had a good effect on the company's balance sheets: the fact that oil was so much cleaner and easier to load. This contributed enormously to a ship's appearance, and consequently to her crew's morale, as a young man named Stanley Algar saw for himself.

Working for another, less forward-looking company, Algar was accustomed to coal-burning ships. Like anyone else faced with the task, he absolutely loathed coaling. The first time he had done it, he had been 15 years old in Scapa Flow, with warships from the Grand Fleet all around. It was slow, cripplingly hard work: shovelling tons upon tons of coal into sacks, putting the sacks into nets, swinging the nets from the collier to your own bunkers, emptying them, then trimming the coal below so that all was level, with as much as possible crammed in – and all done by hand.

Trimming was the worst part, because of the permanent fog of coal dust which got into your eyes, ears, nose and mouth, and penetrated into every part of the ship. It took days to clean up the grime afterwards, and when it was finally clean you knew that in a few more days the whole ghastly procedure would have to be repeated.

Nevertheless, Algar accepted the routine as a necessary evil, until one day when his vessel was in Port Arthur, Texas. What he saw there made an impression which lasted the rest of his very long life.

'The ship was in a sorry mess', he wrote later. 'We were not allowed to throw anything into the dock, and the ashes from the stokehold and the galley refuse were piled high on deck. We looked dirty and smelt so too. On this occasion it seemed worse than usual, because a Shell tanker was lying quite close to us.' It was *Mytilus*, then about four years old, and young Algar stared at her 'in envy and admiration.' Because she was an oil burner,

> *There were no ashes on deck. It was a picture. All the brasswork was gleaming in the sun, the paintwork was fantastically clean, the woodwork on the bridge sparkled with good quality varnish, there was no rust to be seen, not even over the side of the hull, and the wooden bridge deck and poops were as clean as a hound's tooth, being holystoned, I guessed, every morning. The crew were Chinese, and the British officers were in clean uniforms, not in shabby old lounge suits as on our ship. I looked at our ship, and was filled with disgust.*

Limax: *built 1914 as the Canadian train ferry* **Leonard** *by Cammel Laird Birkenhead. She is shown here after conversion in 1920...*

Unwittingly Algar had put his youthful finger on a key factor in the success of Shell – both the Group in general, and the tankers in particular. Put at its simplest, it is pride in the company, and pride in being part of the company. To anyone who has not met Shell people this may sound sanctimonious; yet it is perfectly real, as real as the ships themselves. Although no one can truly say when it began, a measure of its reality (a negative and painful measure, but accurate nonetheless) is the devastating sense of betrayal that members of the company felt in 1986 – a most unhappy year, which will be described in due course.

Back at the start of the 1920s, the causes of this pride were clear enough. The company was successful, strong and global, world-encircling and often world-leading. Its war record was admirable; the farsightedness of its managers (especially Marcus Samuel) was publicly if tacitly acknowledged in 1921, when the Admiralty announced that all new Royal Navy ships would be oil-burners. Pay was good: because of their cargoes, tankers had (in Stanley Algar's words) a reputation of being 'dirty, smelling and dangerous', so in order to get the best men, Anglo-Saxon offered 7% above standard rates for junior officers, and 10% above standard for seniors.

. . . and here, before conversion (see page 79).

In fact, while no one would deny that tankers were dangerous, if their cargoes were handled properly they were not significantly more dangerous than any other kind of vessel; and so far from being dirty and smelly, oil-fired ships were a good deal cleaner than most, and diesel-fired ones even better. A sailor's pride in his ship, which is both his home and workplace, is instinctive – easily awakened, but more easily damaged: no one likes to live and work in a mucky vessel. One that looks dirty and neglected becomes more so; a smart ship is kept smart, generally without any need for coercion. So it was with Shell's tankers, particularly the most modern, built to the company's specification. Other seemingly small, but important, considerations helped keep morale high – decent food, better than average accommodation in the ship, and the provision of bedding, soap and towels, at a time when many shipping companies expected their sailors to buy their own or go without.

Pride in belonging to such a concern, which actually thought of its employees as humans, was further enhanced by Shell's reputation of being a cradle-to-grave employer. Of course people came and went for reasons of their own, and of course the incompetent, once found to be incompetent, were dismissed – one of the commonest causes being drunkenness. But when sackings occurred, they were generally seen to be fair: no one wanted to be shipmates with a man who was a thief, or one who endangered the whole ship by falling asleep on watch. Once they had joined, men often stayed with the company for the whole of their working lives. As time went by, it became quite common for a man's son (and even grandson) to join the company too; so with lifelong friends, sometimes relatives, and sometimes rivals too in a fleet of wide, shared experience, a distinctive family feeling came about, along with the firm conviction that Shell was the best in the world, and *the* place to be.

Having gazed enviously at *Mytilus*, Stanley Algar joined the fleet at the age of 22 as a Third Officer, and was delighted. His pleasure at the time was not because of any sense of achievement, or corporate pride – that came later, and he stayed with the company for more than 30 years. Instead, in 1923, he was simply relieved to have a job. By then the unexpectedly brief post-war boom was over, seamen were being laid off (Algar had been unemployed for ten months) and ships laid up; and to make matters still more difficult, production from Mexico's oilfields was falling, while Mexico itself was in the throes of revolution.

There were moments in those disorganized years which, comfortably viewed from today's greater stability,

sound like something from the Marx brothers. Time and again the company's officers in Mexico ran up against pretentious colonels and self-styled generals, complete with peaked caps, dark glasses and thick moustaches, their uniforms covered with braid and medals of doubtful authenticity. Time and again its ships would leave one port, under temporary government control, and arrive at another, under just as temporary rebel control, to find that the clearance papers issued by one side were not recognized as valid by the other. Guns were freely carried by every Mexican, and as freely used – fortunately, it appears, without much harm to company personnel. Eagle's records carry a report of one Sunday in 1925, typical of the period, from Captain W. S. Smith, master of *San Ugon*. A customs official from Tampico was on board and crew members were doing their weekly laundry when a mail plane flew by, dropped its bags on shore in the usual way, then flew low over the ship. The customs man promptly whipped out a pair of revolvers and blazed away at it; but the only effects were that the crew all dived below decks for cover, the plane continued untouched, and the customs man was left 'supremely pleased with himself, revolvers still smoking, in sole charge of the deserted washing buckets.'

However, the commercial implications, both of political instability and falling production, were far from funny. In the wake of the Russian revolution, production there, and sales to the West, had declined to almost nothing. Similarly, in 1917 Shell's wellheads and installations in Romania had been destroyed, in order to deny them to advancing German forces. The Mexican fields had become correspondingly more important, and in terms of global production were, by 1921, second only to those of the United States. In 1922, Mexico exported 25.2 million tons of oil; but in the same year, Eagle's most productive field, the 'Golden Lane', ceased completely when salt water invaded it, and by 1928 the national

Illustration Simon Williams

export figure had slumped to 4.6 million tons. Shell was doubly affected by this, not only through its interest in Eagle, but through its own existing interest in Mexico, in the form of a subsidiary company called La Corona. The company's Far Eastern concerns (especially in Borneo) were still strong and stable, and it was out there, in often idyllic surroundings, that Stanley Algar spent his first three Shell years. In the New World, however, the focus began to shift from central America and Mexico, to South America and Venezuela.

In the north-west of Venezuela lies Lake Maracaibo, a colossal but shallow body of brackish water covering 5,100 square miles (more than 13,000 square kilometres). This vast lake, 60% the size of Wales, is neither salt nor fresh because, though its river sources are fresh, it is also linked by a comparatively narrow outlet, 40 miles long, to the Gulf of Venezuela, and thence to the Caribbean. With its waters so mixed, the lake may lose out as a supplier of fish; but any such loss is far outweighed by the outstandingly large supplies of oil hidden beneath it.

These were first discovered in commercial quantities by Shell explorers in 1914. Unfortunately, two problems immediately arose. First, there was no local market for the oil, so it would have to be sold elsewhere; but second, at the lake's narrow entrance to the Gulf there was a bar, giving a low water depth of only 12 feet, far too shallow for any ocean-going tanker to cross. Yet with ingenuity and a bit of historical luck, both problems were solved. Compared to most Latin American countries then, Venezuela was politically stable, though in an unsavoury manner: President Gomez, who seized power in 1908, ruled as an absolute tyrant until his death in 1935, using secret police to imprison and torture opponents. Added to the practical difficulties of laying a long pipeline to the Caribbean coast, this repugnant political climate made Shell unwilling to build a refinery in Venezuela itself. Part of the solution

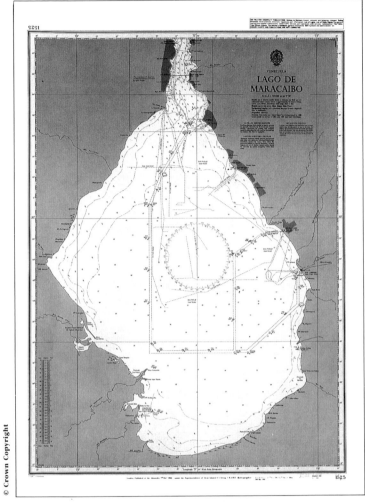

Lake Maracaibo

the Americans. (Indeed, only one island, Cuba, remained under unbroken Spanish rule from the time of its discovery in 1492 until the end of Spain's empire in 1901.) Curaçao was one of those which the Spanish lost fairly early on, in 1634, when the Dutch captured it. Having got it, the Dutch stayed firmly put, resisting all attempts to dislodge them; and thus, nearly 300 years later in 1917, there was an ideal base, close at hand, for the amalgamated Royal Dutch/Shell Group to use in exploiting the Venezuelan finds.

The trade began with two tiny lighters and a pair of tugs bringing oil from Maracaibo to a newly constructed refinery at Willemstad, the capital of Curaçao. In 1920, eight surplus monitors were bought from the British Royal Navy (shallow draught, beamy vessels which converted into good small tankers) and in 1923, the construction began of a dedicated Anglo-Saxon fleet, soon nicknamed the 'mosquito fleet'. This was not only because of the voracious insects their sailors had to endure, but because the ships themselves were such busy little things. By 1928 there were 30 of them, all around 3,000 dwt, with a maximum draught of 13 feet, buzzing backwards and forwards between the lake's terminals and the deep water facilities at Curaçao, and often crowding together, just like a cloud of insects, to cross the bar in convoy.

To people born after World War Two, who grew up with the Middle East as the centre of the world's oil production, the thought of Venezuela as a source of oil can seem improbable; yet its decades as a truly major producer began as early as December 1922, when one of Shell's Barroso wells in the Maracaibo basin blew wild. At a depth of about 1,500 feet, the drill broke through the last crust of rock into a reservoir of oil trapped under such enormous pressure that the whole apparatus shot back to the surface followed by a real gusher, a jetting black fountain which, until it was brought under control, spouted out at 100,000 barrels a day. As Henri Deterding later remarked laconically, 'Venezuelan oil exploration and development

came with a little lateral thinking: big ships could not make the passage through the Maracaibo narrows, but small ships could. So, beginning in 1917, small ships were bought and built for the express purpose of ferrying crude oil out to a deep water refinery; and that was where the historical luck figured.

Only 50 miles off the coast of Venezuela, and just over 200 from the Maracaibo bar, lies the island of Curaçao, part of the Lesser Antilles chain. The first Europeans to land on it arrived in 1499. In 1527, Spanish colonists set up home there. Over the following centuries most islands in the Caribbean changed owners pretty frequently, in wars involving the Spanish, French, British, Dutch, and later on thenceforward made the whole world industry sit up.'

It must be said that, apart from the still continuing employment which Venezuela has provided, it was incredibly lucky for Shell's tankers that Lake Maracaibo emerged just when it did as a major source of oil. Coinciding with the decline of the Mexican fields, the timing was immaculate. Once the problem of getting the oil out over the lake's shallow bar was solved, the deep-sea ships were ready and waiting. Deterding was right to point out that 'we had to spend huge sums of money in developing special vessels for this service, surveying the channel and installing aids to navigation'; but had a replacement for Mexico been found only in some distant part of the world, far more costly problems would have arisen. With new oceans, new routes and new conditions for which they were not necessarily equipped, the Anglo-Saxon and Eagle tankers operating in the Western hemisphere would probably have had to be sold or scrapped, and replaced with new fleets, perhaps with new designs. Instead, as Mexican supplies faded (and in 1938 vanished, when the country's remaining oil assets were expropriated and nationalized), their replacement by what was virtually a neighbouring source meant that the tankers could continue to sail with very little interruption.

By 1927, Venezuela had displaced Mexico as the world's second largest exporter of oil; in 1928 its production of more than 14 million tons was exceeded only by the United States; and in 1929 it exported 19.2 million tons of oil, beating the US into second place. Moreover, it maintained that position, as the world's leading oil exporter, for more than 20 years; so for Shell, the mosquito fleet proved a highly successful operation – indeed almost an ideal one, steady, secure and profitable. Even today, the oil still comes slurping up, with something like 10,000 rigs spread over Lake Maracaibo's 5,000 square miles; even into the 1980s the lake still provided nearly 17% of Shell's oil supplies; and, looking

3 Hamilton Place, where Marcus and Fanny Samuel lived for twenty years from 1907.

towards the future, today the Group has a 30% interest in a joint venture studying the feasibility of a project to export liquefied natural gas from the country as well.

Sir Marcus Samuel retired from the board of Shell in 1920, handing over the reins to his son Walter, and taking the opportunity at the AGM of that year to review the phenomenal growth of his tanker company since its foundation in 1892. After his year as Lord Mayor, his knighthood had been enhanced, as was customary, to the inheritable title of baronet. In 1921, in recognition of Anglo-Saxon's contribution to the national war effort, he was ennobled as the first Baron Bearsted. (Setting the seal on his life's work, this recognition gave him huge but very innocent satisfaction. As soon as he could, he wrote to his children to tell them the news, and said to a friend: 'You can't think what pleasure it gives me to put "The Honourable" on my children's envelopes.') In the same year, Henri Deterding was created a KBE. This was before the days when foreigners could only receive honorary distinctions, and Sir Henri, as he now was, sported his title with equal gratification. Marcus had already been made a Knight Commander of the Belgian Order of Leopold and a *Grand Officier* of the French Legion of Honour; and it did not stop there, for in 1925 he was elevated further in the British aristocracy, from the rank of baron to that of viscount. But by then he was nearly 72 years old, and ill, and on 17 January 1927 (less than 24 hours after his wife Fanny) he died.

Despite the honours piled on their leaders, no one at sea could pretend that the 1920s and '30s were easy decades. At the time of Marcus's death, and even ten years later, many people would have said that he had seen the glory days of Shell and its tankers. The general economic slump of the mid-1920s developed (after the Wall Street Crash of 1929) into worldwide depression, the worst ever known.

As early as 1921, Eagle was forced briefly to lay up one of its brand new ships, followed by others in 1922. In 1923, Anglo-Saxon's sailors had to accept a 25% cut in wages. Jobs became increasingly difficult to find, with many applicants for each vacancy. Rather than face the humiliation and poverty of the dole queue, certificated officers would take work as deck or engine room ratings; men would sign on for the longest voyages possible, and were willing to sign on again immediately they ended. In 1925, 1931 and 1932, the Eagle fleet saw 5-10% of its ships laid up for lack of work. (One might think that to contrive employment at such a time for 90-95% of the fleet should be hailed as a considerable success, but it did not look like that then: these were, in the directors' view, 'the worst

years', ones which they hoped never to see again.) Anglo-Saxon, in 1926, had to resort to the sale and charter back of 28 of its vessels. When unemployment was especially severe, both fleets would run their ships at slow speed, a mere six to eight knots. There were at least three commercial reasons for this policy, firstly because (as remarked by John Lamb, an engineer who served both Eagle and Anglo-Saxon) 'nothing deteriorates more quickly than a laid-up ship'; secondly because a ship bringing in some revenue is better than one bringing in none; and thirdly because with voyages prolonged and more spare time available, more maintenance could be done than usual, reducing repair costs. But there was a recorded social reason as well: the real distress of the unemployed was so painfully evident that the company's managers wanted to do what they could to relieve their plight, and if the ships had not been run slow, they would not have been run at all.

Nevertheless, in the ships themselves, the depression's prevailing mood was aptly summed up by the gloomy habit of one anonymous master in the Far Eastern trades. He would come up to the bridge about midnight, check the planned course, gaze mournfully into the darkness, sigh deeply, then declare: 'And on a reef, she came to grief, my God...'

People remembered such things, especially when the captain then returned to his cabin, leaving an alarmed junior officer in control of the ship. At such times, plotting their courses with dividers, another lugubrious verse would run through their minds: 'Down by the Little Paternosters,' a group of islands in the Makassar Strait, 'down by the Union Bank, in one eighteen East and three degrees South we pricked off where she sank...'

Shell and its tankers were down, as was everyone else; but they were by no means out. Throughout the depression years, only five Anglo-Saxon tankers had to be laid up, a remarkable record for the period, for which the credit must go to Sir Henri Deterding. Everyone acknowledged that he was a fantastically successful leader of business. His early

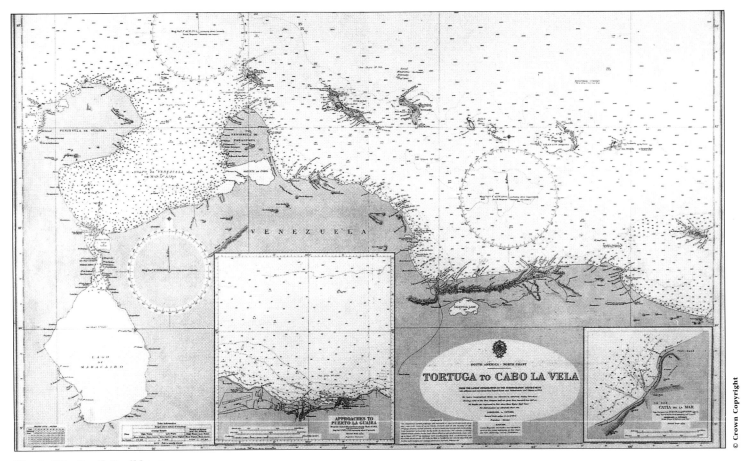

© Crown Copyright

Chart of the South Caribbean.

entry into the Venezuelan concessions (which he later admitted had looked to others like a 'sheer gamble' at the start) was a major factor in the company's survival: by the end of 1932, all the various groups and companies, including Shell, operating in Lake Maracaibo had extracted a total of 110 million tons of oil from it, and of that total, Shell alone had won 52 million tons. Admiral Fisher (who died in 1920) had called Deterding 'the Napoleon of oil'; but he often described single-minded, highly successful people as the Napoleon of this or that. More to the point, it was generally accepted in the Press during the 1930s that only one man in the world, Walter Teagle, was Sir Henri's equal.

Standard's American monopoly had been broken by the Supreme Court in 1911, with 'the Octopus' being divided into 38 components, of which Standard Oil of New

Jersey (known subsequently as Esso and now as Exxon) was the biggest. Teagle, the son and grandson of oil men, was one of its directors at the age of 33, and for 20 years its chairman. The commercial tradition he and Exxon came from could not have been more different from that of Deterding and Shell, the former being rooted in home based monopoly of production and distribution, the latter essentially international. But in addition to their outstanding business skills, Deterding and Teagle shared a likeness of character which cannot be ignored. Both, as they grew older and more powerful, grew increasingly autocratic, and both wanted one simple thing for their respective businesses: global pre-eminence, over all other oil companies.

During the 1920s, Deterding won that position for Shell, and maintained it throughout the 1930s, until

Cliona *(2) 1931-1948, 8,375grt. Survived a mass U-boat attack on a World War Two convoy.*

Exxon overtook around the the beginning of World War Two. Since then, either one or the other has been world leader, each commanding about 13-14% of world production outside eastern Europe and China; and during the 1920s and '30s, depressed as they were, Deterding emphasized his (and Shell's) actual success by an impressive series of newbuildings.

In the inter-war years (in addition to the 17 tankers delivered in 1921, mentioned earlier), Anglo-Saxon took delivery of no fewer than 87 new ships. With only five individual exceptions, these came in just five batches, and so can all be described quite simply.

The first batch, ordered in 1925 and delivered in 1927, was of ten 10,000dwt double-acting diesel-driven tankers, with names old and new – *Bullmouth, Bulysses, Clam, Elax, Goldmouth, Patella, Pecten, Spondilus, Telena* and *Trocas.*

Their engines, John Lamb wrote later, were 'of an entirely new and untried design'. Some people said this was progressive and bold, others that it was foolhardy and rash; from experience, Lamb himself eventually held the latter opinion. The engines turned out to be intensely unreliable. He was an assistant Superintendent Engineer when the ships entered the fleet, and soon became an expert in their repair, with his services on constant call. There was always at least one of these ships broken down somewhere, and for five years Lamb had neither week-end breaks nor summer holidays, as he travelled around fixing one after another; but he was a philosophical man. Acknowledging that they 'cost the owners a fortune in repairs, and many headaches and sleepless nights to us who had to look after them', he reflected that on the other hand, they also brought a lot of work to shipyards on the Tyne and Clyde,

LPG and LNG

Because of their very similar names, lay people often confuse LPG (liquefied petroleum gas) and LNG (liquefied natural gas), sometimes supposing that they are one and the same thing, or else slightly different products of one distillation process. In fact they are very different.

Both are liquefied by being chilled and compressed, but the first distinction is that LNG is as its name suggests *natural* gas, found either in conjunction with petroleum (crude oil) or on its own, and usually composed of 80-95% methane (CH_4). In contrast, the term LPG refers to several refined products of petroleum, including, amongst others, butane and propane.

The second distinction is that in order to liquify natural gas, it has to be made very much colder than gases refined from petroleum. Butane liquifies at $-2°C$ and propane at $-42°C$; before methane becomes liquid, it has to be chilled to $-165°C$. Seen from the other end of the thermometer, those temperatures are the levels at which the respective liquids boil and revert to being gases. For methane in particular, the intense cold at which it must be kept demands an extremely high level of technology at every stage from its liquefaction, at a special plant adjacent to the ship-loading terminal, through its voyage and onward to the point where it can be allowed to re-vapourise for piping to the consumer. Nevertheless, it is a very valuable commodity, its greatest value (both commercially and environmentally) being as a fuel. Unlike toxic coal gas, first used by the Victorians both as an illuminant and a fuel, natural gas is non-toxic and virtually pollution-free. Central to the supply chain, Brunei Shell's LNG ships are designed to allow a small quantity of 'boil off' from their cargoes, which is used to power the vessels' steam turbine engines – an elegant application of very high technology, being effective, economical and clean.

at a time when the noise of building or repair was so unusual that people passing in the street would stop and listen.

These ten and their cussed engines were followed by a dozen at 12,000 dwt apiece, each with twin screws – *Caprella, Capsa, Cardita, Cardium, Circe Shell, Cliona, Conch, Conus, Corbis, Cowrie, Gold Shell* and *Horn Shell* – and all delivered in 1931. In the same year came three of the five 'non-batch' vessels: the oil-fired *Harpa* and *Helix*, both of 4,500 dwt, and the 4,700dwt *Agnita*.

This last was also a first, for she was designed to carry liquefied petroleum gas (LPG), something for which no previous ship had been built. (The Group's Dutch flag *Megara*, built in 1928, also carried LPG, but was converted for the purpose.) Using vertical pressurised cylindrical tanks, *Agnita* could simultaneously handle any two of three different cargoes, gas oil, sulphuric acid, or propane. The gas oil could be carried inside or outside the cylinders; the acid or propane would be inside. Because of her unusual cargoes and appearance (the domed tops of the cylinders protruded above the weather deck), the pioneering *Agnita* was naturally well known in shipping circles; and she became still better known in World War Two.

Before that war began, three more batches of newbuilding came through: a dozen ships nicknamed the 'Triple Twelves' (all motor ships) and delivered in 1935-37; a further 16 delivered in 1936-39; and another 18 of the D-class, also delivered in 1936-39.

At the time the 'Triple Twelves' were being delivered, Shell's British tanker fleet also acquired a new delivery (so to speak) of a sort that no merchant fleet had ever had: its very own padre. The Revd Kenneth Matthews (subsequently, as a Naval Chaplain, to be awarded the DSC and OBE) was Shell's first Chaplain to the Fleet, and from 1934 to 1937 served continuously afloat, bringing spiritual and pastoral guidance and advice to the crews of one ship after another.

As for the 'Triple Twelves': they were so called not

Conch *(3) 1931-1940, 8,376grt. 1940 torpedoed and sunk in mid-Atlantic by U47, U95 and U99.*

Clam *(2) 1927-1950, 7,404grt.*

because there were 12 of them (there were in fact 20, eight being under the Dutch flag) but because each had a capacity of 12,000dwt, a service speed of 12 knots and a fuel consumption of 12 tons a day. The next 16 new-buildings were somewhat smaller, at 9,200 dwt apiece; and there should have been 17 of them. When the Second World War started, the last of them was still under construction, in Denmark, and soon fell prey to German invaders. Likewise, the fifth and final interwar batch should have included 20 ships, but actually, because of the outbreak of hostilities, included only 18, the 12-knot, 12,000dwt D-class. The two which were never delivered were being built in Hamburg, and were snapped up by the German navy.

However, another two newbuildings were safely delivered to the Anglo-Saxon fleet: *Torinia* and *Thiara*, both built on the Tyne and, at 15,260 dwt, the largest (by quite a wide margin) of all the ships under the house flag. Their deliveries, in July and October 1939 respectively, brought the total of new ships built for Anglo-Saxon between the wars to 105 hulls, aggregating a massive 1,164,220 dwt.

Not even that represented the grand total of new tonnage in Shell's British tanker fleet. There were also the 178,811 deadweight tons of ex-Admiralty and ex-government vessels purchased directly after the end of World War One; various further ships transferred at various points from the Dutch to the British flag; and smaller vessels – barges, river craft and the like. To arrive at an absolute figure would have been tricky even then, and much more difficult now; yet in a way, that was not important. The two most important facts were that in the space of 21 years, the Anglo-Saxon fleet had increased by more than 1.3 million deadweight tons, and in 1939 formed about 10% of the whole world's tanker tonnage.

This was a fabulous fleet. No one now remembers who dreamed up Shell's most enduring advertising slogan, but whoever it was, the inventor must have been pleased with

Corbis: *Built by Workman Clarke, Belfast 1931, 12,623dwt.*

his work. Its first recorded use was in 1931. By 1939, with the famous pecten a regular and familiar visitor in every major port in the world, and many of the minor ports too, the phrase had entered common speech: 'You can be sure of Shell.'

Sir Henri Deterding died that year. He had retired in 1936, at the age of 70, by which time he had been chairman of Royal Dutch/Shell for exactly half his life. Of course, none of it would have happened at all without Marcus Samuel, who is still remembered with a certain affection; he seems to represent a kind of enviably grand freedom. Let's have a fleet. Let's search for oil. Don't worry about the nuts and bolts. 'Technical problems solve themselves', he would say with blithe assurance. Such confidence is infectious and attractive; and the pleasure that he derived from his honours – becoming a knight, then a baronet, then a baron, and finally a viscount – the pleasure he derived from these

was so simple and frank that to accuse him of snobbery would be churlish and wrong. On the other hand, it is quite fair to remember too that despite all his vision and energy, the nuts and bolts *do* matter: the problems of running a fleet, technical or financial, do not actually solve themselves, but have to be solved by someone sitting down and thinking them through. By 1939, most of Shell's British tanker fleet had been ordered and built under the vigorous and acerbic chairmanship of the Dutchman with the British knighthood, Sir Henri Deterding. He may not deserve affection – he was too much of an autocrat – but he certainly commands respect. Without him, it would all have gone for nothing at quite an early date; and in the end, it was he who ensured Shell.

'Seamen prefer Shell' by Tristram Hillier.
A 1930's Shell advertisement poster.

Six years in disguise: Though the house flag remained, funnels and superstructures were camouflaged in grey throughout the Second World War.

MAC ship Rapana, built 1935 Wilton Fijenoord, Holland; converted to MAC 9 1943; returned to normal tanker service 1945.

Illustration Steven Rudd

Chapter Seven
Oil in our Tanks
1939-1945

Agnita, **the first British tanker to be attacked from the air in World War Two.**

Captain Stanley Algar

On 17 December 1939, exactly 15 weeks had passed since Britain's declaration of war against Germany. SS *Agnita* was about 10 miles south of Hastings, steaming eastward through the Channel from Cardiff en route for Rotterdam, where she would load a cargo of sulphuric acid for Curaçao. Her Captain was Stanley Algar, in his 16th year with Anglo-Saxon; her Chief Officer was C. H. Hill-Willis, who had been with the company 2½ years. In Cardiff, which they had left the previous day, the ship had been turned into an armed merchantman. Pillboxes of inch-thick steel had been erected on either side of the bridge. The starboard one housed a secondary steering wheel; it also contained a telephone connected to the engineroom, the radio room and the two new gun platforms which had sprouted on the poop. One of these carried a 4.7-inch anti-submarine gun; the other held a 12-pounder anti-aircraft gun. Both weapons were old: the anti-submarine gun was made in 1916, and the 12-pounder was from obsolete stock. Close by them, a pair of magazines had been built, and on the foredeck, gallows had been installed for streaming paravanes, to cut the mooring cables of mines.

With the addition of steel helmets, gas masks, naval signalling equipment, half-a-dozen .303 rifles and their ammunition, the conversion was complete. The Captain declared himself impressed; the Chief Officer, a more cynical man, noted that the 4.7-inch gun could only traverse from one quarter to the other, and that the 12-pounder's arc of fire was similarly restricted by the funnel and mainmast. They might have done well at Trafalgar, he thought, but that had been 134 years earlier.

However, it was typical of the kit given to any merchantman at the time: archaic and simple, but better than nothing, even if its main value was to improve morale; and they made the best of it. Regular gun drills were instituted at once, and both the senior deck officers were surprised and pleased when several of the Chinese crew volunteered for gun training. No one cared much for the idea of going to neutral Holland, feeling it was too close to Germany for comfort; but as they left Cardiff and proceeded up the Channel during the night of the 16th, their main fear was that they might collide with another darkened ship. Having to sail without any lights at all went against every navigational instinct. With no lights on shore and no sounds but the throbbing engine and hissing sea, in taut mood they strained their eyes and ears into the blackness.

At 4.25 pm on the 17th, though, they would have been glad of dark to cover them: for it was then, heralded by a distant droning noise, that a Heinkel 111 bomber appeared through clouds astern of them, and made ready to attack.

It came at them three times, on each occasion dropping a bomb and raking them with machine-gun fire from its front and rear as it passed very low overhead. The Captain estimated it was no more than 50 feet above them. As the ship manoeuvred violently to avoid the bombs, the crew of the 12-pounder managed to loose off two rounds at the aircraft, and, though he knew it was practically useless, the Chief Officer grabbed a .303 and fired several shots as well. None of the bombs hit the ship, any more than the bullets or 12-pound shells hit the Heinkel; but before the aircraft vanished again into the clouds, its bombs exploded close enough to lift *Agnita* bodily in the water. In the engineroom, the concussion split and fractured cylinder jackets, pipes and castings, and ruptured the starting air cylinder; on deck, the machine-gunning pierced some of the steam pipes; in the radio room, the transmitter was destroyed. They could not communicate with anyone, and they could only proceed very slowly (with the added warning from the Chief Engineer that if they had to stop, he would be unable to restart the engines), so they did the only sensible things under the circumstances: they turned for Southampton, prepared the guns for renewed action and distributed brandy.

The Tanker

The stage is set, the ways are greased,
The shattering din in her hull has ceased.
Guests assemble for function and feast
And the speech of a prominent banker.
'God Speed to all who sail in thee!'
The great form shudders as the chocks fall free,
And a noble ship slips down to the sea
At the launch of a British tanker.

Year after year through heat and spray,
Doldrums and hurricanes, the gulf and the bay,
Tropical sunset and daybreak grey,
Never at rest or at anchor;
Carrying potions by devils brewed,
Benzine, kerosene, fuel and crude,
Hurrying slave to the market's mood,
That is the lot of a tanker.

Berth her and load her without delay,
Drive her and sweat her by night and day,
Dock her, discharge her, get her away!
No matter how you may hanker.
'Finished with engines', finished with strife,
Now for a quiet week-end with the wife.
Home for the week-end? Not on your life,
You don't get week-ends on a tanker!

The grey wolf into the convoy slips,
Hunting his prey 'midst the crowded ships.
The U-boat commander curls his lips
In a smile of hate and rancour.
The periscope's twisted spray-washed eyes
The hull of a tanker soon espies,
And the U-boat harries and hunts its prize –
The prize of a British tanker.

Never away from the battle zone,
Never away from the bombers' drone
Or the thresh of a 'sub' on a hydrophone –
We've a lot for which to thank her!
Fuel for the bomber's offensive sweep,
Fuel for the tank, the truck and the jeep,
Fuel for the Navy, their watch to keep:
That is the work of a tanker!

Written c.1942
Quoted from memory by Captain George Griffiths and cited
in British Fleet News, *July 1982. Author unknown.*

When the Second Officer returned to his cabin from his action station on one of the guns, he found a machine-gun bullet had come straight through the deck and across the back of his chair, to bury itself in his desk. Naturally everyone was shaken up by the attack (and as soon as they reached Southampton, all but one of the Chinese resigned their contracts) but at least no one had been killed, or even hurt; and the company gave them all a month's extra pay. Altogether, as Captain Algar said later, this, the first aerial attack against a tanker, was 'a mild affair'. Other Shell ships were far less fortunate.

In the UK, the nation's industrial, domestic and military dependence on petroleum products was greater than ever before. Likewise, a generation after the Great War, its immense losses of merchant shipping were still, for many people, real and harrowing personal memories. The vast majority (85%) of all domestic oil refining, distribution and marketing was controlled by only three companies – predominantly Shell, followed by Anglo-Persian and the British subsidiary of Standard Oil of New Jersey – so when war appeared once again probable, intense secret discussions were held (as early as 1937) between the Government and the companies. These discussions led, in 1938, to an agreement which was perhaps the most radical alteration to the industry that one could imagine – namely, that if or when war came, Britain's whole oil industry would operate as one under the Government, without competition.

Radical as it was, as far as the public was concerned there was only one visible change: in downstream operations (the selling of petrol and so forth) the companies' separate identities vanished. Instead of seeing competing petrol stations with different logos and liveries, motorists found that all stations now sold 'Pool' petrol, from pumps painted a uniform drab dark green. Within company walls, however, the changes wrought by war were considerable. Shell-Mex House, in the Strand in central London, became the operational centre of the united national oil industry. A little to the west of London, the imposing Lensbury Club in Teddington (Shell's private country club, founded in 1921 with new buildings opened in 1938) became the company's main headquarters. About 1,000 staff were transferred there from St Helen's Court, left echoing and almost empty; and virtually the whole management of Anglo-Saxon and Eagle transferred to Plymouth. Though the main headquarters remained outside London for the duration, the shipping management's relocation was short-lived: after about a year, everyone came back to St Helen's Court, because Plymouth was being so heavily bombed that even London appeared less risky.

At sea, scarcely anywhere seemed safe. As the war developed, company vessels were lost in almost every part of the world, from the Caribbean to Singapore, from Scotland to the Indian Ocean. Fifteen months after the hair-raising episode in the Channel, *Agnita* was eventually sunk (22 March 1941) by a surface raider, *Kormoran*, while in ballast half-way between Freetown and the Venezuelan port of Caripito. Algar, Hill-Willis and 36 of the crew were captured and taken to Germany, where they were held as prisoners-of-war until the autumn of 1945. By the time they were liberated, Anglo-Saxon had lost 43 of its ships, totalling 307,375 grt, to mines, fires, torpedoes, gunfire or bombs. Fighting alongside them, the Eagle fleet also lost 17 vessels, and those (being all, on average, larger) totalled

Admiral Graf Spee *(10,000 displ tons)*

Africa Shell. *Sunk by the* **Graf Spee** *15th November 1939.*

Africa Shell – *the wreck.*

211,475 dwt. The human loss under the two flags was proportionately severe: a total of 1,434 men were killed, of which 668 were British officers and 766 Chinese ratings.

Before *Agnita* was first attacked, at least three Shell ships had been sunk already. The small, brand new tanker *Africa Shell* (Captain Patrick Dove), owned by the Shell Company of East Africa, was captured on 15 November 1939 by the surface raider *Admiral Graf Spee* (Captain Hans Langsdorff). Dove was certain that, at the moment of capture, his 706dwt vessel was in the neutral territorial waters of Portuguese East Africa. Notwithstanding his protests, the little ship was taken and destroyed, adding to the raider's tally (which by 7 December would reach 50,000 tons); but Dove was luckier than he realized, for Langsdorff was that rarity in modern warfare – a sailor who still believed that his enemy was another ship, not its personnel, and that once he had disposed of the ship, the personnel should be rescued and cared for. Even Churchill acknowledged this (though somewhat grudgingly), calling Langsdorff 'a high class person', and Dove, after 29 days of ship-board captivity before his release into neutral Uruguay, found that he could feel only respect for his captor.

Meanwhile, Eagle endured its first two sinkings. The curtain-raiser came at about midday on 2 December 1939, when the 12,150dwt *San Calisto* (Captain A. R. Hicks), en route from Hull to the US Gulf, struck a mine and went down in the northern part of the Thames Estuary. Six

men were killed. Exactly one week later, the 11,054dwt *San Alberto* (Captain George Waite) became the company's first U-boat victim, when she was torpedoed in heavy seas 150 miles south of the Fastnet Rock. One man died when the crew abandoned ship, and many more would certainly have died of exposure, but for an odd event. As the survivors watched, their ship split in half. The entire for'ard section, from stem to abaft the central bridge, sank swiftly; but the after section stayed afloat. When Waite was sure it was in no immediate danger of sinking, he ordered his men back on board. This they achieved with difficulty; and they managed not only to restart the engines, but also to keep the wreck stern to sea throughout the night. Waite hoped to bring his half-ship back to port. This proved impossible, for the bad weather was getting worse; but over the following two days, first a neutral Belgian merchant ship and then a Royal Navy destroyer found the hulk, and

Captain Patrick Dove

SS San Demetrio *miraculously safe again in the Clyde – note distress signals painted on her bridge and poop.*

between them took off all the survivors, the last being Captain Waite himself, who left the remains of *San Alberto* only when it began to break up.

But George Waite's war was far from over. With extraordinary luck (good or bad, depending on how one viewed it), he was sunk twice more, and survived both times. The last occasion was on 15 June 1943, in the Indian Ocean. His ship then was the 12,180dwt motor vessel *San Ernesto*, the attacker a Japanese submarine. A single torpedo broke the ship's back and destroyed its engines. One man was killed, and the order to abandon ship was given as a second torpedo hit them. The submarine surfaced and opened fire on the blazing wreck, but let the three lifeboats go. Shaping course for the nearest land (the Maldive Islands, 900 miles away), the boats were soon separated. In the middle of the Indian Ocean, in the hottest part of the year, their chances looked very poor; yet they lived through it with only one death from exposure. The boat under Waite's command was picked up after eight days by a merchant ship bound for Australia, and the other two, commanded by the Second and Third Officers, actually reached the Maldives: the longest lifeboat voyages made by any Eagle men, and, by any standards, an astonishing achievement of seamanship.

An unusual footnote to the *San Ernesto* episode (and a tribute to her builders) is that although she was left broken-backed and in flames, she did not actually go down. Instead, she stayed afloat for more than five months, and ended up aground on Pulau Nias, an island off the west coast of Sumatra. Her probable track was subsequently worked out, and it was estimated that she must have drifted about 2,000 miles – a strange and ghostly sight.

However, it was Waite's second sinking which gave rise to one of the most famous stories of merchant ships at war. To be strictly accurate, it was not a sinking, nor did Captain Waite have any direct part in the events which led to the vessel's ultimate rescue; but that does not diminish his role, for it was by his example with *San Alberto* that *San Demetrio* was brought safely back to port.

Laden with gasoline, the 12,132dwt *San Demetrio* was only 11 months old when, on 5 November 1940, she was crossing the Atlantic in convoy with 37 other merchantmen, escorted by the armed merchant cruiser HMS *Jervis Bay* – originally a 14,000dwt passenger liner. In mid-ocean the convoy was intercepted by the pocket battleship *Admiral Scheer*, sister to *Admiral Graf Spee*. With the third of their class, *Deutschland* (later renamed *Lützow*), these warships were (from a purely professional point of view) exciting and unconventional. Built in the 1930s, they were really heavily armoured cruisers, circumventing the restrictions placed on German naval building between the wars. Basically, they combined the small displacement (10,000 tons) and high speed of a cruiser with the firepower of a battleship: in theory, they could catch and sink any single weaker ship, and escape from any stronger one.

HMS *Jervis Bay* (Acting Captain E. S. Fogarty Fegen, RN) was unarmoured, and armed only with seven 6-inch guns; *Admiral Scheer*'s main armament consisted of six 11-inch guns. Facing such a formidable warship, *Jervis Bay* was in an impossible situation. If she abandoned her convoy and fled, which was inconceivable, the pocket battleship's greater range would find and sink her nonetheless, and the convoy would be destroyed piecemeal. If she stayed and fought, she would just as certainly be sunk, but the convoy might escape; and so she stayed. Under cover of smoke, the convoy scattered, and for a little more than 20 minutes, Fegen and his men fought an inevitably suicidal action.

Some of *Jervis Bay*'s men survived; Fegen was not among them. Five ships from the convoy were sunk as well, but it would have been far more otherwise, and for his outstanding gallantry the acting naval captain was posthumously awarded the VC.

Survivors returning to **San Demetrio**.   **Painting by Norman Wilkinson**

Shelled by *Admiral Scheer*, *San Demetrio* was severely damaged, immobilized and set ablaze, with the loss of three lives. 'We were then in an unhappy position,' wrote the Chief Engineer, a Mr C. Pollard, in his subsequent downbeat report, 'because our ship was burning furiously and we feared she might blow up almost at any time. We were therefore anxious to get as far away as possible. The position at the time was what might be described as very dangerous.'

Accordingly, Captain Waite gave the order to abandon ship. All four lifeboats got away, but one overturned with

The German 'pocket battleship' Admiral Scheer (10,000 displ tons)

SS Dorcasia (1938-1960) 8,053grt.

some loss of life. During the ensuing night, the three remaining boats were separated. The men in two of them were later saved, with Waite's boat being one of the lucky ones (as later happened again in the Indian Ocean with *San Ernesto*). The third surviving lifeboat was not rescued; but, two days after the attack, its men sighted what was left of *San Demetrio*, still afloat, miraculously in one piece, and with most of the fires out.

Remembering Waite's effort with *San Alberto*, the three officers (Second Officer A. G. Hawkins in charge, Third Engineer G. P. Willey and Apprentice J. L. Jones) and their 13 men decided to try the same thing; and despite their small numbers and their physical condition, much weakened by burns and exposure, they succeeded brilliantly, coaxing the shattered vessel back to harbour in the Clyde, where they arrived on 14 November. Five days later, operating under her own steam, the ship discharged what was left of her cargo: a full 10,000 tons of gasoline.

There can have been very few experiences more constantly frightening than sailing in an oil tanker in wartime. The ships were excellent targets: comparatively slow, easily recognized and virtually defenceless, with cargoes which were highly combustible and of great strategic value. Their lives could be very short. The 11,866dwt *San Victorio*, built by Blytheswood Shipbuilding in Scotstoun,

was launched on 20 January 1942 and delivered on 16 April. On 16 May of the same year – only 30 days after she had joined the company – during her maiden voyage in cargo, while sailing independently through the Caribbean Sea from Aruba to Freetown, she was twice torpedoed in a double submarine attack to port and starboard. She was carrying refined oils, and of the 52 men in the ship's company, only one (Gunner A. Ryan) survived: everyone else on board was killed either by the first volcanic explosions or by the intense fires which immediately followed.

No one could say that one crew was braver than another: every vessel was equally vulnerable, yet the sailors continued to man them, despite all the destruction of tonnage and lives. Many of the sailors were, of course, very young men, often under 20 years old. At that sort of age it is hard to believe in one's own mortality. Perhaps because of that, they could sometimes display remarkable *sang froid* – as, for example, in 1940, shortly after the evacuation of the British Expeditionary Force from Dunkirk, when 19-year-old Apprentice Douglas Carr (later a Captain) was in Petit Couronne, up the river Seine, about ten miles south of Rouen. His ship, *Dorcasia* (Captain J. O. Evans), was loading a cargo of extremely volatile industrial alcohol. Simultaneously, on the other side of Rouen, German forces were advancing rapidly towards the city;

but since it was a place he had never visited, Carr decided to go and have a look at it. Strolling around with another apprentice, he admired the cathedral and the statue of Joan of Arc. Together, they bought a bottle of champagne (which cost them half a week's wages each), then, in a café by a bridge over the Seine, sat sipping the wine as an unbroken stream of French refugees poured over the bridge; and the only thing which struck them as unusual was the huge amount of baggage that could be carried on a bicycle.

However, in wartime (if they are lucky) young men grow old fast. That summer of 1940 was a beautiful one, but, as *Dorcasia*, with 11,000 tons of industrial spirit loaded, made her way through a channel swept free of mines and turned west for the Loire, the sun was completely obliterated by the smoke from blazing oil tanks on shore. As the ship approached the Loire, France fell; *Dorcasia* was ordered back to the UK with the destroyer HMS *Wolverine*; and then, off Aberdeen, heading for the Thames around the north of Scotland (since the Channel route was too dangerous) she was straddled by a stick of bombs. She had already been unsuccessfully attacked once by bombers in Le Havre, and she survived this second attack too, though the bombs were close enough to spring her rivets loose.

After repairs in Tilbury came the all too short relief of a voyage round the world: relief because, once through Panama, *Dorcasia* had apparently returned to peacetime; all too short because, before the end of the year, she was back in Liverpool, and there she was mined.

The weapon was an acoustic mine, against which there was at that time no means of protection. Lifted bodily in the water by the force of the explosion, the ship came to a stop; yet though she was crippled, her luck still held. The engine room was destroyed, the pump rooms were flooded to the top with cargo, the cargo

pipeline system was fractured. The surrounding surface of the sea was covered with petrol leaking freely from her damaged tanks, its smell mixing with the stink of burning materials from the mine, but she did not explode or even catch fire.

Carr would be the first to emphasize that his experiences were by no means unusual: that more or less every Shell sailor in wartime – literally thousands of others – endured the same, or similar, trials. Each who survived had his own story, his own memories; and as a representative here of so many others, Carr's adventures were far from finished. Sometimes there was a break, a magnificent respite in an area seemingly miraculously free of war, as in 1943, when Carr (by then a Third Officer) had three blissful months in the Seychelles, helping to fuel the Royal Navy from SS *Pellicula*; but such times were the exceptions. Afterwards, he returned to the 'real war', serving in the Mediterranean, Alexandria, Malta and the invasion of Sicily; and before going to the Seychelles, he had taken part in one of the most gruelling aspects of the Merchant Navy's war: the supply convoys to Russia.

With *Dorcasia* being repaired, he had been transferred to the 9,000dwt MV *Elona* (Captain J. C. Nettleship), where he joined Don Mitchell, another young apprentice who later became a Captain. After loading aviation spirit in Houston, Texas, they were kitted out with Arctic clothing in Halifax, Nova Scotia, and from Iceland joined convoy PQ6. The date was 8 December 1941. Twenty-four hours earlier, the Japanese had attacked Pearl Harbor, the Philippines, Hong Kong and Malaya, and the Allies, now including the United States, had declared war against Japan. The war had become truly global, with no safe passage after Panama, or anywhere else.

Today, several Japanese companies are

Captain J. C. Nettleship

103

important partners with or customers of Shell and its British tankers, and have been for 20 years or more: co-operation has long replaced conflict, a most welcome change for all concerned. However, it does not alter that period in history, from the last days of 1941 to the autumn of 1945, when Shell sailors and their dependents in south-east Asia faced the ordeals, whether by sea or overland through jungle, of trying to escape from the enemy. It would be wrong not to mention them, for Shell ships were involved in many dramatic and terrifying rescues, carrying evacuees from major and minor ports through the Dutch East Indies. Some succeeded; others died in the attempt; and yet others, who were captured, suffered permanent mental and physical scarring from the atrocious conditions and treatment given to prisoners of the Japanese Army.

But having mentioned them, by the same token this is not the place to describe their experiences in detail, because (at the risk of sounding parochial) they were almost all Dutch, and therefore not really part of the tale of Shell's *British* tanker fleets. Their story belongs elsewhere, but here they can at least be accorded a respectful salute.

For the Russian supply convoys, slogging through the Greenland Sea in mid-December presented multiple hazards, natural and man-made: perpetual darkness, almost perpetual storms, encroaching ice to the northward, predatory U-boats to the south. The convoys would push as far north as they dared, their upperworks growing thick and heavy with frozen spray which sometimes, by its very weight, threatened to capsize a ship. In the aptly-named White Sea, PQ6 came to a halt for two days as the sea itself froze. Released by Russian icebreakers, they reached Molotovsk just before Christmas, where they were promptly frozen in again, solid as a rock, for two months.

Those long, dark weeks of intense cold left Carr and Mitchell with a profound hatred for Stalinist Russia: not because of the weather, which was a thing of nature, but because of the deeds they saw carried out in the name and with the authority of that grotesque regime – the open executions of thieves and political criminals. Within sight of the ice-bound ships, these men would be either shot, which was at least instantaneous, or forced to strip and sit naked on the ice until they froze, which did not take take much longer. Yet it was impossible to intervene; the young apprentices, growing old very quickly indeed, could only pray for the downfall of such tyranny.

Summer convoys were little improvement on winter ones. While the threat of ice was reduced, the danger (and cover) of darkness was removed altogether, and daylight was constant. Then, convoys often faced attack not only by U-boats but by surface ships and aircraft – as in July 1942, when, after being ordered to scatter, the tragic and infamous PQ17 was picked off piecemeal, with only 11 out of 35 ships reaching Russia. At any season of the year, of all the convoy routes – including those to Malta – the runs to Murmansk and Archangel were always the most feared, by Royal Navy and Merchant Navy alike; and considering all the perils they faced, the Shell ships that helped form these convoys were outstandingly fortunate. Not one of them was lost at all. Elsewhere, however, it was a different tale.

Anglo-Saxon's first loss came on 29 May 1940, when *Telena* was bombarded and set on fire by a U-boat off Cape Finisterre. Eight more company vessels went down that year: *Thiara*, torpedoed 170 miles SW of Rockall, 27 July; *Pecten*, torpedoed 75 miles N of Tory Island, Ireland, 25 August; *Torinia*, torpedoed 450 miles W of Tory Island, 21 September; *Caprella* and *Sitala*, torpedoed 150 miles SW of Rockall, 19 October; *Dosinia*, mined in the Mersey, 26 October; *Conch*, torpedoed 450 miles W of Tory Island during the night of 12 December; and *Arinia*, mined five miles ESE of Southend, 19 December.

The following year, 1941, was still worse, with ten Anglo-Saxon losses: *Clea, Simnia, Agnita, Chama, Conus, Auris, Horn*

MS **Simnia** *(9,233dwt) under fire from the guns of the German heavy cruiser* **Admiral Hipper** *in the Atlantic.*
Reported sunk by **Gneisenau***, 15 March 1941.*

Shell, *Turbo*, *Bulysses* and *Cardita*. Most were torpedoed, and all except one (*Turbo*, victim of an air attack off Port Said) were in the Atlantic. In the 12 months following Japan's entry into the war on 7 December 1941, the company lost a further 17 vessels. Tragically, one of these, the small MV *Harpa* (Captain C. A. Howarth), was blown up on 27 January 1942 by an Allied mine in the Singapore Straits. Ten of the others were torpedoed, and on 3 February 1942 *Pinna* was bombed. She survived that attack, but was bombed again the following day, after which she ran aground and was lost.

Nevertheless, a turning point was approaching. In south-east Asian waters – to the enormous relief of every Allied sailor, civilian or naval, from the American Chief of Naval Operations (Admiral Ernest J. King) down – the once completely dominant Japanese Navy did not think to apply the German strategy of systematic attacks on merchant shipping. Meanwhile, in the Atlantic theatre, the menace of the U-boat was gradually brought under control in 1943, with the Allies' introduction of new weaponry: Asdic, VLR (very long range) aircraft, escort carriers, and the Hedgehog and Squid – depth charges

thrown forwards rather than aft, which enabled a submarine killer to track its prey without interruption. Thereafter, in common with all other merchant fleets, Shell's losses plummeted dramatically: only four Anglo-Saxon vessels were sunk in 1943, none at all in 1944, and only two in 1945. The very last to go was *Gold Shell*. Ironically, she was a German-built vessel, completed by Bremer Vulkan in 1931 – German-built and, on 16 April 1945, German-sunk: she hit a mine while on passage from Thameshaven to Antwerp with a cargo of high octane spirit. Thirty-five men died, and many were dreadfully injured – amongst them, a Geordie with what later seemed the fateful name of Billy Burns. He had just been made up to Chief Engineer; the ship had been in need of a Chief; and at short notice Burns was telephoned by Jerry Walters of Anglo-Saxon's personnel division, to see if he could fill the billet at once. Burns accepted. He took the night train the evening he was called, and arrived at Thameshaven just in time to join *Gold Shell* for his first, and last, voyage in his new rank. The explosion blew him into the oil-covered, blazing sea around the ship. He was rescued alive; but by then he had been so terribly burned that he was permanently disfigured and blind.

He lived another 46 years, an honoured member of and regular attender at 'the old boys' club', Shell's society of retired Masters and Chief Engineers, and died shortly before their annual reunion in 1991. Of course, war is war until peace is signed; yet somehow, coming only 22 days before VE Day, the end of the war in Europe, the dead and injured from *Gold Shell* seem among the most tragic of all Shell's losses in those years.

For Eagle, though the numbers of losses were smaller, the pattern was similar, with 1942 being by far the worst year: two ships in the last months of 1939, two more throughout 1940, three in 1941, seven in 1942, one each in 1943 and 1944, and, mercifully, none in 1945.

Naturally enough, not all the harrowing details were made public knowledge at the time; but some of the voyages were undeniably spectacular achievements, which, for their value as propaganda and sustainers of national morale, received the full publicity treatment, including films. The rescue of *San Demetrio* was one such, and another – perhaps the most spectacular of all – was the voyage, in August 1942, of *Ohio* to Malta from the Clyde. *Ohio* – a 14,000dwt tanker, property of the Texas Oil Company (today's Texaco) and on loan to the Ministry of War Transport – was managed and manned by Eagle. As a British colony since 1814, and autonomous since 1939 (though not independent until 1964), Malta's location was strategically critical in the war: lying at the crossroads of the Mediterranean, it formed a base from which Allied forces could interdict Axis supply lines to north Africa. Axis forces besieged the island for three years, inflicting dreadful carnage on it and its people; but, defended by the Royal Navy, the Royal Air Force, the US Navy and the Maltese themselves, and sustained by the Merchant Navy, it never surrendered.

The battles surrounding the merchant convoys were among the bitterest of the war, and one of the most savage of all was fought over Operation 'Pedestal', the code name given to the convoy of which *Ohio* (Captain D. W. Mason) and her 13,000 tons of kerosene and fuel-oil formed part. From many volunteers, Captain Mason, Chief Engineer J. Wyld and all the other men in *Ohio* were specially selected for the task. With them were a naval liaison officer and 23 extra gunners. Before they set sail, Mason assembled the ship's company and read them a letter written to him by the First Lord of the Admiralty and the First Sea Lord. It said, in part:

Malta has for some time been in great danger. It is imperative that she should be kept supplied. These are her critical months, and we cannot fail her. She has stood up to the most violent attack from the air that has ever been made, and now she needs your help in continuing the battle. ... We know that Admiral Syfret [commanding the naval escort] will do all he can to complete the operation with success, and that you will stand by him according to the splendid traditions of the Merchant Navy.

From left: *Captain R. S. (Bob) Allen, Captain David Williams; C/E W. W. (Billy) Burns; Mr. Jerry Walters; C/O I. M. L. (Ian) McLean; Rev. Kenneth Matthews, DSC, OBE; Cdre J. R. (Jimmy) Rumbellow.*

MS Sepia, product carrier, en route from Madagascar to Seychelles in 1942.

After leaving the Clyde on 2 August 1942, the convoy headed north-west and then south around Ireland, entering the Strait of Gibraltar under cover of darkness during the night of 8-9 August. The merchantmen were exceptionally heavily defended: transatlantic convoys might frequently have only one or two warships escorting them, but Pedestal was screened by destroyers, cruisers, battleships and five aircraft carriers. They continued into the Mediterranean for two more days, covering 500 miles; then on the morning of 11 August, when they were about 60 miles off the north African coast, between Bougie and Philippeville, HMS *Eagle* – one of the aircraft carriers – was torpedoed. She was only a mile and a half from *Ohio*, clearly visible from the tanker, and she went down so suddenly that men watching saw, in a terrible cascade, the planes falling from her flight deck as she turned over and sank.

From then on the daylight air attacks were almost continuous. One merchant ship was fatally crippled; one destroyer was severely damaged and had to be scuttled. As the convoy approached the Sicilian Narrows, between Marsala and Cape Bon, where the heavy naval units could no longer accompany them, the merchantmen and their close escort were mauled by air, submarine and torpedo-boat attacks. The cruiser *Manchester* was sunk by an Italian torpedo-boat, the anti-aircraft ship *Cairo* by an Italian submarine; and at dusk on 12 August *Ohio* was torpedoed. The explosion ripped a great hole in the main deck, silenced the engineroom, laid the pumproom open to the sea, and started fires in several places.

For several hours the ship lay dead in the water. Ahead of her, another merchantman blazed steadily – five were sunk altogether – and, as they had to, the rest of the convoy continued on their way. Nevertheless, Wyld and his colleagues managed to restart *Ohio*'s engines, and by six in the morning of 13 August they had caught up with the convoy – just in time for the attacks to be renewed. One enemy aircraft, shot down, crashed on deck and lay there burning; two simultaneous sticks of bombs, exploding on either side of the ship, lifted her bodily from the sea; and at 10.30 her engines stopped again. Astonishingly, the engineers got them going once more, but they could now make only three to four knots. Before noon both boilers were blown out. This time they could not be restarted; the only remaining hope was to be taken in tow by some of the

Ohio *in her Texaco colours*

escorting vessels.

Air attacks interrupted their efforts again and again. In one of these attacks, a bomb penetrated into and exploded in the boiler room. At last, however, with a destroyer lashed on either side and a minesweeper towing ahead, they got under way, but desperately slowly. Again, the rest of the convoy was obliged to keep going, but now some air support was reaching *Ohio* from Malta. Even so, the attacks against her carried on: on the morning of 14 August she was holed aft, her rudder was blown away, and she began to sink. As the battle overhead continued, below decks the battle was to keep her afloat. Part of the cargo was jettisoned and replaced by compressed air. By 8 pm Malta was in sight, and naval tugs came out to take over from the destroyers. Struggling on through the night, the ship settled steadily into the water; and when the gallant vessel crept at last into the relative safety of Valetta's Grand Harbour, she had only 30 inches of freeboard (the distance from main deck to waterline) left.

That terrible voyage brought deserved honour: *Ohio's* crew became one of the most decorated of all, with a George Cross for Captain Mason and a DSO for Chief Engineer Wyld, as well as five DSCs and seven DCMs for other members of the ship's company. Today, remembering and saluting those extraordinarily brave men, there is scarcely a better tribute than the signal sent to them from the Vice Admiral commanding Malta:

I am very glad to see you after such a hazardous and anxious passage. Your cargo will be invaluable.

So it was; for though *Ohio* herself was a total loss, she still had 11,500 tons of oil in her tanks.

There was another side to the tankers' war, a side which did not achieve great fame, but which was nonetheless crucial. Without the compressed air that helped keep her up, *Ohio* might well have sunk before reaching Malta; and that was only one of five inventions which, originating from the combined staff of Anglo-Saxon and Eagle Oil, saved many

Captain D. W. Mason

ships and many lives.

The men at the head of the teams were Lynn Nelson of Eagle and John Lamb of Anglo-Saxon. Nelson first thought of using compressed air to keep torpedoed ships afloat in 1940, after another Eagle ship, *San Delfino* (Captain S. Perry), was mined in the Humber on 28 December 1939. With her back broken, Perry beached his ship. As successive tides weakened the hull and the after part began to sag, it seemed likely that she would split completely in two. Different methods of keeping the stern up and relatively straight were tried, and compressed air turned out to be the most effective. *San Delfino* was eventually drydocked for permanent repairs, and Nelson, supported by the Shell directors, began experimenting. The system he and his team eventually devised, which enabled compressed air to be fed into any part of a ship, was found to have many uses: it could power sea water pumps for firefighting, shift cargo from a damaged tank, even steer the ship; and, as they had originally envisaged, it could help keep a sinking ship afloat, by simultaneously forcing water out of a ruptured tank and by providing buoyancy.

By mid-1941 this valuable system was standard in all tankers. Two years later, Eagle and Anglo-Saxon boffins turned their skills to another problem, and solved it with equal success. The problem was that if sailors were escaping from a sinking tanker, more often than not the surrounding sea would be covered in oil, perhaps inches thick. Anyone who fell or jumped into it, or surfaced through it, found he was covered in it. It would fill a man's ears, eyes, nose and mouth: blinded, deafened and unable to breathe properly, he might not realize that a life-raft was only a few yards away. Many lives were lost simply by men swimming in the wrong direction, but even if an oil-covered survivor made it to a raft or boat, his troubles were far from over: eyelids stuck together, nostrils clogged, mouth filled with filth, lungs seared – it is no wonder that life-rafts were sometimes found bearing nothing but corpses.

The answer was two-fold. First, as much oil as possible had to be kept off the survivors, especially their faces; but they had to be able to breathe and see. Second, if they did get oil on them but reached a raft, they had to be able to remove the oil. Working in conjunction with another Shell company, Anglo-Saxon's technical division

Illustration Steve Rudd

invented a soap that worked in salt or fresh water to remove oil; and Eagle's Reginald Mitchell came up with an ingenious device to stop the oil getting on a man in the first place.

Simple but effective, this was a mask or hood, covering the whole head, rather like a diver's mask. The ingenious aspects were these: a valve in the forehead position, which, activated by being tapped after surfacing, gave the man air without allowing either oil or water inside the hood; and the eye pieces. Looking like nothing so much as an optician's diagnostic lenses, these had four separate, individually removeable discs over each eye. Surfacing through oil, the top discs would inevitably be covered and the man in darkness, but by taking one disc out, he could see for a few minutes, at least until an oily wave slopped over his head again. If that happened, the process could be repeated; and provided he remembered to take out only one disc at a time, he had eight chances of getting a good clear look at his surroundings – eight chances where otherwise he would have had none.

One of the few positive things to be said about war is that, by concentrating years of experience into months or even weeks, invention leaps ahead. Unhappily, this is usually the invention of still more efficient ways of killing people; but John Lamb (who was not only an employee of a shipping company, well versed in the hazards of the sea, but also happened to have a strong Christian faith) was a good deal more interested in saving people's lives.

Before the introduction of the Eagle hood, blindness, deafness and scorching of the lungs were in some ways the least a man had to fear when he plunged into an oil covered sea; because, as happened to Billy Burns, there was every chance that the oil, and consequently the surface of the sea itself, would be ablaze. Boats, if

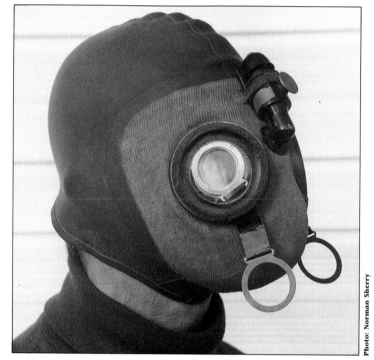

Eagle hood

Photo: Norman Sherry

there had been time to launch them, might well be on fire too; and even if they were not, then all oxygen could be stolen from the superheated atmosphere. If survivors were not burned to death, suffocation could all too easily follow, even in the open air.

What was needed, therefore, were fireproof, covered lifeboats. Lamb conducted a lengthy series of experiments to achieve this aim – and did so personally, putting himself into his prototypes while they were surrounded with flames so hot that thermometers, on reaching 2,400° Fahrenheit, simply exploded.

Through trial and error, he learned that steel lined with asbestos formed the best hull. Under the urgent demands of wartime, though, he also found that wood was best in the short term: wooden lifeboats were readily available for conversion; steel was in short supply; and wood alone was actually better than steel alone, because wood charred and formed an insulating layer, whereas steel just melted.

John Lamb OBE

He and his colleagues then devised hand-powered water sprays to cool the top of a collapsible canvas and asbestos hood, covering the whole of the boat. 'To see the flames licking round the canvas hood was rather alarming,' Lamb admitted later, 'especially when the fire got going and began to roar like a dozen jet-engined aeroplanes passing overhead.' But they found that however fierce the blaze outside, the temperature inside never exceeded 116° Fahrenheit.

Fearsome as they were, these experiments were thoroughly successful, with wooden lifeboats soon being converted wholesale; and since it would be impossible to compute the number of lives saved by them, perhaps the

San Adolfo (1935) 11,335dwt

Fireproof lifeboat under test.

best and simplest tribute to this invention was one from a boy who watched the experiments. Sitting on a wall near the trial basin, he was joined by a girl who wanted to know what was going on. Down below, John Lamb's lifeboat was engulfed in fire. 'They're trying to burn that boat', said the boy contemptuously, 'and they can't.'

It is often forgotten that the first (and, really, the last) reason for the existence of an armed navy in peacetime is to protect the merchant navy as it goes about its lawful occasions on the seas. In wartime, the situation, though of course not reversed, is altered. The two fleets (the one armed, the other virtually unarmed) then operate in even closer and mutually vital roles of defence and supply; and throughout the Second World War, Shell tankers supported and supplied the warships of the Allies in every theatre of operations, from Greenland to Tobruk, Norway to Australia, Ceylon to Iwo Jima. A shining example was Eagle's 11,335dwt *San Adolfo*. Completed by the Furness Shipbuilding Company in 1934, she was requisitioned by the Admiralty on 5 November 1939 (Fireworks Night – perhaps an apt date), and served for the entire war as a Fleet oiler, going practically everywhere. In the West Indies station she helped salvage a captured German tanker; thereafter, she oiled the Russian convoys, the forces invading North Africa, and the British Pacific Fleet.

This last force is often forgotten. By the time it was formed (November 1944), the Pacific War had been fought very largely by American forces, and the presence of the BPF brought inevitable tangles to inter-allied politics – yet it was more than a tail-end Charlie. Designated Task Force 37, its operations (nominally independent of the Americans) were in practice a full part of Admiral Halsey's Third Fleet. Ten vessels owned or managed by Shell were involved: *San Andres*, as a naval store carrier; *Empire Crest* and *Seven Sisters* as water carriers; and seven of the BPF's 22 oilers, namely, *Carelia*, *Darst Creek*, *Golden Meadow*, *Loma Novia*, and the San's *Adolfo*, *Amado* and *Ambrosio*.

Here, essential as they were, it is possible merely to mention the tankers' Pacific service, without elaboration.

Likewise, space permits only an outline of their service in yet another operation: Overlord – the liberation of Europe, beginning on 6 June 1944 with the D-Day landings in Normandy.

To walk those beaches today, mile upon mile long, is a very moving experience. It does not matter whether you are in the quiet and empty parts, or in the bustling sections near the famous resorts: everywhere, you can imagine how it was that morning, the dawn of D-Day, when every part of the sea in front of you was covered with Allied warships and merchant ships – for the occupying enemy, a complete surprise provoking the utmost consternation; for us today, a memory for which we can only be grateful.

It was the largest amphibious operation ever undertaken. In the Allies' armed forces of sea, air and land, a total of 2,876,439 officers and men were involved, and a total of 3,567 major naval combat vessels, landing craft and special vessels, all supported and supplied by the Merchant Navy. *Dolabella*, *Goldmouth*, *Opalia* and (less than a year before her sad demise) *Gold Shell* were there; so

were the little 900dwt *Empire Settler*, and 50 of her sisters. Their function was not glamorous: the large tankers supplied fuel and (by means of filters and distillation units) fresh water to landing craft and others at sea, and the little ships, with their shallower draft, did the same for units close in shore. To be among the suppliers of fuel and fresh water for D-Day may not sound like much – the equivalent of a theatrical spear carrier, perhaps – but a moment's thought of the huge numbers of warships and men will adjust that. This was the largest amphibious operation in history, and without fuel and fresh water not one of those ships or men could have moved far. Even Shell's British fleet, which in a 1942 register of ships was described as 'this vast enterprise', could play only a small part in such a great undertaking. Nevertheless, it was a vital part, as were the parts played by Shell's tankers in their supply of the armed Allied navies across the world; and with this 'Mention in Dispatches', all can fairly take their place in the fleet's gallant war record.

Long before those events, Shell tankers were intimately and actively involved in an area which, to conclude this brief account of the fleet's role in the Second World War, deserves some detailed attention: the winning of the Battle of the Atlantic.

It is not too much to say that if that battle had not ultimately been won by the Allies, D-Day and the liberation of Europe could not have taken place. Victory on the ocean was an essential prerequisite, for without it the enormous quantity of transatlantic supplies that drove the Allies through to Berlin simply could not have been carried across with any certainty or safety. Shell's contribution was imaginative and unusual: the MAC ships.

John Lamb had enjoyed his experiments with fire-proof lifeboats: in his later writing, he described them, engagingly but realistically, as 'playing with fire'. In recognition of his contribution to the safety of merchant ships, he was awarded the OBE, an honour which he said had been earned not by him alone but by the team that worked with him. Together, they had overcome some of the perils

Illustration Steve Rudd

facing a sailor from a sunken tanker; but the ultimate protection was to guard them from being sunk at all.

For transatlantic convoys (which, throughout the war, were the most important for Britain's survival), the most dangerous part of a voyage in either direction was the middle of the ocean, the so-called 'Black Gap' or 'Black Pit'. From either side of the ocean, convoy escorts, destroyers and cruisers, could usually go only part way, shepherding their charges through the first or last thousand miles or so. In the intervening gap, the convoys' greatest (and often sole) protection was the wide expanse of the ocean itself; but the wolf packs lurked in that gap, and were dreadful predators. To bridge the gap, with defences that kept the packs at bay, was consequently a matter of the utmost concern, not only for Great Britain as a whole, but also for the thousands of individual merchant sailors who crossed it. Some of the Allies' anti-submarine measures have been mentioned above, but the one which, for a sailor, was the most reassuringly visible (and which was highly effective as well) was the escort carrier.

In the latter part of the war, American shipyards churned these out, purpose-built and mainly for use in the Pacific. Earlier on, British yards could not hope to provide all that was needed for the Atlantic. The first expedient, fitting launch catapults on large merchant ships, was too wasteful of aircraft: unless a pilot were close to shore, he would eventually have to ditch, and his machine (and maybe he himself) would be lost. So was born the concept of the MAC ship, the Merchant Aircraft Carrier. To begin with, the Admiralty considered converting general cargo ships for the purpose. The main drawback of this was that, because a flight deck would make cargo winches unusable, each conversion would mean one less cargo-carrying hull. Simultaneously, however, John Lamb and his team were working on the same problem, and their solution was to use tankers. Some capacity would be sacrificed, but not much: needing pumps rather than winches to load and discharge, a tanker could still work

as a tanker, even with a flight deck on top.

The Admiralty were interested, but unconvinced, reasoning that if an aircraft crashed on landing, it could blow up the whole vessel; the ship and her crew would be destroyed, and the blazing wreck would be a homing beacon for U-boats. Sure that he was right, Lamb took his rough, unfinished plans home in disappointment; but time and the U-boats forced the issue. In June 1942 conversions began on two grain ships, *Empire MacAlpine* and *Empire MacAndrew*, which, with a below-decks hangar aft, would be able to carry four Swordfish biplanes with their wings folded. Grain handles in a very similar way to oil, so in September Lamb was asked to resubmit his plans for converting tankers, this time in detail; and this time they were accepted, virtually without change.

Between February 1943 and November 1944, nine Shell tankers were turned into MAC ships. Unlike the grain carriers, they had no below-decks hangars, because the entire tank space was needed for oil, so each carried three Swordfish on the open (and, as one pilot said, 'truly minuscule') flight deck. Despite their antique appearance, these open-cockpitted 'Stringbags' were amazingly effective aircraft. It was Stringbags which on 25 May 1941 helped seal the fate of the German battleship *Bismarck*, and which on 11 November 1940 crippled the Italian fleet when it lay at anchor in Taranto.

Anglo-Saxon's *Rapana* was the first tanker to become a MAC ship, followed by six more – *Acavus*, *Adula*, *Alexia*, *Amastra*, *Ancylus* and *Miralda* – from the same fleet. (Two of the Group's Dutch flag ships, *Gadila* and *Macoma*, were also made into MAC ships, and were the first aircraft carriers in the Royal Netherlands Navy.) All were members of the 'Triple Twelve' class of 1935-36, and, being virtually identical (12,200 dwt, 465 feet length overall, 59 feet beam), their conversions could be standardized, each one taking about five months to complete.

***MS Standella, 9,233dwt. This tanker was twice torpedoed (August 1942 and June 1943) but survived the war and was eventually
scrapped in 1959.***

This did not mean the job was easy; all kinds of
technical difficulties had to be overcome. The tanker's
superstructure had to be removed and replaced by a
prefabricated sectional deck of 461 by 62 feet. This was 'less
than a cricket pitch', a pilot pointed out ruefully, and there
were no steam catapults – they 'would have been a big
help,' an engineer acknowledged, 'but we needed our
steam for the steering gear'. With hydraulic arrester wires
to halt the incoming aircraft, and a crash barrier ('a wire
hawser net affair like an outsize tennis net') in case they
missed the arresters, the whole structure weighed nearly a
thousand tons, leaving aside the girders which supported it
underneath.

Upright funnels had to be replaced with horizontal
ones; an island structure on the starboard side had to be
installed, incorporating navigating bridge, aircraft control
and signal top; gun sponsons, for two Bofors and six

Oerlikons, had to be mounted on the sides; lifeboat davits
had to be relocated; and finally the accommodation space
had to be increased, because the usual crew complement
was nearly doubled by pilots, gunners, observers,
maintenance men and others from the Fleet Air Arm.

Despite all the alterations, a typical MAC ship was only
half a knot slower after conversion than she had been
before, and still had 90% of her pre-conversion cargo
capacity. However, the changes could cause confusion.
Fifth Engineer John Main was a new Anglo-Saxon recruit
when, in 1943, he arrived in North Shields to join *Rapana*.
No one had told him she was now an aircraft carrier, and
he naturally expected to find a conventional tanker with
three islands – poop, bridge and fo'c'sle. Instead, 'no
funnel, no masts, the bridge and wheelhouse gone...' He
was thunderstruck, and thought a terrible mistake had
been made; but sure enough, it was *Rapana*, and he had to

Nassarius (1944-1959), 8,246grt, in a North Atlantic convoy. Note armament at the latter stages of the war.

get used to it quickly.

So, of course, did the Fleet Air Arm boys. Collectively, they formed 836 Squadron, with a total of 92 aircraft. With very few exceptions, they were 'Wavy Navy' – Royal Naval Volunteer Reservists, active during hostilities only, with their volunteer status indicated by wavy gold braid around their cuffs, instead of the straight gold rings of the career Royal Navy. Lieutenant John Godley (later Lieutenant Commander Godley, DSC, and subsequently Lord Kilbracken) was one of them, serving for a year and a half in *Acavus* and *Adula*. His father was a peer and, at 23 years old, he himself was one of the squadron's most highly skilled pilots, but in the working of the ship, these were minor facts; and though he and John Main never served together, their memories overlap and confirm each other, most importantly, in the crucial area of relationships between the fliers and the merchant sailors.

In a transatlantic convoy (which could include anything from 40 to 100 merchantmen), a MAC ship had a unique status. Royal Navy escort vessels were commanded by the senior RN officer present, the Senior Officer (Escort) or SOE. Merchant Navy vessels were under the direct, sole command of the Convoy Commodore, usually a retired RN or RNR officer who had volunteered for the job. MAC ships, though, came under both, being commanded by the Convoy Commodore or the SOE as appropriate to the circumstances.

This strange hybridity extended within the ships themselves, for – although convoy was a tradition well established by the First World War and earlier conflicts – the mix of RN and MN crews in one vessel under a Merchant Navy Master had never occurred before. In everything that pertained to the safety of his vessel, a MAC-ship Master had absolute control over his crew, whatever their role or rank. To formalise the arrangement, the Fleet Air Arm contingent was obliged to sign ship's articles as deck hands, nominally on a daily pay of one shilling and a bottle of beer. No one knew if it would work out happily, and if so, how. Though it was obviously vital that harmonious relations should be established swiftly and maintained well, customary attitudes between the two fleets seemed likely to be a serious hurdle; merchant sailors usually found the Royal Navy snobby, bossy and over-organized, while the Royal Navy usually

John Main

MAC ship **Rapana. Built 1935 Wilton Fijenoord, Holland: converted to MAC 9 1943; returned to normal tanker service 1945.**

saw merchant sailors as uncouth, loutish and ill-disciplined.

There was, in short, every possibility for (even likelihood of) discord; yet if ever any occurred, no one seems to remember it now – indeed, very much the opposite. From the beginning, while testing, training and working up to operational status, everyone was infected by the barely-suppressed air of excitement on board, and by the knowledge, obvious at first sight of the ship, that here was something really different and new. Like everything else which is done repeatedly, it all became routine after a while; but by then the crews had come to know each other well, respected each other's different but complementary skills and, off duty, enjoyed each other's company socially. If the weather was bad, poker was a favourite pastime; if not, deck hockey. Main reckoned later that with the combination of arrester wires and narrow, low-level side walkways instead of proper shipside rails, deck hockey became more hazardous than U-boats.

Whether intended or not, that is a considerable tribute to the Stringbags and their pilots. The aircraft were each armed with eight rocket projectiles, and a skilled pilot could place a rocket inside a semi-submerged target only four feet square. Until commanders became wary, the aircraft did actually destroy U-boats; in Kilbracken's words, their rockets were so powerful that a submarine could be sunk by 'a single hit in the right place, let alone eight.... A pair of well-aimed rockets would pass clean through a U-boat, making bloody great holes below water-level where each of them entered and exited. That should be enough.'

After four years of horrible suffering at the hands of U-boats, sinking one was immensely satisfying for all concerned; but what was no less important was keeping them away, so that the convoys with their life-giving supplies could pass in safety. Weather permitting, the Stringbags would patrol at least twice daily, at dawn and dusk: 'The strategy', as Main recalls, 'was to force the U-boats off the surface for at least a full day's steaming distance around the convoy.'

The operational achievement of ships and aircraft may be judged by a few simple figures. MAC ships collectively made 323 transatlantic crossings in the two years of their service, escorting 217 separate convoys; the Stringbags flew 4,177 sorties; and only one of those convoys was successfully attacked.

That exemplary record was not the only achievement of the MAC ships. Another, which in the longer term some might say was just as important, was the almost unheard-of degree of harmony established between the two halves of the crews, the merchant and the armed sailors. Both sides contributed positively to this. Thinking of *Adula* ('a happy ship if ever there was one'), Lord Kilbracken still affectionately recalls her Master, Captain J. F. Rumbellow – 'an officer of the old school, always perfectly turned out, spick and span in full uniform, with eagle face, gold peaked cap, and some of a Captain's exclusiveness' – and 'above all, Bob Allen, the three-striped Chief Officer, life and soul of

MAC ship Amastra *under conversion. The flight deck was carried above the tank tops on a 'giant set of meccano'.*

*Swordfish landing on MAC ship **Amastra**, North Atlantic, 1943. The Swordfish were armed with eight anti-submarine rockets and a machine-gun.*

his own never-ending party, enveloping us in his laughter and high spirits, welding in friendship our whole ship's company with its Merchant Navy and Wavy Navy contingents.'

For their own part, the pilots and their assistants – being members of a young and only half-acknowledged part of the Royal Navy – knew all too well what it was like to be cold-shouldered by their stuffier colleagues. From the start they showed every respect to their new shipmates, proudly wearing the silver 'MN' badge in their uniform lapels, and greatly enjoying the rage that this entirely legitimate act caused in more hide-bound naval officers ashore; and before long they hit upon another very visible method of showing their regard. It was quite simple, completely illegal, and one of the most pleasant tributes that could have been paid. The Stringbags used in the MAC ships were painted pure white, being the best camouflage for day-flying over the sea, and were otherwise entirely standard Fleet Air Arm planes – 'except that', says Kilbracken with a twinkle, 'in many flights, so great was our MN loyalty, we would paint out ROYAL NAVY on their sides and substitute MERCHANT NAVY.'

That Family Feeling

Shell has long had a reputation as being a cradle-to-grave employer, and over the decades many employees have indeed spent their entire working lives within the Group. This is, of course, a two-way transaction; the Group is not a machine, but a very large number of like-minded individual people, and employees would not stay in the Group if they did not like it, any more than the Group would employ them if they were not liked.

The mutual loyalty that develops over the years has often extended from one generation to another, with fathers, then sons, and sometimes grandsons too joining. With Shell's British tanker fleets, this has been just as true in the East as in the West. From the earliest days of the Samuel fleet, Hong Kong Chinese crews were recruited to serve at sea and ashore. Unfortunately, today there are too few young men from Hong Kong available for sea service; the last of STUK's all-Chinese crews served in SS *Bekulan* during the rescue of the castaway Filipino fisherman Camilo Arcelao in April 1991, and were paid off when the ship went into dry-dock that September. However, one example which may stand for many, being both long-serving and Chinese, is the Lee family of Hong Kong.

Lee Mun Ting, born in Canton province in 1909, moved to Shanghai in 1925 with hopes of becoming a marine engineer. A three-year apprenticeship in a workshop led to five years with a small shipping firm as a ship repairing engineer. From there he joined a larger, international company, learned English and (in 1936) successfully applied for a job with Anglo-Saxon. This was the beginning of a life-long association, interrupted only by the Second World War.

Engineer Lee Mun Ting in uniform . . .

From 1936 to 1940, Lee served as Second Engineer in inland tankers, sailing along the Yangtze Kiang river. By the time Japan entered the war, Lee was married and serving in ocean-going tankers, working between Malaysia, Sumatra, Borneo and Singapore. On 3 February 1942, in position 0° 52′S 104° 19′E, while on passage from Pladju in Sumatra to beleaguered Singapore with a cargo of aviation fuel, his ship, *Pinna*, was attacked by a Japanese bomber. By good fortune, the highly volatile cargo remained untouched; but after several passes, the plane scored a hit on *Pinna*'s forecastle, and then, seeing his victim apparently beginning to sink, sheered off and left the vessel to her fate.

Second Engineer Lee helped to shore up the damage, and, severe as it was, the flooding was brought under control. Trying to avoid further air attack, the ship

. . . and more relaxed.

began to zig-zag, but, while approaching Singapore the following day (4 February 1942), was bombed again and had to be beached. A total of 20 crew were killed; a further 23, and two passengers were taken prisoner. On 15 February Singapore fell to besieging Japanese forces, and Lee remained in the captured city for the rest of the war.

Though he was not behind bars, he was a prisoner, obliged to do as his captors said, and was made to work for the Kwong Soon Engineering Company – which was likewise made to produce technical equipment for Japanese military aircraft. With the return of peace, however, Kwong Soon switched to ship repairing, and found Lee's knowledge and experience very valuable. He was at once made their Chief Foreman, helping to set up their still flourishing marine business.

In 1947, Lee was able to return to his family in Shanghai; then, back in Hong Kong, he picked up the traces with Shell once more, becoming a Marine Engineering Foreman in 1948. His family joined him in 1951 and he worked for Shell for 17 years more, rising to be Marine Engineering Supervisor. He retired from that post in 1968, at the age of 59; but that was still not the end of the link. Almost immediately, he was taken on again, this time by the new department, to act as an examiner of Chinese candidate fitters and mechanics.

In 1971 – 35 years after he had first joined Anglo-Saxon – Lee Mun Ting retired permanently from Shell. He lived another 20 years, proud to see how 'that family feeling' continued: in 1970 his eldest son David Lee joined Shell Hong Kong, and remained with them for 18 years before transferring to another company within the Royal Dutch/Shell Group.

Together, the Lees, father and son, have given well over half a century's service to Shell. In itself, the example demonstrates the high degree of two-way loyalty and support very often found between Group companies and their employees; and it should be remembered that the Lees were, and are, by no means a unique, or even an extreme example. It is not a question of 'jobs for the boys': if it was ever true, companies today certainly do not survive (far less grow to the stature of Shell) by employing incompetents merely because of a family connection – rather the contrary. Those whom Shell employs are employed because of their competence (often, indeed, their world-leading expertise) in their field; and those who work all their lives with Shell do so not least because it is so satisfying to work with people as able as themselves.

'Fitting-out basin, Harland and Wolff, Belfast', *by Pamela Drew.*
Left: **Patella** *(1946-1967) nearing completion. Centre:* **Lepton** *(1947-1960) commencing fitting-out.*

Chapter Eight
Peaceful Waters
1946-1957

MV Lyria (1946-1955), 9,240dwt.

Captain Sam Harland

The port of Okha lies at the mouth of the Gulf of Kutch in north-west India, just where the gulf opens out into the Arabian Sea – hot, dusty, fragrant, and, as the site of one of Shell's many Eastern shore installations, a place visited regularly by the company's tankers. In the late 1940s and early 1950s, Anglo-Saxon's MV *Lyria* (Captain E. Jacob) was often seen there, discharging cargoes from the great Iranian refinery at Abadan. Built by Harland and Wolff in Belfast in 1946 with diesel engines, the 9,000dwt *Lyria* was graceful in appearance, with tall masts and an attractive sheer, and immaculately cared for. In Abadan, the first time he saw her, Sam Harland (her then Chief Officer) described her as 'easily the smartest ship in the harbour'. Later, in Okha, she outdid herself, dressed overall for a rather special occasion. Looking at the bright bunting stretched from stem to stern, anyone who could read flags would have seen a long name spelled out. On board there was even more activity than usual. In the saloon, decorated with flowers and flags, a white cloth was being laid on a sideboard; in the engineroom, the inside of the ship's bell was being polished on a lathe; in his workshop, the Chinese carpenter was shaping and polishing a piece of teak to make a frame, so that the bell could be stood upside down and used as a font; and when the church minister arrived, summoned from his parish 200 miles in the interior, everything was ready for a christening.

Such events are rare in tankers; this one was a favour to the local installation's manager and his wife, whose baby it was. There was only one slight difficulty: the baby's name was so long, *Lyria* did not have enough flags to spell it out completely. But as far as the running of the ship was concerned, the occasion presented no problem at all: throughout

the ceremony and the subsequent party, the pumps unobtrusively continued discharging cargo. Their deep, distant throbbing did not disturb the guests at all, but the officers, half-hearing it in the background, were constantly reassured that all was well.

When Stanley Algar and his prisoner-of-war comrades were liberated and returned home in 1945, they began to learn how terrible were the changes wrought by the war. On the personal level (though Algar's marriage remained happily strong), many men found their families had become strangers, and, feeling themselves to be intruders in their own homes, they could not stand the strain of trying to reconstruct a relationship. On the professional level, there was almost as much heartache to bear, when they read the long lists of their colleagues who had been killed and the ships which had been sunk. Compared to its size at the outbreak of war, nearly 40% of the fleet had been lost; but there, at least, the task of reconstruction was rather easier to understand.

During the war, ships requisitioned by the Government had been painted a uniform dull grey. With the return of peace, their bright pre-war colours returned too, and a significant (though seemingly minor) change was made to the Anglo-Saxon livery. The house flag had been altered in 1932, from the 1907 'amalgamation' design (white background, blue diagonal cross, and red central ball) to one much more like the emblem we know today: a red background with a white central ball, on which a yellow pecten – the classic scallop shape – was superimposed. Beginning late in 1945, wartime drabness faded as the company's traditional smart black hulls and sparkling white super-structures made a welcome return. The ships' funnels were likewise restored to their cheerful pre-war yellow with a black band around the top; and they had

San Fernando (1953), 18,032dwt. Built by Cammell Laird and Co. Ltd., Birkenhead.

something extra, and new. In that year the Shell pecten was added to their sides, in red.

In such small, almost subliminal ways, the fleet's Shell identity was made ever stronger. Similarly, on 8 January 1946, the Group's old marketing arm, the Asiatic, was renamed the Shell Petroleum Company, and at the same time the fleet's reconstruction galloped ahead: by the end of 1946, through purchase or newbuilding, almost all its wartime losses had been replaced.

In the four years immediately after the war (1946-49 inclusive) Anglo-Saxon acquired a total of just over 700,000 dwt of new shipping. Placed alongside almost any one of today's fleet, these ships were still small – *Lyria*, at only 9,000 tons deadweight, was a middle-sized ship for the time. However, there was an enviably grand exuberance in their numbers: in those four years, no fewer than 71 ships were bought by or built for Anglo-Saxon. On average, a new ship joined the fleet every three weeks.

Lyria's class, the L's, included a dozen vessels completed between 1946 and 1950; in 1946, the small (5,100dwt) B-class provided the fleet with eight new names; and the 12,000dwt N-class, which included 16 war-built ships, swiftly swelled to 26 ships. Together, the

30 new members of these three classes aggregated nearly 270,000 dwt; and then came the 16,600dwt T-class.

Class initials are generally used to designate ships of identical or similar type, ordered in one batch, and generally each ship in the class has a name beginning with that initial. So it was with the T-class. During the Second World War, these were mass produced (rather like the Liberty dry cargo ships) in America, where they were known as T2 tankers. Producing 14 knots, their steam turbo-electric machinery plants were far ahead of equivalent British designs, where development had been virtually stopped by the war. The T2s were a first-class engineering job, but their hulls – all welded, for speed of production – gave some problems, and needed reinforcing. However, when peace returned there was a great surplus of these ships, and in 1947 Shell bought 19 of them. They brought two major new design factors into the fleet. Firstly, they introduced centrifugal-type cargo pumps in a single pumproom located aft, replacing the aft cofferdam. Secondly, though no less importantly, they also introduced the creature comforts of individual cabins with private showers and toilets for all deck and engineering officers.

Cargo Handling

Efficient cargo handling has always been one of the most important factors in determining the profitability of a crude oil tanker. To minimise the time spent in loading or discharge, the crew must of course know precisely what they are doing, and their equipment must be the best possible.

For deck and engine room staff alike, it quickly becomes a routine but unforgettable part of the job. Power demands are usually very great; the noise levels could be as well. Senior and retired personnel today remember how 'in the old days' the pre-1939 'Triple Twelves' could be heard a long way from the jetty, their big horizontal reciprocating cargo pumps in the two inter-tank pumprooms slamming and banging as they laboured to get the 12,000 tons of cargo out. At something better than 300 tons an hour, one complete discharge could take 36 hours or more.

With higher discharge rates, centrifugal-type pumps – electric-driven in the T2s, steam-driven in subsequent ever-larger crude carriers – can drain the ship well within 24 hours. Nevertheless, the power demand is formidable: when one of today's 320,000dwt L-class ships discharges cargo at full rate, one of her two main boilers must steam at near full rate, the ship securely moored at the terminal. These enormous power requirements for cargo discharge have been a significant factor in keeping steam turbine propulsion in VLCCs.

Helicina *(1946-1962), 18,002dwt.*

Having studied the ships already, Shell produced the 18,000dwt *Helicina* (1946) and *Hyalina* (1948), both built in Wallsend by Swan, Hunter & Wigham Richardson Ltd, with service speeds of 16 knots. All told, these two and the the 19 ships of the T-class added another 351,400 dwt to the re-forming post war fleet. Compared with them, the tiny F-class vessels (eight, of about 1,200 dwt each, aggregating a mere 9,600 dwt) could almost be overlooked, but a ship is a ship; large or small, she still needs to be manned, maintained, and provided with cargoes and trading routes.

Even that was not the end of the immediate post-war acquisitions, for in the same period there were also a number of one-offs. Bought from Government stock, *Ficus* (ex-*Empire Grenadier*) was not one of the F-class, despite her name; she was much bigger, being able to carry 14,900 dwt. However, her sea career was short: in 1951 she became a company oil storage hulk at Gibraltar.

Paludina of 1949 was very like the L's, sharing their 12,000dwt size; but she was built to carry bitumen, and so (in order to keep her cargo from solidifying) had more extensive steam heating coils in her tanks.

Finally, *Auricula* of 1946 and *Auris* of 1948 must be remembered, because, though they too were of about 12,000 dwt each, they were both experimental ships. Ordinary motor ships used a distillate fuel, only slightly more viscous than kerosene, in the pumps and injectors of their diesel engines. In contrast, *Auricula* was designed to burn high viscosity fuel (HVF). This, one of the final fractions of crude oil, was coming from the refineries in ever-increasing quantities, and was so dense that hitherto it had only had limited commercial viability. It could be used as a fuel in conjunction with lighter fractions, but not alone, except in the boilers of steam-ships and power stations. On the other hand, if it could be used by itself as a fuel in large marine engines, then – being abundant and needing very little treatment to provide the same energy content as distillate – it could offer enormous cost benefits. Compared to diesel, it was reckoned that heavy fuel-oil could save the company half a million sterling a year: a

Auris (1948), 12,290dwt: the first merchant ship to be propelled by gas turbine

figure which in 1991 was equivalent to comfortably more than £9 million, and consequently well worth pursuing.

A degree of success was apparent in *Auricula*'s maiden voyage from the UK to Curaçao in 1946. This was the first time any motorship had operated on HVF alone, and *Auricula*'s consumption was exactly the same as if she had used diesel; but the fuel was of course markedly cheaper.

Over the next few years, experiments and improvements continued under the leadership of John Lamb, comparing the efficiency of the two fuel types, testing the high viscosity fuel in manoeuvring and at slow speed, modifying and strengthening the pre-treatment and injection systems; and (though *Auricula* was sold in 1955) by the time her tenth birthday came around in 1956, every motor ship in the fleet had been altered to use HVF. Not only that, but many other shipping companies had again followed Shell's lead, so that something like 500 other vessels worldwide were using HVF too.

Crossing the bridge from the 1940s to the '50s was *Auris*, built in 1948 as a diesel-electric ship and, in 1951, fitted with the world's first marine gas turbine engine,

which replaced one of her four diesel engines. Trial, error and correction brought her to the point where in March 1952 she achieved another historic first, making a transatlantic voyage on gas turbine power alone. It seemed sufficiently promising to warrant the removal, in 1955, of her other diesels and the installation of one large gas turbine. This had some distinct advantages – it was lighter than the diesels, simpler to operate and maintain – but, per unit of power produced, it was no cheaper than the diesels, and it cost so much more to put in that other savings were cancelled out; so the project was eventually abandoned, and the onus of developing this particular system was taken up by the world's major armed fleets.

Even if the ambitious *Auris* experiments were overall less successful than the heavy fuel-oil in *Auricula*, everyone acknowledged that, once more, Shell tankers had shown the way; and throughout the 1950s, the fleet continued to expand. Between 1950-52 the first four of the V-class – *Velletia*, *Velutina*, *Verena* and *Volsella* – were completed. At 643 feet length overall and 28,000dwt each, these were the largest tankers that had ever been built in Britain.

Helix *(1953-1962), 17,780dwt.*

The trend towards an ever-closer identification of Shell and its ships continued: on 26 October 1953 a new company, Shell Tankers Ltd., was registered in London, and, at the beginning of 1954, was given management of Anglo-Saxon's vessels. The crude-oil-carrying V-class was already being followed by the ships which, until the mid-1970s, became the company's backbone: the 30-strong, 18,000dwt H-class. The first was *Harpa*. Built by Harland & Wolff, and replacing the tanker of the same name blown up by an Allied mine in 1942, she came into service in the summer of 1953; the last of the class, *Hima* (built by Cammell Laird), joined in January 1957. Two of the H's (*Helix* and *Helcion*) had turbo-electric drive; all the rest had geared steam turbines, producing a service speed of about 14.5 knots, and their number was a measure both of how well they served and how highly they were regarded. Indeed, it could be said that with the H's, Shell had evolved a good tanker for its time: sound and reliable, fairly easy to operate and (in fleet jargon) 'good pumpers',

they became the training ground for a whole generation of Shell sailors.

However, when compared to some other types of merchant ship, there was also something odd about the H's, and most oil tankers of the time: they were really still pretty small. When *Harpa* was building in 1952, exactly 60 years had passed since the launch of Marcus Samuel's first ship, the 5,010dwt *Murex*. True, at 28,000 dwt apiece, any two of the V-class together had as much deadweight capacity as all ten of Marcus's first ships, but the V's were exceptional. Likewise, Eagle ships had always tended to be larger than Anglo-Saxon ones: the first *San Fernando*, of 1918, had been an 18,530dwt ship, and was then the biggest tanker in the world. But even they had scarcely altered in size – Eagle's major post-World War Two additions (*San Leopoldo* and *San Leonardo*) were no more than 16,000 tons deadweight, and after the Anglo-Saxon V's had been built, Eagle's largest vessels were the 18,000dwt *San Florentino* and the second *San Fernando* (1953), of 18,032 dwt.

Considering the way in which the world's appetite for oil had increased, with the internal combustion engine common on sea and land, and increasingly so in the air as well, this stability of tanker size over so many years seems strange – especially today, when 300,000dwt tankers are not particularly unusual; when tankers exceeding 500,000 dwt have been delivered; and when tankers as huge as 800,000dwt (which have been designed) remain unbuilt only because of market requirements.

The design of the second *San Fernando* originated with Shell rather than Eagle; she was in fact an H-class ship, and by the standards of 1953, was the last word in modernity. She had a main address or loudspeaker system throughout, along with echo-sounding equipment, radar, direction finder, radio telephone, gyro compass and autopilot. As usual, there was not much space for carrying passengers; that has never been a part of Shell's targeted trade, and their ships have always been designed as strictly cargo-carrying. (As a quick aside, however, it is worth noting that every ship usually has a spare cabin or two, and in the past Shell ships would occasionally take two or three fare-paying passengers at a time. Terry Medley, who retired in 1990 as Shell International Marine's manager of corporate and economic analysis, began his career in the early 1950s doing freight accounts and sending invoices to the passengers in question; they were charged ten shillings a day. Such passengers – 'favoured friends and notables', as Medley described them – always took the risk that the ship's intended destination might be changed during the course of their voyage. Partly because last-minute changes have become more frequent, the practice of carrying paying passengers, even occasionally, has been discontinued.)

In parallel with her modern equipment, the crew's accommodation in *San Fernando* was a good deal more spacious and comfortable than most. Every member of the ship's company had his own cabin; every officer had his own bathroom; the furnishings of individual cabins were even colour-coordinated, the whole ship (as the owners proudly said) being 'designed and built with the same guiding principle of maximum comfort.' Altogether, it was a far cry from the simple – most people would say primitive – conditions that had obtained in most tankers, even as recently as 1939; and yet modern as she was, the *San Fernando* of 1953 actually had marginally less deadweight capacity than her namesake of 1918. This slow growth in almost all tankers of the time is such a noticeable phenomenon that it and its reasons are worth a much closer look.

The first natural thought is that it must have been a question of design limitations. In 1938, the whole world's tanker fleet had aggregated 16.6 million dwt, without one single ship being more than 25,000 dwt. By 1950, the world fleet had grown to 27.6 million dwt, yet of that total, still only 1.5 million dwt was made up of ships larger than 25,000 dwt; but this was not because bigger ships could not be built. They could be: witness Cunard's beautiful sisters, *Mauretania* and *Lusitania*. Both were launched in Britain in 1906; both could attain 25 knots or more (at least double

San Florentino (*Later to become* Hemidonax). *Built in 1959 –* 18,003dwt.

the speed of any contemporary tanker), and, at nearly 32,000 gross registered tons, both were physically as big as a tanker of 70,000 deadweight tons – not that there was such a thing in those days.

Those large ships were passenger vessels; so one might suppose that the tankers' size limitations were caused by their liquid cargo. That had indeed always been a serious consideration, because, as any sailor knew, you could not safely put a large quantity of unrestricted liquid into an ordinary hull. If you did, then as soon as the ship began to roll or pitch, the liquid would begin to surge (moving uncontrolled either from side to side, or fore and aft) and the ship could become dangerously unstable.

However, even in early tankers, this particular problem had been largely overcome by measures to limit the oil's free surface movement. First, of course, the inside of the hull was divided with longitudinal and transverse bulkheads, giving a number of separated tanks; second, because oil's actual volume alters with temperature, increasing with warmth and shrinking with cold, each tank was given an expansion trunk on top. This was supposed never to be brim-full: if it were, then with warm weather the expanding oil would overflow. Sometimes this did happen, if loading was over-enthusiastic; but given that the oil's surface was normally limited to the area within the trunk space, any destablising movement of the cargo was very much restricted.

Even so, the sheer weight of the cargo and its dividing bulkheads limited the vessels' overall size. Tankers built on the traditional pattern (ribs mounted in a strong keel, plates put over the ribs and bulkheads placed between) simply could not sustain an infinite load: the optimum size was around 12,000 dwt.

A key development in tanker design came in 1906. Invented by Sir Joseph Isherwood, 'longitudinal framing' turned the traditional pattern on its side. Basically, instead of having ribs (or 'frames') going upwards from the keel, the frames in Isherwood's design were horizontal, running fore-and-aft parallel to the keel. They in turn were joined together, and to the keel, by transverse vertical bulkheads spaced at intervals – the intervals being the tanks – and, in the centre, by one continuous bulkhead running fore-and-aft. Seen without its outside plates, the skeleton of a tanker built thus was very different from the traditional, and possessed far greater longitudinal strength while using less steel.

By 1918 more than 80% of the world tanker fleet was built to this design. The maximum safe size was still less than 20,000 dwt, but in 1925, Isherwood modified his design further, enabling the construction of tankers of 20,000 dwt and more. In the same decade, the single central bulkhead, running continuously fore-and-aft, was replaced by a pair of parallel bulkheads positioned one to either side of the centre line, giving a row of central tanks and a row of smaller wing tanks to port and starboard.

Despite all these design developments, tankers of more than 20-25,000 dwt remained mysteriously rare well into the 1950s – indeed, when Sam Harland joined the 9,000dwt *Lyria* in 1949, he was still able to say that she was 'reckoned a fairly large ship'. So with design a very interesting but by now evidently mistaken approach to the question of the limitation of tankers' size, one must consider another tack; and suddenly all becomes clear. Obviously tanker operators do not plan to work at a loss. Given that, it is equally obvious that for the whole period from the 1890s to the 1950s, the very large numbers and relatively small dimensions of Shell ships were the most profitable mix. In other words, it was not problems of design but patterns of trade and dimensions of ports which dictated the shape of the fleet.

As far as the size of tankers was concerned at that time, economies of scale did not necessarily apply, for in both hemispheres, east and west, there were practical trading limitations. In theory, it could be more economical, and

Velutina (1950-1971), 29,648dwt; the first supertanker on sea trials.

hence more profitable, to move large cargoes across the oceans in single ships. In the real world, that depended on port facilities at either end of the voyage. This was a real chicken and egg problem. In the west, the American coast was naturally dominated by American tankers, with the majority making short coastal voyages between US ports. These were not generally equipped to handle large crude-oil-carrying vessels. To do so meant considerable investment by the port authorities, dredging deeper and wider channels, building longer jetties, constructing larger storage tanks and so on. Such costs could no doubt be offset by higher port charges; but from the tanker owner's point of view, port charges were quite high enough anyway. There was no incentive to encourage their further increase; and if the owners were not going to build bigger ships, there was in turn no incentive for American authorities to spend money on unnecessary facilities.

Similarly, though the ports throughout the south-east Asian area might be separated by long sea voyages, and might not be dominated by American traffic, they nonetheless remained coastal stops rather than deep-sea

terminals. In the eastern hemisphere, therefore, essentially the same conditions obtained as in the west; and between the two lay the Suez Canal.

No one who wished to carry oil or anything else profitably to and fro between Europe and the Far East would dream of going round the Cape of Good Hope if they could go through the Canal instead: the distances and time were so much less. That, of course, had been one of the cardinal principles underlying Marcus Samuel's original creation of the Shell tanker fleet, and it remained just as true in the mid-1950s as it had in the early 1890s; and that in turn meant that the optimum size of a tanker was something that could pass through Suez. The Canal, it was true, had been enlarged since the first *Murex*'s pioneering voyage. When her 5,010 deadweight tons were towed through (she was not allowed to make the passage under steam), the maximum size the Canal could admit was 7,000 dwt. By 1954, dredging and widening had increased that limit to 32,000 dwt. Over a period of some 60 years, the dimensions of tankers and of that crucial Canal kept pace with one another. Which was chicken and

MS **Bursa** *(1946-1961) 3,738grt*

which was egg is another question; but in the end it is not too much to say that, if one is looking for a single central reason for this strange slowness in the crude oil tankers' growth in size, it was simply Suez.

So there it was: for the first sixty-odd years of Shell's British tanker fleet, it was neither technology nor design factors which kept the size of the ships so unadventurously small compared to ocean liners. Rather, the technology was available; designs could swiftly be made when necessary; and without a doubt, in either the eastern or the western hemisphere, if port authorities and tanker owners alike saw the benefit of enlarged facilities and enlarged ships, then both would come, each nudging the other forwards. But what lay between was the crucial Canal, the key to it all. From time to time Canal and tankers gave each other a prod to grow, but there was no rush: the Canal was there, would always be there, could be enlarged if prompted, and could prompt tankers to be enlarged.

With all that, there was an area in which the Suez Canal was not a matter for consideration: Shell's 'Eastern Fleet'. Of course, Shell's tankers have traded in the Far East ever since the first days of the Samuel fleet, but for a brief and indeterminate period – roughly the 20 years after World War Two – the Eastern Fleet was a more or less separate entity, composed of very small ships which worked *only* in the Far East, enjoying a high degree of independence. No such thing existed before, nor does it today; and it probably never will again.

In one sense this has no place in the history of Shell's

British tanker fleets, because (until 1959, when Singapore ceased to be a British colony) Eastern Fleet vessels were registered locally, in their region of operations, and were managed from a branch office in Singapore: even after 1959 London had little to do with their day-to-day administration. Nevertheless, the Eastern Fleet is firmly embedded in the individual and collective memories of Shell Tankers' senior personnel, many of whom trained in its vessels; and that is why it figures here.

Its economic logic was that there was quite enough trade within the zone east of Suez to support a semi-autonomous fleet with shore-based office headquarters not in London, but in Singapore. Larger ships, sent in or out as necessary, were never regarded as part of the Eastern Fleet; instead, that included vessels like the minute 305dwt MS *Lang*, the 947grt *Fossarina* (ex-*Empire Tedassa*, completed in 1947 by Laing & Sons of Sunderland) and the 3,738grt (5,000dwt) B-class tankers like *Bursa*. (This last, another Sunderland product completed in 1944 by Doxford & Sons, was built to supply the Royal Navy with oil at sea during the war, and post-war became the first command held by C. H. Hill-Willis, former Chief Officer in *Agnita*.) Taking the trade to places which their larger sisters could not reach, these little ships worked all over the region – Singapore, Balik Papan, Pladju (not so attractive), Pontianak, Bukom, Morotai, Surabaya, Bali, Hong Kong, Haiphong, Macassar, Tarakan, Benoa...

The list of ports is far from complete, but begins to give an indication of why the Eastern Fleet has such a powerful emotional existence in the memories of those who served in it. The age of jet-propelled mass tourism had not yet arrived. The region was still genuinely remote from Europe, romantic, and, at every turn, redolent of the writings of Joseph Conrad and Somerset Maugham. Voyaging in areas unfrequented by ordinary travellers, the ships had the chance to stop, sometimes for long periods, in exotic ports, occasionally large and famous, more often obscure and tucked away up some river; and though routes and cargoes were programmed, Masters were to an extent left to their own devices, with greater freedom of action and fewer pressures than were found in the global fleet. Last but not least in the Eastern Fleet's attractions, the distances and time involved meant that pay was better than in the West – a particularly important factor if one was trying to support a family at home in post-war Britain.

Of course, all this was even better if you were young and single. But the Eastern Fleet had its down-side as well, especially for those who were then its senior officers. Again because of distances and time, postings were long: anything from 18 months to four years. Often, its seniors were men who had served in the region before 1939, and who had endured the terrors of the Second World War there – not so much the attacks and sinkings at sea, as had been the case in the Atlantic and Mediterranean theatres, but the attempted flight, the capture, and the sustained degradation of life in Japanese prison camps. With the return of peace, these men became a breed apart: they had suffered in a way which, however awful the experiences of those in the west, remained utterly foreign. Nevertheless, they remained Shell people too; and when the war was done, the company did not forget them, but found them work. They knew the job and the area; they often knew the individuals ashore who ran the reconstructed ports and installations. From one point of view they were the obvious men to fill the post-war need; from another, they could scarcely have been less obvious a choice. At every port, whether loading or discharging, these survivors recognized how much had changed, saw how many familiar faces had gone, remembered (not that they could ever forget) the horrors of their war. Trying to forget those things, they retreated into silence, or, more often, into their cabins, and drank, leaving the running of the ships to their younger Chief Officers: men out from the west who did not know what it had been like in the east before the war, whose wives and children, if they had them, had never been forced to flee through jungles in fear of their lives – whose wives and children had not died.

Young as the Chief Officers were, they and their still younger subordinates were neither wholly inexperienced, nor completely insensitive. When the Old Man was overwhelmed by dark depressing memories, even the youngest officers knew enough about war to feel sympathy, and they treated their Masters with a degree of respectful indulgence that is not commonly seen in merchant ships. Perhaps it was not the right way to do things, but it was the instinctive human way, and the best that anyone knew. Occasionally it turned up some tales which can seem amusing, but which are at base desperately sad. One such was the time when a Master, habitually never seen on the bridge, was found – to everyone else's astonishment – awaiting his ship at its port of arrival. He had fallen overboard without anyone noticing. So accustomed were his crew to operating the ship without him, they had carried on without worrying overmuch that he did not emerge from his cabin; but luckily he was rescued by another, faster vessel, and reached his own ship's destination first.

The very freedom of the period and place could bring misfortune too, as in the cases (one comic, the other tragic) of two sister ships, the 305dwt *Lang* and *Landak*. These little motor vessels, typical of many in the Eastern Fleet, had only a handful of European officers and a dozen or so Malaysian, Singaporean or Chinese crewmembers, with nothing but the simplest technical equipment – not for them the luxury of a transmitting radio, for example. Being incommunicado was part of the joy of working those ships: once at sea, no one knew where you were. By the same token, though, if you got into difficulties there was no way of summoning help, apart from the traditional methods. Thus it happened that one day when *Lang* broke a rudder pintle, her crew (after trying unsuccessfully to mend it) decided they needed outside assistance. There was no immediate danger, because although they were drifting, there was plenty of sea all around; and because they were on a regular shipping route, there were frequent other vessels passing, any one of which could help. It should have been no great problem; but the result was farcical.

Making the simplest traditional signs of distress, the sailors turned the ensign so it flew upside down, and as soon as another ship came in sight they all began waving madly to attract attention. Men on the other ship saw them – and waved back cheerfully, no doubt thinking to themselves, as they passed on their way, what a friendly lot *Lang* had on board.

Puzzled, but not very much dismayed, *Lang's* crew then resorted to the next and more drastic traditional sign of distress. With suitable precautions, an open tar barrel was placed on deck and its contents set ablaze. Feeling sure that no one could mistake the meaning of the billowing column of thick black smoke (not to mention the ensign, which continued to fly upside down), they awaited results with confidence. Another ship appeared; once again, they began jumping up and down, all waving; and once again, the other crew waved back happily and sailed on.

It continued like that for two whole days – ship after ship came by, every one close enough for its answering waves to be seen, but none close enough to hail. However, in the event of a ship being two days overdue, it was company practice to send a search plane along its expected track. That was done, and in due course *Lang* was found, repaired, and taken to port, with her crew cross but safe

MS Lang (305dwt) *at Singapore.*

and well, and none the worse for their adventure.

No such luck attended *Lang's* little sister *Landak*. There is no point in speculating about the cause, but one day she just vanished. When she was noted as being overdue, an aerial search was made for her, first along her expected track and then in widening circles; yet only an empty lifeboat was found. No one knew precisely where *Landak* had been, and, with a communications fit as rudimentary as in *Lang*, she had had no way of letting anyone know what had happened. Eventually the search had to be abandoned, and the loss of *Landak* became one of the many unsolved mysteries of the sea.

Nevertheless, when the Eastern Fleet is talked of, it is not so much the individual unhappiness and occasional sad accidents which are mainly remembered now, but the carefree independence of that way of life. Memories of the (sometimes great) physical discomforts fade: the extreme heat, the all-night racket of a generator thumping away immediately beneath one's bunk, the inescapable stink of the cargo, the awkwardness of navigating up and down narrow rivers – those who knew it might not like to repeat it, but are glad they had the chance then. Travel, adventure, excitement and good pay: a young man could ask for nothing more, and it is no surprise if the young men who served in Shell's Eastern Fleet think of it now, when they are older and rounder, with such nostalgic affection.

Over the dozen or so years following the war, a list of key events affecting the oil industry reads almost like a summary of contemporary world history. In November 1948, Venezuela demanded and received a 50:50 split, between the country and the oil companies, of its national oil profits. In December 1950, Saudi Arabia did the same. Over April and May 1951, Prime Minister Mossadegh and his immediate predecessors in Iran expropriated and nationalized the entire oil industry within their borders. In August of the same year, Iraq followed the example of Venezuela and Saudi Arabia; in September, so did Kuwait. In 1952, Western sanctions against the Iranian national-isation brought about an economic crisis in that country; in Egypt a coup d'état brought in a new government; and in the December, Bahrain played the Venezuelan card for an equal split. The year 1953 brought a general rise in the prices of Middle Eastern crude oil, a coup in Iran, and (in November) the discovery of oil in Nigeria. In 1954, while the world's largest oilfield was found in Ghawar (Saudi Arabia), the newly independent Indonesians – until before the war, colonial dependents of the Dutch – pushed forward their own programme of oil nationalisation; and in 1956, the Suez Canal was closed.

All the earlier events had had their effects on Shell and the world's other oil companies; but it was this last which, more than any other, affected the tankers. To sketch in barest outline the causes of the Canal's closure, suffice it to say that in 1955, Egypt's revolutionary President Nasser had turned to the USSR for his country's defence needs; on 19 July 1956, the USA cancelled a proposed loan to Egypt for the construction of the huge Aswan dam across the Nile; and one week later, in direct response, the Egyptian military seized control of the Suez Canal Zone. To politicians in Britain and France, this brought back all too vivid memories of Hitler's behaviour in the mid-1930s, starting with the annexation of the Rhineland; to politicians in the newly created state of Israel, who had already fought one war against Arab states, it seemed an unambiguous threat. Their combined reaction, ill prepared and completely ineffective, was military intervention, beginning on 29 October with an Israeli attack across the Sinai, and followed the next day with an Anglo-French ultimatum to Egypt.

One of those who saw the immediate effects for himself was Don Mitchell. Fifteen years earlier, he had been an apprentice, sailing in the wartime convoys to Russia; now he was Captain of the 8,246grt MS *Nassarius*, and early on 31 October he received an urgent message, including quoted Admiralty advice, from his Head Office in London:

> *Quote...Merchant shipping is advised for the time being and until further notice to keep clear of the Suez Canal and Israeli Egyptian territorial waters Unquote Ends Stop...View foregoing you should endeavour put to sea as soon as possible even though partly loaded and proceed point in vicinity 23° North 37° 45 minutes East* [the middle of the Red Sea] *Stop Acknowledge with ETA that position and bunker and water remaining...*

Fortunately news of the fighting had already reached the ship. Her Chief Engineer, J. H. Mortimer, had been keeping her engines ready for the past 24 hours, and Mitchell himself had arranged with the local British Consul to evacuate 19 shore staff: ten from Anglo-Egyptian Oilfields Ltd., five from the Khedivial Mail Company, three from the British School at Suez and one from Lloyd's Register. Just after 11 am the ship left for Suez Bay, where the evacuees were to be taken on. For the entire afternoon *Nassarius* was detained in the bay by Egyptian officials who removed everyone's passports and said the ship must discharge its remaining 1,500 tons of oil. Mitchell refused, citing his owners' instructions and firing off cables saying (as he told the officials) that his ship might be detained. At 6 pm this skirmish of nerves ended with *Nassarius* being allowed to sail. With his navigation lights on but the ship otherwise darkened, Mitchell tagged onto the tail end of a southbound convoy, which he presumed to be neutral, and *Nassarius*, with the Dutch and British evacuees, male and female, became one of the last vessels to pass through the Canal.

A few hours later, British attacks on airfields began; in

Vexilla: *(1955-1972), 31,465dwt*

Worldscale and New Worldscale

The business of trading tankers worldwide is beset by many variables – not least the spot-market negotiating of mutually acceptable charter rates. For both parties, such negotiation have to take into account many fluctuating factors, such as bunker prices and currency exchange rates.

To simplify the trade, a standard measure of cost called 'Worldscale' was used for many years. This evolved from a system set up in November 1952 by Shell and BP, called the London Tanker Nominal Freight Scales. Published by the Worldwide Tanker Nominal Freight Scale Association Ltd (or Worldscale Association). Worldscale provided a comparatively straightforward reference gauge for owners and clients alike; in a phrase often heard in the tanker world, it was 'a simple index for a complex market'. Following World War Two, Worldscale was based on the American T2 tanker, against which all other ships were measured – for example, a VLCC might be measured as 20 T2s. This gave a fast and accurate guide to such things as the anticipated time for given voyages, the cost of tugs for the vessel in question, its agency costs in different ports such as New York and Liverpool, and so forth. Similarly, bunker capacities were correlated to those of the T2s. By the late

1980s, however, the T2 scale had become too small to be of further use, and on 1 January 1989 'New Worldscale' was introduced.

New Worldscale is based on a completely revised set of nominal factors. The basic reference has become a vessel of 75,000 dwt, with a speed of 14.5 knots using heavy fuel oil of 380 cst (a measure of the oil's viscosity) and a daily fuel consumption of 55 tonnes. Bunker price is to be given as an average of recent worldwide prices; port costs are treated similarly, and port time has been standardised. Likewise, a fixed hire element, and standard times for transitting the great canals, Suez and Panama, are included; and finally, both simple and multi-port loads and discharges can be covered.

As *Lloyd's Shipping Economist* magazine observed in December 1988, just before New Worldscale was introduced, the new formulae were not designed to answer every problem: 'only the market can establish the going rate for a particular voyage.'

However, by using the formulae, in most instances owners seeking to charter a tanker on the spot market may readily arrive at an appropriate rate, expressed as a percentage of New Worldscale and priced in US dollars per tonne, for round voyages between stated load or discharge ports.

Hatasia (1956 - 1973), 18,000dwt, passing the Opera House at Sydney during its construction.

the middle of the night, gunfire was heard ahead, with tracers and searchlights, apparently from Egyptian vessels controlling outward traffic. Proceeding gingerly onward, they thought they had passed the control point, when a simple but shocking signal was received: STOP OR I FIRE.

Mitchell stopped. In an exchange of signals, he identified his ship, obeyed an order to switch on his deck lights, and then, to his astonishment, received the message PROCEED SOUTH AT YOUR BEST SPEED. Without more ado, *Nassarius* got going again, and a final message came through from the mystery ship – apparently a British warship – saying WELL DONE GOOD LUCK WILL BE TO SOUTHWARD OF YOU.

Just one year previously, Eagle Oil directors had remarked: 'The most startling post-war development in the oil trade is the rapid strides which the Middle East has made as an oil producer.' Lacking American support (indeed, with active American diplomatic opposition), the Anglo-French-Israeli intervention at Suez was worse than useless. Nasser's forces blocked the Canal thoroughly, scuttling dozens of cement-laden ships in the waterway. It remained closed until April 1957, provoking Europe's worst fuel shortage since the Second World War, and adding thousands of miles to tanker passages from the Middle East. By the time

it re-opened it was irrevocably Egyptian, and in Western eyes deeply suspect. This was far more than merely an oil company view; it was also the view of many Western governments. Knowing how heavily dependent they had become on oil from the Middle East, they were determined to avoid a repetition of the supply crisis caused by the closure of Suez. In March 1957 President Eisenhower and Prime Minister Macmillan met in Bermuda, with the interlinked subjects of oil and Middle Eastern security high on the agenda.

Apart from the traditional route through the Canal, established 65 years earlier by Marcus Samuel, there were only two ways to bring oil from east to west: by pipeline – but the existing lines through Syria had proved vulnerable to sabotage – or around the Cape of Good Hope. That made the voyage so long that, in the smallish quantities which existing tankers could carry, it was uneconomic; but it was secure from the political risk that faced any other method

of transport. Over a game of golf, the two statesmen discussed the problem candidly, and one option which occurred to them was that they might encourage the building of bigger oil-carrying ships than the world had ever known. In the age of Superman, the comic-book hero, anything larger than life was swiftly given the prefix 'super'; in Britain, Macmillan himself was nicknamed SuperMac. Why not supertankers?

Captain D. H. Mitchell

137

Chapter Nine

Black, Blue and Green
1958-1972

The third Murex (1968-1974), 208,800dwt: 41 times larger than
Marcus Samuel's original ship.

Left: *Launching of* **San Gregorio** *(later to become* **Vitta***), 31,910dwt*
26 July 1957. Built by Vickers-Armstrong (Shipbuilders) Ltd,
Barrow-in-Furness. Delivered 30 November 1957.

In a kind of historical shorthand, it is often said that the 1956 closure of the Suez Canal led directly and rapidly to the creation of those giants of the seas, the supertankers. Actually, there was already a spur towards building larger ships than the 10-15,000 deadweight tonner typical of the interwar period. That spur was the Iranian nationalisation, in 1951, of its oil assets. The direct effect was on BP alone, but indirectly the shape of the oil industry and its shipping began to be altered. By the time Iran's Prime Minister Mossadegh was ousted in 1954 and the Shah came to power, it was clear to every oil company that all of their refineries which were close to the sources of oil, were potentially vulnerable to expropriation. After all, it had happened before, in Mexico in 1938; so now moves began towards building refineries in secure locations, close to the markets of western Europe. This was not entirely new – there had been refineries in Europe for decades, and the choice of their location, anywhere in the world, had always been a matter of balancing various factors. What was new, though, was the perception of potential political instability elsewhere. Put that into the scales, and Europe became the preferred choice. Refineries there would not only be relatively safe from nationalisation, but could also be supplied from any source. This in turn meant that only one grade of oil, crude, would need to form the tankers' primary shipments. So economies of scale in newbuilding had already begun to be attractive, even before Suez was closed: rather than initiating the idea of building bigger ships, the closure gave added impetus to an existing idea.

Even so, it did not mean that all of a sudden, everyone was charging around in tankers the size of the Houses of Parliament. That day would come, and the closure of 1956 certainly brought it closer; but no ship can be built overnight, or on a whim, and for a full ten years afterwards, the term 'supertanker' meant something much smaller

than it does today.

On 1 December 1955, The Shell Petroleum Company Ltd acquired most of Anglo-Saxon's assets, keeping Shell Tankers Ltd as the managers of the fleet. This, since the preceding August, included the 33,000dwt *Vexilla* from Cammell Laird's Birkenhead yard, the first of a new eight-strong V-class. It was also in 1955 that the British fleet was joined by two specialized vessels, the 11,000grt bitumen carriers *Plagiola* and *Platidia*, destined to work out of Curaçao and the neighbouring island of Aruba; and in that year too, the directors of Eagle spoke about their own forthcoming 'supertankers'. Two had been ordered for delivery in 1957, of 31,000 deadweight tons apiece. At the same time, two 38,000dwt ships, *Zaphon* and *Zenatia* would be delivered to Shell. These V's and Z's (all with geared steam turbine propulsion) were significantly larger than the average tanker then, and for their era they deserved the 'super' label. It did not last very long, however. In 1966, the two Z's were taken to Kure in Japan for 'jumbo-ising'. Keeping their engines, they returned to

Platidia *(1955-1974), 15,100dwt.*

Plagiola *(1955-1974), 15,100dwt.*

service at 70,000 dwt, nearly twice their previous size, yet lost less than a knot in speed. As for the V's, long before their working lives were finished, instead of being supertankers they would have become some of the smallest vessels in Shell's British fleet, which by then would include vessels eight and nine times their size.

The Suez closure had led to an extremely lucrative but brief boom in the existing tanker market. One might imagine that the Canal's re-opening in April 1957 would simply have restored the *status quo ante*, but not so: in fact, rates slumped to a frightful low, and over the following three years Shell Tankers had to lay up over 40 of its ships. This was not necessarily because of age – most of them were built post-war – nor because of lack of investment in them: *Auris*, one of the victims, had just had gas turbines installed. It was simply because of their size: at an average 12,000 dwt, they simply could no longer pay their way,

141

and could not be sold – there were very few buyers for uneconomic ships.

Over the same three years, however, the company was also acquiring new hulls. Apart from the 13,000dwt *Pallium* and *Partula* (two new additions to the specialised bitumen-carrying P-class, built by Deutsche Werft AG in Hamburg and completed in 1959), all were significantly larger than those laid up. First came ten members of the new 19,000dwt A-class, completed 1958-60, the design of some of them indicating the shape of things to come. By then, the three-island design had long been customary: poop, bridge amidships and fo'c's'le divided the main deck. In all newbuildings immediately post-war, seamen were accommodated on the main deck level in the poop; engineer officers one deck higher; and deck officers below the bridge. In contrast, two of the A-class had the navigating bridge and *all* their accommodation aft.

The all-aft design was vigorously promoted by Captain Henry Russell, then Staff Director, and Alex Logan, then Technical Director and later (as President of the Institute of Marine Engineers) awarded the OBE. Jerry Walters (a member of the British fleet's shore staff from 1918 to 1962) remembers well how Russell justified the design: it would, he said, stop complaints from engineers that the kippers served to deck officers in the midships saloon were bigger than their own. Though it was only a joke, in a sense this was true (all-aft accommodation services were more efficient, and therefore cheaper) but as far as captains were concerned, the design took some getting used to, and not just because the engineers were closer at hand than usual. With the bridge placed amidships, the captain was at the vessel's turning point. With it aft, he was correspondingly distanced from that point, and in manoeuvring had to adjust his calculations accordingly – not an easy skill to

San Ernesto *(1960), 18,317dwt. Later to become* Alinda.

Partula *(1959), 18,675dwt*

acquire when one was accustomed to something completely different.

The company's other new acquisitions were, however, still more dramatic than the all-aft A's. These, in 1960, were the startling new S-class, and no fewer than 14 of Eagle's *San* ships.

Ever since 1919, seven years after its formation, the Eagle fleet's relationship with the Royal Dutch/Shell fleets had been close but separate, with the Group holding only a minority stake in Eagle. As recently as 1952, a new concern, the Eagle Tanker Company, had been formed alongside Eagle Oil and Shipping; but in July 1959, the Group acquired the assets and business of Canadian Eagle Oil Ltd, which included both the tanker company and the oil and shipping company, and on 1 January 1960 the control and management of their vessels passed to Shell Tankers. After 48 years, overnight, the Eagle fleet ceased to exist.

Who had taken over whom was not, however, entirely clear, at any rate in the minds of the Eagle sailors. Though their flag and their livery had gone, their actual ships remained, absorbed into parallel classes under the Shell flag, and some of the people stayed as well; and since many of these were senior Masters and Chief Engineers, they

brought with them an immeasurable amount of knowledge and experience. To this day they will assert, cheerfully and with total confidence, that even if (legally speaking) Shell Tankers took them over, practically speaking it was they who took over Shell Tankers.

There were nine 18,000dwt vessels involved (the *San's Edmundo, Emiliano, Ernesto, Fabian, Felipe, Fernando, Florentino, Fortunato* and *Patricio*) and five at 33,000dwt (a new *Calisto, Conrado, Gaspar, Gerardo* and *Gregorio*). Whichever way one looked at it, it meant that 14 ships totalling 327,000 deadweight tons had come under the Shell flag at a stroke; and within the same year Shell Tankers introduced into the combined fleet the extraordinary S-class.

These represented a quantum leap in Shell's British tanker fleet, and indeed in the entire national tanker fleet. Ordered as standard 33,000-tonners, they were radically redesigned in 1958. The first, *Serenia*, built by Vickers Armstrong in Newcastle, was launched there on 18 October 1960, and was more than twice the size of any ex-Eagle ship. In fact, she was the biggest tanker built in Britain to that date: 817' 9" length overall, 112' 6" beam, and every ounce of 71,250 tons deadweight.

Hemifusus (1954-1976) 18,102dwt

John Main (who had been so surprised to find his first tanker was also an aircraft carrier) was superintendent in charge of specifications and new construction, and regards *Serenia* and her sister *Solen* as 'his'. Becoming Technical Director of Shell International Marine in 1971, he took Shell's new tonnage designs into the second generation of VLCCs (270-320,000 dwt), the L-class, the LNG G-class (later renamed the B's), and the diesel-engined 32,000dwt F- and E-classes.

Solen (the second of that name) was built in Wallsend by Swan Hunter & Wigham Richardson Ltd, and launched in the summer of 1961. Both she and *Serenia* had a loaded service speed of 16.25 knots, with accommodation more like that of an ocean liner than a tanker – grand curving staircases and extremely comfortable cabins. There were another couple of minor unexpected aspects to these two ships: first, as an experiment (which some people loved and others hated), their hulls were painted *eau de Nil* green; second, they retained the three-island design of superstructure. Given the greater efficiency of the all-aft design seen in the preceding A-class, this surprised some people. Today it looks almost anachronistic; but it represents well the transition through which ship design was then passing, for with the S-class it was not the hull colour or the superstructure that was important, but the sheer size. In 1959, an American firm had launched a tanker named *W. Alton Jones* of 68,840 dwt, and within five years of the launches of *Serenia* and *Solen*, Shell Tankers themselves would send a 115,000dwt tanker down the slips, making even the S-class look small; but it is probably fair to say that, with the first of that class breaking the 70,000dwt barrier, Shell launched the age of the supertanker as we know it today.

The unification of Eagle and Shell ships under one flag was not the only remark-

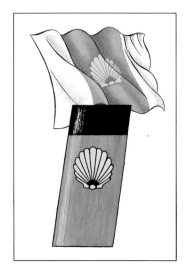

able event in the world of tankers in 1960; for that was also the year in which OPEC, the Organization of Petroleum Exporting Countries, was created by the combination of Iran, Iraq, Saudi Arabia, Kuwait and Venezuela. In the subsequent 30 years, until the dramatic changes in the USSR, the ending of the Cold War and the collapse of Communism, no other single event affected the world as much as this; and yet at the time, it passed relatively unnoticed.

One reason why OPEC was not taken terribly seriously at first was that, just then, African nations (particularly Algeria, Libya and Nigeria) were emerging as sources of oil, apparently with as great potential as the Middle East. Shell had been searching for oil in Nigeria since 1937; in 1956 it was found at last, in the delta of the River Niger, and in 1958 *Hemifusus* (Captain G. A. C. Nelson) brought the first test cargo for refining in Rotterdam.

Meanwhile, over in Venezuela, the shallow narrows leading into Lake Maracaibo had been extensively dredged, enabling ships larger than the traditional 'mosquito' vessels to carry the crude out for refining. This provided part of the trade which kept the H-, K-, and V-classes out of lay-up, while the surviving pre-war mosquitoes – strengthened by 11 of the ex-Dutch 6,250dwt G-class, now under the British flag – went off to Nigeria and the Far East.

These small ships could count themselves lucky that there was an appropriate trade for them to serve; if there had not been, they would probably have become part of

Oscilla *(1963-1969) 52,500dwt*

the sale of the century. On 1 April 1960, Shell Tankers Ltd acquired the marine assets of The Shell Petroleum Company Ltd. This meant they became the actual owners, not just the managers, of those assets, which of course included the fleet; and they promptly sold 18 of the ships. *Trochiscus*, one of the American-built wartime T2 tankers, went for scrap in Hong Kong, but all the others (*Helicina*, *Hyalina* and another 15 T2's) were sold to the British Iron and Steel Company: a total to the one purchaser of about 185,000 grt of shipping, the biggest such sale there had ever been.

A clearing of the decks had certainly been needed. Low freight rates in the early '60s continued to force the average size of tankers upward. The two S's alone replaced more than 75% of the scrapped capacity, and were followed in 1963 by the completion of a new three-ship class, the O's. At 52,500 dwt each, these – *Otina*, *Oscilla* and *Opalia* – were the last ships to be built which, when designed and ordered, had been as Eagle ships. From the drawing board to completion they were given all-aft bridge and accommodation, the pattern followed by every subsequent newbuilding. Three hulls may be a trifling number, as

hulls; but added to the S-class, the O's brought the fleet's deadweight tonnage to a level higher than before the great sale, and there was no intention of stopping there. People who were young in the '60s remember the excitement of the time – good jobs and plenty of them, money to spare, independence, fashions and a way of life that provoked a gratifying degree of overt shock, and possibly covert envy, in their elders. There was no reason for a shipping company to stay aloof from the surging optimism, and Shell Tankers did not.

In 1961, the company moved from its base at Ibex House in The Minories to Shell Centre's more commodious 'Downstream' building on the south bank of the Thames; and in 1963 the colours of the fleet's flags and funnels were changed. Since the end of the war, the flags had had a red background, with a white central ball and a yellow and black pecten inside. From 1963, this changed markedly: now the flag had three vertical stripes, white-red-white, the outer (white) stripes occupying about a quarter of the whole width, with a simplified yellow pecten in the wide red central stripe. Likewise, since 1945, the funnels had been yellow topped by a black stripe, with a red and black pecten on the side. From 1963, this was switched around: the black stripe remained, but the body of the funnel became red, while the pecten became yellow and black. Compared to the sensational colours of Carnaby Street clothing, a change of livery was perhaps a small thing, but to a sailor it was just as memorable – not least because, in many ships, the switch created a temporary shortfall of red and a large surplus of yellow paint. This had to be used somehow, and soon anything that needed a dab of undercoat was being undercoated in brilliant yellow.

Almost as if someone had said, 'Well, while we're at it...', the company form and name changed too. In January 1964, Shell Tankers Ltd was separated into two. For the one part, Shell International Marine Ltd (SIM) was created, its basic brief being chartering and the care of Group marine interests beyond the actual running of Shell's British ships. For the other part, the British fleet's operating company became (and still is) Shell Tankers (U.K.) Ltd. It is that company whose history forms most of the balance of this book; and appropriately, when it was brand new, one of its first tasks was to manage two new ships in a new international trade – the bulk carriage of liquefied natural gas (LNG).

LNG was first made (by the chilling and compression of natural gas) in West Virginia in 1917, but it was not until 1959 that refrigeration and bulk containment technology was sufficiently advanced to allow the first LNG shipments. The vessel involved (*Methane Pioneer*, a converted cargo ship) was owned by Constock International Methane Ltd, and successfully carried seven trial cargoes from Lake Charles in the States to Canvey Island in the UK. Early in 1960, Shell acquired a 40% interest in Constock, which was then named Conch International Methane, and in 1964, Shell Tankers accepted the management of the world's first two purpose-built LNG carriers – *Methane Progress* and *Methane Princess*, built, respectively, by Harland & Wolff and

Vickers Armstrong, and the property of Methane Tanker Finance and Conch Methane Tankers.

Sailing from Arzew in Algeria to Canvey Island with cargoes chilled to approximately -165°C, the ships were unlike anything there had ever been. The very novelty of the bulk cargoes, and what seemed to be their potential hazards, produced considerable unease in Canvey Islanders – as someone said, 'The bigger the cargo, the bigger the bang.' But this was not a trade to be entered into lightly. With extensive research and development carried out by the Group's Thornton Research Centre, and full-scale tests (on MoD land at Maplin Sands) of the consequences of an LNG leak, every conceivable safety precaution had been taken, as an exhaustive four-year public enquiry confirmed. Today, whether for domestic or industrial purposes, LNG is universally recognized as one of the cleanest possible fuels. *Methane Progress* is long gone, and *Methane Princess* is laid up, but for more than 20 years – first as owner, later as manager – Shell Tankers (U.K.) Ltd has run a fleet of LNG tankers on a regular shuttle from Brunei to Japan without any of the seven ships, or any of their thousands of cargoes, being involved in any accident at all.

From its beginning in 1964 – and despite its rather ungainly acronym, STUK – the new Shell Tankers (U.K.) was an enthusiastic body, promptly ordering some new ships for delivery over 1965-67. These were the seven strong D-class. They included five motor ships, the Sunderland-built *Daphnella* and *Donacilla*; *Donovania* and *Dorcasia* from Malmö in Sweden; and *Donax* from Belfast, as well as two steam turbine ships, *Drupa* and *Darina*, from Hamburg. (Alone of these, *Drupa* still remains in the fleet, converted for North Sea work – a hard-working and much-loved old lady, never ill-tempered and always reliable, even at 27 years of age.) The seven could handle 70,000 deadweight tons each, aggregating a cool 490,000 dwt. Naturally, each order was the fruit of long thought and deliberation, but in our more straitened days, it is hard

Captain D. Still and his crew on **Methane Princess (1990).**

Methane Princess, *27,400m³ (LNG carrier) by Vickers Armstrong (Shipbuilders) Ltd., Barrow-in-Furness in 1964.*

Darina (1966-1983), 71,917dwt, with Yokohama fenders on port side of deck used in lightening operations.

to restrain a pang of envy for such seemingly breezy exuberance; there is a distinct echo of Marcus Samuel's grand attitude, so much so that one almost wonders why STUK stopped short of ordering a full half million dwt.

The restraint, if that is the right word, had two reasons: the great canals, Suez and Panama. In response to the growing size of ships, both canals were being enlarged. In Panama, the most significant limitation has always been on the Pacific side, in the channel known originally as the Culebra Cut, and nowadays as the Gaillard Cut (after Colonel David DuBose Gaillard, who masterminded its enlargement). Even today, the Canal authorities describe the Cut as 'an enormous ditch'. When first opened in 1914, it was 300 feet wide; during the period 1957-71, it was increased to 500 feet, with a maximum draft of 39½ feet. This, together with the lock size, dictated 'Panamax', the maximum size of vessel that can squeeze through. It truly is a squeeze, with only a few inches to spare between the hull and the walls of the locks to either side; but it will be no surprise that a Panamax vessel is one not exceeding 70,000 dwt – precisely the size of the D's.

Similarly, the Suez Canal had been enlarged at periodic intervals ever since its opening in 1869. From then until 1900, the largest vessel it could accommodate was 7,000 dwt; *Murex* of 1892 was of course 5,010 dwt. Gradually this maximum had been stepped up until, by 1964, it had reached 65,000 dwt – too small for a fully laden D-class ship to pass through, though a part-laden one could make the passage if necessary. But the men who designed and ordered the D-class were not too bothered: for one thing, the fleet still contained numerous vessels which could use the Canal; for another, under nationalized Egyptian control, the Canal no longer inspired confidence. Who could tell if it might not suddenly be closed again, as it had been in 1956? Better to be safe than sorry; better, too, to use the economies of scale afforded by carrying a single grade of oil, simple crude, to be refined near the market rather than at source. Following the logic through, when designing really big tankers, the size limitations of Suez could be ignored; and henceforward they were.

The Start of OPEC

OPEC's eventual effect on the tanker world was so drastic that it is worth knowing something about how and why it began. Between them, its five founding members – Iran, Iraq, Saudi Arabia, Kuwait and Venezuela – were the source of more than 80% of the world's oil. Although, with Iran and Venezuela, it included two non-Arab countries, the general reason for their banding together was the rise of nationalist aspirations throughout the Arab world; the immediate reason was that Arab or not, they all saw their national incomes under threat. Since before Suez, the 50 : 50 agreements had been calculated from an official 'posted price' for oil. To increase their incomes, throughout the 1950s the oil exporters exported more. The USSR did the same, for the same reason, and a global glut developed, forcing the oil companies to lower their downstream selling prices, though the posted buying price remained the same. To consumers in the western world, oil was virtually as cheap as water; for the notorious American gas-guzzler cars, eight miles a gallon was a perfectly acceptable consumption figure. Consumer demand rocketed; production rocketed even faster; downstream prices remained low; and then in 1959, BP unilaterally cut the posted price by about 10% (18 cents a barrel), triggering a general cut by the companies. In the same year, worried that the States might become over dependent on 'unreliable sources' of oil, the US government began import quotas, designed to freeze America's annual oil imports at about 1959 levels.

That governmental decision has been described as 'one of the most crucial events in the whole history of both oil and tankers', the source of 'a torrent of crises over the next 20 years.' The judgement may be overstated, but to the Middle East exporters the decision certainly appeared to be targeted directly against them, and at the Arab Oil Congress of 1959, Iranian, Iraqi and Kuwaiti reached an unofficial 'Gentlemen's Agreement', recommending their governments jointly to defend prices. On 9 August 1960, Exxon knocked another 14 cents a barrel off posted prices. The other companies followed suit with marked reluctance; John Loudon of Shell called it a fatal move, and on 8 September restored 2-4 cents of the posted price. But by then the exporters were congregating, and in the space of five days (10-14 September) reached agreement between themselves. OPEC was born; and, though consumer nations thought it would soon fizzle out through its own internal competition, it was there to stay.

Zidona (1989), 69,500dwt – a Panamax in the Panama Canal.

Even before the 70,000dwt D's had all been completed, STUK were planning their largest ship to date: the 117,206dwt *Naticina*, a full 65% increase in deadweight tonnage over any single vessel the company had ever had, and equivalent to any three of the ships which Eagle, in the late 1950's, had called supertankers. Already the nomenclature was changing, and *Naticina* had to be called a 'giant', because she was so much bigger than a 'supertanker'; yet within five years of her completion, she would become a lightening ship, used to take part of the cargo out of an even bigger tanker.

The Danish yard of Odense Staalskibsvaerft had been selected for her construction, and her completion, in September 1967, could not have been more timely, nor a greater vindication of her planners' forethought. Just three months earlier, as a result of the Six Days' War between Israel on the one hand and Egypt, Jordan and

MS Naticina (1967) 117,206dwt by Odense Staalskibsvaerft A/S, Odense.

Syria on the other, the Suez Canal had been closed again; and this time it would turn out to be shut not for a matter of months, as in 1956-7, but for eight years.

Never before had there been such a need for big ships. Oil was still in real terms a cheap fuel. For more than 20 years its cheapness had driven the whole world's post-war economic recovery, with a constantly escalating demand for every oil-based product. The system had reached a point of such dependence that without cheap oil, it would seize up; tankers had become essential to the maintenance of an entire way of life. At the same time, though, the ever-larger vessels provoked great concern, often bordering on fear; and on 18 March 1967, suddenly and vividly, those fears were justified. That was the day the 119,000dwt Greek tanker *Torrey Canyon* approached Land's End, and, laden with a cargo of Kuwaiti crude belonging to BP, ran onto the Seven Stones rocks.

Tankers had often accidentally spilled oil into the sea. For decades, too, when cleaning out their tanks, crews had habitually discharged their waste overboard, just as sailors of every period in history had disposed of any rubbish. In all the centuries of sea-faring, 'ditching gash' this way had never mattered very much: the quantities were small, the sea was large, and the rubbish in general would rot away unnoticed. But virtually from the beginning, oil and its derivatives were viewed differently, as Captain Hocken, Chief Officer in the first *Murex*, had found:

From time to time protests have been made by various seaside resorts, and, as a matter of fact, at fishing centres, against what is stated to be contamination due to oil floating on the surface of the sea. This is not a new incident, because I remember that when I first discharged bulk oil on the second trip, part at Kobe and part at Yokohama, we went out to the breakwater and cleaned our tanks before taking in general cargo. Mr Foot

Mitchell [later Sir William Foot Mitchell, MP, and then in charge of the Samuel family's Japanese-based firm] *at the time drew my attention to an article in a European newspaper published in Japan, complaining about oil contaminating sea water and preventing people from bathing, and also stating that it was killing the fish in the Gulf of Tokyo.*

Fair enough, we today might think; but, backed by centuries of maritime custom and several years of personal observation, the good Captain would have none of it.

I said, "Tell the people who are putting such trash in the newspapers that they do not know what they are talking about, because at Batum, where I have been loading oil for 10 or 15 years, there were no difficulties of that kind." It was suggested to me that the articles were inspired by our competitors...

Drupa (1966), 71,917dwt – still going strong in 1992.

As far as Hocken was concerned, whether the cause was dastardly underhand trickery or ignorant prejudice, his robust reply put an end to it:

At any rate, what I had to say seemed effective, as nothing more was heard on the subject.

But of course it was. By 1954 the effects of pollution had been sufficiently well observed for more than 30 nations to ratify the International Convention for the Prevention of the Pollution of the Sea by Oil. This important agreement was further tightened in 1962; yet there had been very little to prepare anyone for such a large-scale, public and visible disaster as the wreck of *Torrey Canyon*. In their newspapers, on television, or with their own eyes, horrified Britons saw their holiday beaches covered in brownish-black sludge, and witnessed the distress of innocent, bewildered seabirds, as, with their feathers irretrievably fouled, they tried uncomprehendingly to clean themselves.

Very few people (and certainly no one immediately at hand) knew quite what to do. Something which was bad enough already was made worse by well-intentioned but ill-informed attempts to clean up, in which very toxic solvents were used, killing still more wildlife. Eventually, knowing no better, the government sent aircraft to bomb the wreck, in the hope that it and its suddenly repulsive cargo would burn away. However, because of the combined action of gravity and water's surface tension, oil spilled on the sea spreads rapidly into a very thin film. On a clean, flat calm sea, 1,000 cubic metres of crude will, within an hour, form a roughly circular slick of about 600 metres diameter and 3.5 millimetres average thickness; and by then, the cooling action of the water is such that the oil simply will not burn. If wind or waves are present, they add to the cooling effect.

Such was the case with the *Torrey Canyon* bombing. The wreck remained; the entire cargo was lost, with 80,000 tons of it going into the sea. There it stayed for some considerable time, little by little evaporating, washing away, breaking down, and by one natural means and another, gradually dispersing. At the time it seemed to some people it would never go; yet it has, and there is today no obvious sign that the oil was ever there at all.

But no one could be complacent. Recognizing this, Shell brought some very positive good from the episode. The physical effects of the wreck were local and (comparatively speaking) transitory, but its mental effects were global and permanent. Though it was unarguably a disaster, it gave added credibility to the concern already being voiced by people, all round the world, for the safety of the natural environment; and though neither the vessel nor the cargo belonged to Shell, from then on, constantly increased safety and the greater protection of the environment became a major concern for the Group as a whole, and Shell International Marine in particular.

Safety of individual personnel, of ships and of the surrounding environment – they all go together, as do the reasons. It would be naive to suggest that Shell's environmental sensitivity springs only from the goodness of its collective heart without any commercial prodding. Equally, it would be ignorant and unjust to suggest that only government pressure had caused improvements in safety measures. Oil is a contentious commodity, with associated politics as complex as a chain of hydrocarbons, and this is not the place to try and unravel them. However (as Huub van Engelshoven, then one of the Royal Dutch/Shell Group's managing directors, put it), rather than being part of the problem, 'business should become part of the environmental solution'; and as another senior Shell person said recently, in the months and years following the *Torrey Canyon*, 'Governments were too slow for us.'

This is one area in which the histories of Shell's British tanker fleets and of the Group are inseparable. Environmental responsibility and good business go hand in hand, and form a central part of the Group's *Statement of General Business Principles*:

> It is the policy of Shell companies to conduct their activities in such a way as to take foremost account of the health and safety of their employees and other persons, and to give proper regard to the conservation of the environment. In implementing this policy Shell companies not only comply with the requirements of the relevant legislation but promote in an appropriate manner measures for the protection of health, safety and the environment for all who may be affected directly or indirectly by their activities.
>
> Such measures pertain to safety of operations carried out by employees and contractors; product safety; prevention of air, water and soil pollution; and precautions to minimize damage from such accidents as may nevertheless occur.

Despite the rather legal-sounding language, the importance of the policy is self-evident. If they ever existed as more than an individual's reaction to criticism, the days of defensive bluster are long gone: 'Increased public awareness of environmental issues is entirely legitimate,' Sir Peter Holmes, Chairman of Shell Transport and a Group managing director, said recently, 'and must be met by openness.' Captain Hocken would have been amazed.

Focusing down again from policy to tanker specifics, the Group has a really outstanding record of successful applied research into safety matters, with the results in many instances becoming industry standards. Much of this is centred in Shell International Marine, and a few items from its record will

Sir Peter Holmes, MC

give the flavour of its technical achievements.

Applied to hulls and propellers, SPCs, or self-polishing co-polymers, reduce fuel consumption; following Shell trials, these have been widely adopted in the industry. Autopilot course instabilities of as much as plus or minus 15° were corrected some 20 years ago by Shell with a system which was adopted by all major manufacturers of autopilots, and is the basis of the modern autopilot. In the late 1970s, as part of a concerted fuel-saving effort, Shell developed a Ship Performance Monitor which was so successful and offered such an edge over competitors that it was initially classified 'Company Confidential'; now it is sold under licence to others. When the International Maritime Organization first proposed a limit on the oil content of water discharged overboard, there was no equipment available which could measure accurately enough. With the manufacturers, Shell developed this to certification level, and the equipment is now in common use. Likewise, Shell identified Crude Oil Washing and Load on Top as optimum environmental operating practices, and evaluated the potential of inert gas as a fire extinguisher. All of these are now used industry-wide.

Even if it were limited to Shell's safety and environmental developments for tankers alone, this list could go on a very great deal longer. The above will give a good idea both of the time and effort expended continually by Shell to this end, and of the success those efforts have achieved and do achieve; but none of it has come easily, and some has been the result of very bitter experience.

In January 1968, STUK began publishing a new in-house newspaper, *British Fleet News*, conceived, designed and, throughout its 19-year lifetime, edited by Norman Sherry. The front-page article in its first issue described *Naticina*'s maiden voyage: 'uneventful, with the ship settling down well.' The second issue opened with a report of the acceptance, on 19 January, of the company's biggest ship to

Marinula (1968-1974). One of the 195,500dwt 'M'-class.

that date, the 205,800dwt *Megara*, first of the M-class. Alongside her, the 38,000dwt ex-Eagle 'supertankers' were dwarfed; even the 115,000dwt 'giant' *Naticina* looked small; and a new term was coined to describe this kind of ship: Very Large Crude Carrier, or VLCC. Despite her huge size (1,066' long and 155' in beam) *Megara* needed a crew of only 32.

The class grew steadily towards its planned size of 15 hulls, one being the third *Murex*, 41 times larger than Marcus Samuel's original ship. Sherry reported each new addition, and by October 1969, 13 had been completed: not only *Megara* and *Murex*, but also *Marisa*, *Marinula*, *Mangelia*, *Medora*, *Meta*, *Melania*, *Mitra*, *Mactra*, *Mytilus*, *Mysiax* and *Melo*. Together they could carry over 2,665,000 dwt, and there were still two more to add to the class. The issue of January 1970 marked the second anniversary of *British Fleet News*; but, far from any celebration, the front page of this second birthday issue carried a shocking report.

On 29 December 1969, *Mactra* had a tank explosion. Her Third Officer, R. W. Gardner, and a Grade I Seaman,

J. S. Lincoln, had been killed and several people seriously burned, including the wives of the Second and Fourth Engineers. An aerial photograph showed that, though the ship could still steam under her own power, a colossal hole, something like 50' wide and 400' long, had been ripped in the centre of her deck. An H-class ship could have sat in it as neatly as an egg in an egg cup. Worse: on 14 December, only 15 days before the *Mactra* explosion, *Marpessa* – one of her sisters from Shell's Dutch fleet – had blown up in a similar manner, and sunk on her maiden round voyage. Two Chinese Petty Officers were killed; the ship herself had

the terrible distinction of being the largest vessel ever to sink. Nor was the awful catalogue complete, for on 30 December, *Kong Haakon VII* (not a Shell ship, but a Norwegian vessel very like the M's) had also suffered a huge explosion and fire.

All had exploded while performing tank-cleaning operations. Exhaustive internal and legal inquiries followed the tragedies. In the legal inquiry, John Rendle, then STUK's Operations Superintendent, was the company's main representative in court. In retirement over 20 years later, he remembered this as a 'chastening

*The giant **Mitra** (1969-1974), 195,900dwt, dwarfing a refuelling vessel alongside.*

Mactra (208,560dwt) badly damaged by a gas explosion during tank cleaning in 1969.

atmosphere inside the empty tanks, were fatal. However, the gaseous atmosphere became potentially explosive only when mixed with a certain proportion of air. A higher proportion of air made the mixture too 'lean' to explode, and a lower proportion made it too 'rich'. Either would render the cleaning safe, and both were tried; but the final answer was to flood the tanks, during cleaning, with inert gas which simply could not explode.

It sounds straightforward put like that. So, too, do two other Shell developments at this time – lightening ship, and single buoy mooring. Neither was a new idea: lightening ship is the process of taking some of a ship's cargo off while she is at sea, so that her draft is reduced enough to let her enter a given port; single buoy mooring is essentially the system that the skipper of any small yacht will use. Here, though, the problems were not only of technology but also of sheer scale, and for those involved they were nerve-racking at first, because no one had tried to do them with such big ships before. It would have seemed incredible just a few years earlier, but (from 1968) the 70,000dwt *Drupa*, and (from 1972) the 117,206dwt *Naticina* were used primarily not as independent tankers, but as lightening ships serving the VLCCs – and still larger vessels.

For Shell's British tankers, the 1960s could be summarized as a decade of constant expansion and exponential growth in the size of ships, with all the attendant risks and rewards, disappointments and satisfactions; and as years in which environmental duty and responsibility came consciously to the fore. The 1970s could be summarized in a single word: OPEC.

By 1969, a quarter of all oil consumed in Western Europe came from Libya. It was close at hand, not even having to pass through Suez to reach its market; it was also of high quality, with little sulphur in it, which, in a more environmentally-conscious market, added further to its value. But on 1 September 1969, a military coup d'état took

and revealing experience. We were certainly not slap-happy before, but this focused minds.' There was no government pressure to find a solution, but, if only from the commercial point of view, one clearly had to be found, and, with assistance from other sources, Shell's Dutch laboratories worked for two years to that end.

Eventually, it appeared the central problem had been that in the washing, the cleansing water spray in every ship had created an electrically-charged mist. In very simplified terms, this meant that within a VLCC tank, a cloud could be formed large enough to give rise, under certain circumstances, to electric sparks, which, in the gaseous

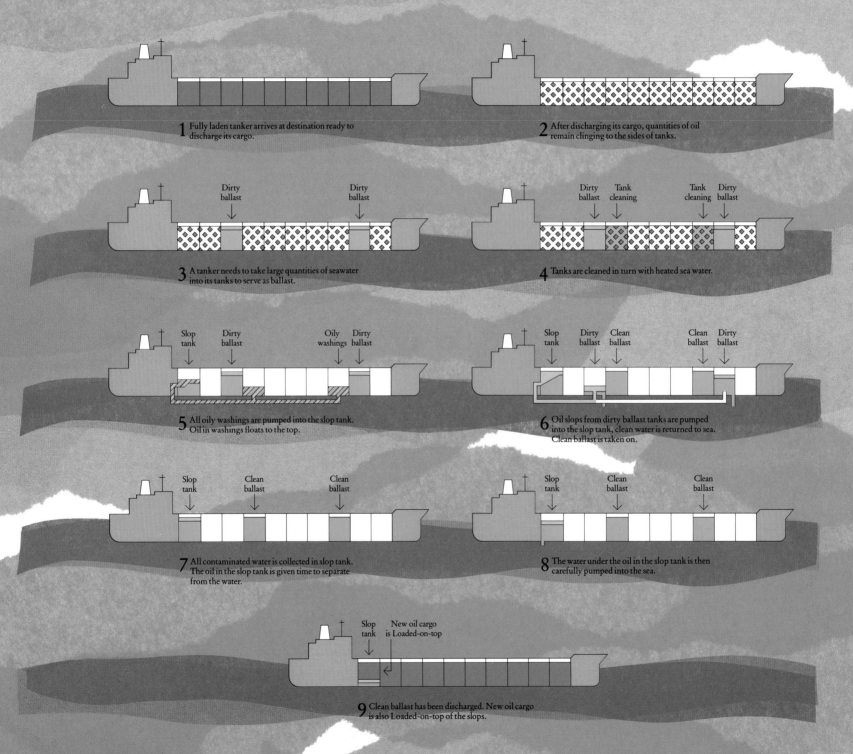

LOAD ON TOP
The first serious effort to deal with oil pollution caused by the operations of tankers was Load-on-top developed by Shell International Marine. Although now superseded by crude oil washing and segregated ballast requirements Load-on-top prevented several hundreds of thousands of tonnes of oil a year from being discharged into the sea.

1 Fully laden tanker arrives at destination ready to discharge its cargo.

2 After discharging its cargo, quantities of oil remain clinging to the sides of tanks.

3 A tanker needs to take large quantities of seawater into its tanks to serve as ballast.

Dirty ballast   Dirty ballast

4 Tanks are cleaned in turn with heated sea water.

Dirty ballast   Tank cleaning   Tank cleaning   Dirty ballast

5 All oily washings are pumped into the slop tank. Oil in washings floats to the top.

Slop tank   Dirty ballast   Oily washings   Dirty ballast

6 Oil slops from dirty ballast tanks are pumped into the slop tank, clean water is returned to sea. Clean ballast is taken on.

Slop tank   Dirty ballast   Clean ballast   Clean ballast   Dirty ballast

7 All contaminated water is collected in slop tank. The oil in the slop tank is given time to separate from the water.

Slop tank   Clean ballast   Clean ballast

8 The water under the oil in the slop tank is then carefully pumped into the sea.

Slop tank   Clean ballast   Clean ballast

9 Clean ballast has been discharged. New oil cargo is also Loaded-on-top of the slops.

Slop tank   New oil cargo is Loaded-on-top

Tankers and the Environment

World opinion on this question tends to focus on what goes wrong rather than what goes right. This is not surprising, because no amount of statistics about the quantity of oil carried safely and without problems can repair the damage done when accidents do happen.

Nor is it any kind of answer for any fleet operator to say 'It wasn't one of our ships'. The whole shipping community bears responsibility for environmental protection.

TANK WASHING

After a tanker has discharged its cargo and put to sea on the return voyage, it washes some of its tanks in order to be able to take on clean ballast which can be dishcarged at the next loading port. Regular washing also prevents the build-up of scale and sludge on tank surfaces and in the pipe networks. The washing is carried out by machines fixed in the tops of the tanks, which eject rotating high-pressure jets of water into the tanks.

In the early days, dirty washing water was pumped directly into the sea, resulting in considerable pollution. The answer to this problem was a technique, initially introduced in Shell tankers, called the Load-on-top system. In Load-on-top, tank washings are all pumped into a slop tank where oil which has emulsified into the washing water is allowed to float to the top. Once separation has taken place, most of the water is pumped out from below leaving the oil behind. If the vessel is loaded before that oil can be discharged, fresh crude is loaded on top – hence the name. Tank cleaning is usually scheduled so that all tanks are cleaned in rotation in the course of three voyages.

The Load-on-top system became mandatory in the 1960s, but, as the diagram opposite shows, Load-on-top vessels still produce pollution, although the system itself, properly applied, should produce no discharge of free oil to the sea at all. Unfortunately, not every vessel implements the system as carefully as it might, and although major operators like Shell companies may keep their houses in order, it is virtually impossible to enforce foolproof international regulations.

For this reason, the latest initiatives are more concerned with avoiding contact between oil and water. The washing method of the future, which is being installed in increasing numbers of tankers, uses crude oil itself to rinse deposits from the tank walls and floors. Crude oil washing has proved very effective in reducing tank residues and, as a bonus, it has the effect of maximising the amount of crude discharged.

BALLAST

Unless a tanker is brand new or has just undergone a major refit involving complete cleaning, there is always a residue – albeit a small one – of petroleum in tanks which normal washing procedures cannot eradicate. Thus any time that water is put into a tank, it may become contaminated and cannot be pumped into the sea without the risk of pollution.

Water ballast is taken on board to keep an unladen vessel deep enough in the water for the propeller and rudder to operate properly. Certain cargo tanks are designated as ballast tanks, chosen to maintain the trim of the ship and to avoid over-straining the hull.

During the voyage, tank cleaning and transfer of ballast is carried out in such a way that the ship arrives at the loading port with clean seawater ballast in some cargo tanks, the oil washings from these tanks having been pumped into slop tanks. However, a risk of pollution remains – especially if the procedure is not followed with absolute care

The solution to this problem, which is being made compulsory for various classes of tankers during the 1980s, is to increase the use of Segregated Ballast Tanks (SBTs): tanks which are used solely for ballast, and never for cargo. The system achieves the objective of ensuring that oil and water never meet – but again at a higher cost.

INTERNATIONAL REGULATION

The formulation and enforcement of international regulations governing the operations of tankers is the result of cooperation between governments and shipping interests worldwide, operating in various international forums.

Of these, the foremost is the International Maritime Organisation (IMO), an agency of the United Nations based in London which has more that 100 member nations. IMO's regulations do not have the force of international law, but the organisation has achieved great success in getting regulations passed as legislation in member countries. Such provisions have recently included SBTs, standards for steering gear, navigational aids including the fitting of collision avoidance devices, and equipment for monitoring the oil content of discharged water.

Other organisations involved in international control include those representing the tanker operators themselves: the Oil Companies' International Marine Forum (OCIMF), whose membership comprises 45 companies, and the International Chamber of Shipping (ICS), the organisation of shipowners, which has an active tanker section. Both these organisations are involved in developing procedures and policy on safety and marine pollution, and both have consultative status with IMO.

Shell companies play an active part in both OCIMF and ICS, and take pride in the fact that every item of equipment or practice which has become mandatory in tankers as a result of international action, was installed in the Shell fleet well before the regulations.

COMPENSATION FOR ENVIRONMENTAL DAMAGE

However strenuous the efforts to eliminate the causes of tanker pollution, the risk still exists. In 1967 the crude carrier *Torrey Canyon* ran aground off Cornwall and broke in two, causing substantial pollution of English and French coastlines. This incident, the worst ever at the time, brought home to governments and oil companies alike the need for schemes to compensate those who, through no fault of their own, found themselves having to spend large sums of money on shoreline decontamination.

The first such schemes to come into operation were created voluntarily by the oil and shipping companies. The very first, known as TOVALOP (Tanker Owners' Voluntary Agreement Concerning Liability for Oil Pollution) came into operation in 1969. Member companies involved in a pollution incident are obliged either to organise and pay for the clean-up themselves, or to reimburse the cleaning-up costs of the responsible authority. Members finance these liabilities through special insurance arrangements, and the extent of their liability is laid down by a formula related to tonnage, which is revised regularly to ensure adequate funding.

TOVALOP is in force today, and virtually every tanker in world trade today is contracted to the scheme.

CRISTAL (Contract Regarding an Interim Supplement to Tanker Liability for Oil Pollution), begun in 1971, represents the owners of cargoes rather than the owners of ships. Member companies make payments in proportion to the amount of oil they transport, in order to meet situations not covered either by the law, or by TOVALOP. The scheme effectively covers 95 per cent of the oil cargoes carried by sea.

These two voluntary schemes are gradually being superseded by mandatory equivalents created under the auspices of IMO. The first of these was the Civil Liability Convention (CLC), which came into operation in 1975. It imposes much the same liability on tanker owners as they had undertaken voluntarily under TOVALOP. TOVALOP no longer applies in incidents occurring in countries which are signatories of the Convention.

CLC was followed in 1978 by the International Fund Convention (IFC) which is the mandatory equivalent of CRISTAL, relating to the liability of the cargo owners.

Between them, these four schemes, operating either singly or in combination, ensure that any state, local authority or in some cases, individuals suffering loss as a result of tanker pollution, can obtain fair compensation.

Compensation, though, is no cure. However well compensated an authority may be, it would still have been better if no pollution had taken place at all. For this reason, the efforts of the industry and community will continue to be devoted to eradicating the sources.

Zenatia (1966) 70,000dwt: The first completely off-shore oil field and export system at Idd el Shargi off Qatar.

place in Libya, hurtling a young army officer with mystical leanings and Nasserite politics into power: power which, over 20 years later, Colonel Muammar Qaddafi still retains. In May 1970, a rupture of Tapline (the trans-Arabian pipeline from the Middle East to the Mediterranean) contributed to a tripling of tanker freight rates. By the end of September 1970, Qaddafi had succeeded in forcing on the western oil companies working in Libya a division of oil proceeds amounting to 55% for the nation, 45% for the companies – a new base line for OPEC nations. In November, Iran gained the same, and OPEC nations began leap-frogging each other in their demands on the companies. 'The avalanche', said Shell Transport's head, Sir David Barran, 'had begun.'

In 1971 it gathered pace, with the Tehran agreement of 14 February promising annual increases in the price of crude. 'The buyer's market for oil', said Barran, 'is over.' At the end of that year – despite voluble protests from the smaller states around the Arab Iranian Gulf, and despite their offers actually to pay for the maintenance of British troops – all British forces were removed from the Gulf, ending Britain's historic role as guardian of the region, and creating there instead a vacuum of military and political power, into which any ambitious adventurer could try to step.

The following year, a new concept began to gain credence – an idea more revolutionary than anything Qaddafi could have dreamed up. For some time, the Club of Rome (a then influential group of economic forecasters) had been studying a project they called *The Predicament of Mankind*. In 1972, their report on the project was published in book form. In four words encapsulating its theme, its title challenged the whole of humanity's customary thought. It was called *The Limits to Growth*, and its central message was that bigger was not always better; that traditional and existing patterns of consumption, of all sorts, could not continue indefinitely; and that if they continued without restriction for as little as 100 years more, no further growth would be possible thereafter. Mankind, the report alleged, would have used the world's entire natural resources.

Though the report ignored the price mechanism, its message could scarcely be overlooked, and certainly not ignored; but roller-coasters have their own momentum –

Marisa (1968-1974) 208,560dwt.

they cannot be stopped in an instant without an inevitable series of concertina crashes. Everything in the civilized world was on that roller-coaster, and had been since the dawn of civilization; all that had altered since the Industrial Revolution was the pace, which, in those couple of centuries, had been constantly increasing. Shell's British

tanker fleet was no exception at all: STUK, a full-blooded child of the industrial age, was (one might say) stuck in a rut, a kind of Cresta Run – hurtling onward with a sense of breath-taking exhilaration, and all the time only an unseen and narrowing hair's-breadth from disaster.

Single Buoy Mooring, FSUs and Lightening Ship

The technique of single buoy mooring (SBM) originated with the Danish Navy, as a means of mooring small warships, and in the 1960s was developed for tankers by Shell engineers in The Hague, with maritime expertise provided by Shell International Marine.

Although tankers usually moor to quays or jetties, it is sometimes necessary to load or discharge some way offshore – for example, when the oil is produced well offshore, or when the water is too shallow near the shore. Before the introduction of single buoy mooring, a typical large tanker would be moored, during offshore loading or discharge, to a minimum of four buoys (one off each side of the bow and one off each side of the stern), with its cargo being pumped through a flexible hose running over the side and along the seabed. The drawback to this arrangement was that when the ship was light, either at the beginning of loading or the end of discharging, she was vulnerable to the weather: an unexpected squall could blow her out of her berth.

The original Danish version of SBM was like a much-enlarged form of the buoy used for a typical yacht: moored to the buoy, with sufficient depth of clear water all around, a small warship could swing freely around the buoy as dictated by wind and tide. Shell's development of this was a highly complex piece of engineering. For loading, oil had first to be delivered by pipeline to a point on the seabed below the SBM; then it had to be brought through a swivel joint in the SBM on the surface, and carried to the ship by a flexible hose; and the SBM itself had to be extremely strong, to bear the weight of the ship as wind and tide moved her around it. For discharge through the system the same principles applied, except (of course) in reverse.

Shell first used an SBM at the port of Miri, in Sarawak, and later at Idd el Shargi in Qatar – the world's first completely offshore oilfield. Using the SBM there gave Shell an immense technical advantage over its competitors. Moored to an SBM, the STUK vessel *Zenatia* received crude direct from the field. On board, some of the oil's impurities (primarily high density water) were separated out prior to export. For export, a regularly trading tanker would come alongside on the starboard side, receiving the partly purified crude in what was the beginning of ship-to-ship transfers. *Zenatia* remained on station for two years, until facilities on the nearby island of Halul were built to accommodate the oilfield's increasing production. Thereafter she returned to normal service, but the SBM remained on site and in use.

SBMs demonstrated that the offshore transfer of oil to or from very large ships could be safely undertaken in deep water sites. Using the system, such large oil ports as LOOP and Ju'aymah now handle enormous quantities of crude oil. The system operated equally well in such difficult locations as the Amlwch SBM off Anglesey. There, where not only the winds and currents of the Irish Sea but also a very large rise and fall in tide had to be taken into account, an SBM was used for more than ten years, from the summer of 1977 to the end of 1987, without major accident or oil spillage throughout its life.

Floating storage units, or FSUs – that is, permanently moored tankers – have played major roles in the initial phases (and sometimes throughout the life) of offshore oilfields, and the development of offshore oil ports. The 105,252grt *Fulmar FSU* (ex-*Medora*) fills this role on the North Sea Fulmar field, moored to a large SBM. In order to load from her, offtake tankers moor onto her stern in the so-called 'sniffing dog' technique. Perhaps the most sophisticated unit in Shell's part of the Tazerka project in Tunisia is the 104,722grt *Tazerka FSU*, formerly the third *Murex*, which not only exports oil, but also controls the entire oil field of five separate wells.

With VLCCs – and even more with ULCCs such as the 554,000dwt *Batillus* of Shell Française – single buoy mooring provided part of the answer to a navigational problem posed by the vessels' great size. Despite their economies of scale, some of these ships were too large to enter European and American ports. (Some, indeed, were so large that when fully laden, they could not navigate the Dover Strait.) Deep-water SBMs enabled them to discharge cargoes successfully: *Batillus*'s sister *Bellamya* used the Amlwch SBM in this way for the first time on 11 August 1977.

A further Shell development with a similar purpose is the technique of lightening ship. Essentially, this is a very old idea: lightening barges – small vessels which take part of a ship's cargo outside a shallow port and thus enable the ship to enter the port – have been used for centuries. However, after developing the principle with *Zenatia*, Shell not only increased its scale enormously, but also began its application in the open sea. This meant that much new equipment, and even new operating practices, had to be developed experimentally.

A good deal of justifiable caution attended these developments. Bringing a large oil tanker close alongside an even larger one at sea risks contact between steel and steel, which can bring sparks and explosions. To ensure such contact does not occur, mooring, hoses, and the handling of hoses are all specialized, and every operation requires scrupulous supervision. Large, strong fenders – at first, the tyres of earth movers; now, giant inflatable fenders – keep the hulls three metres apart. It has been found that with two ships which are not actually made fast (unlike the tethered *Zenatia*), it is safer and more practical to join them when both are still moving. The lightening ship comes alongside the larger one, both vessels steaming just fast enough for the larger one to maintain steerage way. When they are made fast one to the other, the larger drops its anchor; and when both have come to rest, the actual work of lightening proceeds.

Lightening developed significantly in the period 1968-76, when much of the crude oil consumed in Europe and the USA was imported from the Gulf. After carrying the oil through the long ocean voyages, VLCCs and ULCCs would be lightened near their destinations. This not only enabled the VLCC or ULCC to enter a deep European port such as Rotterdam, but also permitted parcels of crude oil to be taken from the large vessel in smaller ones to other ports. Combined with the economies of scale offered by the large vessel, this paid handsome economic dividends. Environmentally, the record of such operations has been excellent too, and it has been found that when other tankers are in trouble, one of the first calls now usually made is for a lightening ship to relieve the distressed vessel of her oil. As well as reducing the potential pollution, it also plays a most significant part in the salvage and rescue of the distressed vessel.

Drupa *lifting Brent crude from the Brent Spar in the central North Sea.*

Distant Conflicts: Indonesia and Vietnam

It is not only in the two World Wars and the 1982 Falklands War that Shell's British tankers have been exposed to the violence of battle. As trading ships of a non-combatant nation, they were present during uprisings in Indonesia and during the Vietnam war, and suffered in both.

After three centuries of Dutch colonial rule, the Indonesian archipelago, containing something in the order of 13,700 islands, became independent on 27 December 1949 under the presidency of Dr Ahmed Sukarno. Independence did not, however, bring peace to the 16 united states of Indonesia, and on 28 April 1958 the 18,000dwt Eagle tanker SS *San Flaviano* (Captain J. Bright) became an unexpected victim of the turbulence in the new republic.

Ernie Wilkinson – now a Captain himself, then a deck apprentice – remembers vividly what happened. On this, her final voyage, *San Flaviano* was carrying crude oil from Mina al Ahmadi for discharge at Balik Papan. On arrival they learned that rebels operating from the Celebes (present-day Sulawesi) had acquired some Second World War aircraft, and pilots to go with them, and so loading and discharge periods were limited. From 4 am to 8 am each day, all ships had to leave the refinery berths and anchor in a nearby river.

San Flaviano did this for two days, and on the third morning (with about 1,500 tons of cargo remaining in her tanks) returned to the anchorage, close to the Shell tanker *Daronia*, for the last time. Wilkinson had been on duty until 6 am, and about 6.30 went gratefully to his bunk. Fifty minutes later he was thrown out of it by an enormous explosion, and woke to find himself on deck.

The Chief Officer and his wife were on the bridge at the time. They were the only people who saw the Mitchell B-25 bomber coming – flying low over the Balik Papan signal station, then releasing some black objects which plummetted towards the ships.

The first bomb struck *San Flaviano*'s No 7 Starboard tank; the second fell some way off on her port side. But, with the very explosive gas/air mixture in the tanks, one strike was enough: a series of shattering explosions began, rapidly followed by fire. Running to his starboard-side boat station, Wilkinson found his boat had disappeared. With Captain Bright and five others, he managed to get the portside boat launched – not without difficulty, for the ship was already listing heavily to starboard, and her port side had been bulged outwards.

With flames preventing those in the after part of the ship from going forward, most other people had to clamber into the No 4 boat, aft. This became very heavily loaded – so much so that the sole casualty of the episode was sustained when the Chief Cook, unable to move for the crowd, was hit on the head by the last rung of the boarding ladder. Simultaneously, the Second and Third Officers abandoned ship via a forward porthole, the hawsepipe and the anchor cable, and after some delay were picked up wet but unharmed. (The delay was because No 4 lifeboat was so packed that the rowers on one side could not see those on the other. With both sides doing opposite strokes, the boat went round in circles for a while.)

Meanwhile, as the aircraft strafed the shore facilities, there was nothing to do but row for the shore and watch the poor ship blazing. She broke her back; the entire section aft of the bridge front sank, and settled on the bottom with funnel and upper works above water. With the turn of the tide, the forward section, still anchored and floating, swung round and faced the stern – 'A strange sight', Wilkinson recalls. Nor was the story of *San Flaviano* quite finished. Her front half was eventually sold for scrap, and, while on tow to Hong Kong, broke adrift in a typhoon and grounded in the Philippines: as Wilkinson observes, 'Not a lucky ship, to say the least!'

As for the war in Vietnam, the origins and outcome of that conflict are too well chronicled to need repeating here. Suffice to say, then, that throughout the war – from the time when it was solely a French colonial war, through the period of American involvement and on after the American evacuation – companies of the Royal Dutch/Shell Group, including Shell's British tankers, were involved as commercial members of neutral nations. However, it was scarcely business as usual, not least because two of Shell's British tankers were mined and sunk, both in the harbour of Nhatrang. First was MS *Amastra*, in March 1967. While she was discharging at a buoy mooring, a limpet mine attached to her hull exploded, blowing a hole 12 feet square in her engineroom. The hole was just below her waterline, but, though there was a heavy inrush of water, there were no casualties; everyone was able to evacuate the engineroom safely. Nevertheless, within a very short time the ship was awash from her poop to her No. 10 cargo tank, with her engineroom and aft maindeck accommodation completely flooded. At dawn it appeared she must be a total loss, but she was in fact still clear of the bottom. Over a period of 25 days, with the help of the USN salvage ship USS *Current* and further assistance (steam, water and other services) from the Dutch Shell ship *Kara*, *Amastra* was successfully patched up and pumped dry. Her remaining 15,000 tons of cargo were then discharged; she was taken to Singapore for permanent repairs; and it was not until 30 April 1985 that *Amastra* was finally scrapped at Chittagong, by which time she had become the last of the A-class.

Just under two years after the *Amastra* mining, in December 1968, SS *Helisoma* became the second of Shell's British tanker fleet to be mined in Vietnam. This time the ship was fully laden and awaiting berth, but again, the location was Nhatrang, and again the mine struck on the waterline. Fortunately no one was injured, and the damage was less than before; being close to the forehold and cofferdam, the No. 1 cargo tank (containing jet fuel) was broached, yet there was no fire, and, after being lightened by the Dutch Shell ship *Korenia*, once more the US Navy – this time in the shape of USS *Safeguard* – provided the necessary salvage expertise. Like *Amastra*, *Helisoma* was taken to Singapore for permanent repairs, and remained in the British Shell fleet until June 1973, when she was sold to African Coasters Pty Ltd and re-named *Africa Shell*. She was eventually scrapped in Kaohsiung on 26 September 1977.

Amastra (1958-1985), a victim of the Vietnam war. Mined and sunk in shallow water 1967. Later repaired.

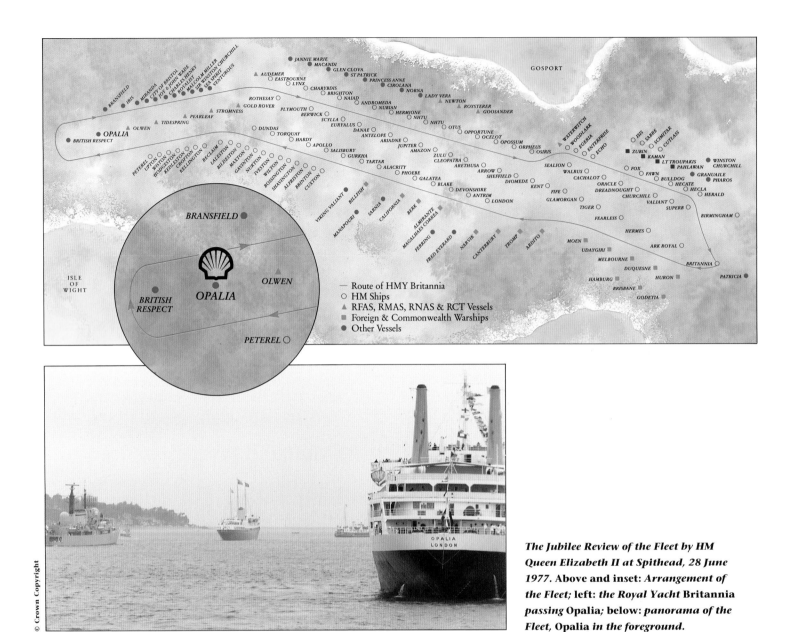

The map labels (top panel):

GOSPORT

JANNIE MARIE
MACANDI
GLEN CLOVA
ST PATRICK
Princess Anne
CIROLANA
NORNA
LADY VERA
NEWTON
ROYSTERER
GOOSANDER

BRANSFIELD
IRIS
MIRANDA
CITY OF BRISTOL
JOY & JOHN WADE
CHARLES HENRY
ROYAL EAGLE
MALCOLM MILLER
SIR WINSTON CHURCHILL
SEA SPIRIT
VENTUROUS

AUDEMER
EASTBOURNE
LYNX
CHARYBDIS
BRIGHTON
NAIAD
ANDROMEDA
NUBIAN
HERMIONE
NHTU
NHTU
OTUS
OPPORTUNE
OCELOT
OPOSSUM
ORPHEUS
OSIRIS
WATERWITCH
WOODLARK
EGERIA
ENTERPRISE
ECHO

ROTHESAY
PLYMOUTH
BERWICK
SCYLLA
EURYALUS
DANAE
ANTELOPE
ARIADNE
JUPITER
AMAZON
ZULU
CLEOPATRA
ARETHUSA
ARROW
SHEFFIELD
DIOMEDE
KENT

GOLD ROVER
STROMNESS
PEARLEAF
TIDESPRING
OLWEN

OPALIA
BRITISH RESPECT

DUNDAS
TORQUAY
HARDY
APOLLO
SALISBURY
GURKHA
TARTAR
ALACRITY
PHOEBE
GALATEA
BLAKE
DEVONSHIRE
ANTRIM
LONDON

PETEREL
UPTON
WISTON
HODGESTON
KEDLESTON
CROFTON
KELLINGTON
RECLAIM
LALESTON
BILDESTON
MAXTON
NURTON
IVESTON
WILTON
BOSSINGTON
SHAVINGTON
ALFRISTON
BRINTON
CUXTON

VIKING VALIANT
BILLFISH
MANAPOURI
SARNIA
CALIFORNIA
BERK
ALMIRANTE
MAGALHAES CORREA
FERRING
FRED EVERARD
NARVIK
CANTERBURY
TROMP
ARDITO

SEALION
WALRUS
CACHALOT
ORACLE
DREADNOUGHT
CHURCHILL
GLAMORGAN
TIGER
FEARLESS
HERMES

ISIS
SABRE
SCIMITAR
CUTLASS
ZUBIN
KAMAN
LT TROUPAKIS
PAHLAWAN
FOX
FAWN
BULLDOG
HECATE
HECLA
VALIANT
SUPERB
HERALD
BIRMINGHAM

MOEN
UDAYGIRI
MELBOURNE
DUQUESNE
HAMBURG
BRISBANE
HURON
GODETIA

WINSTON CHURCHILL
GRANUAILE
PHAROS

ARK ROYAL
BRITANNIA
PATRICIA

ISLE OF WIGHT

Inset circle:
BRANSFIELD
OLWEN
OPALIA
BRITISH RESPECT
PETEREL

Legend:
— Route of HMY Britannia
○ HM Ships
▲ RFAS, RMAS, RNAS & RCT Vessels
■ Foreign & Commonwealth Warships
● Other Vessels

© Crown Copyright

The Jubilee Review of the Fleet by HM Queen Elizabeth II at Spithead, 28 June 1977. **Above and inset:** *Arrangement of the Fleet;* **left:** *the Royal Yacht* Britannia *passing* Opalia; **below:** *panorama of the Fleet,* Opalia *in the foreground.*

© Crown Copyright

Chapter Ten
The World Engulfed
1973-1982

Opalia (1963), 53,739dwt

Captain Simon Darroch RD RNR

It all seemed so splendidly right: bigger was better, more was merrier; and why not? It always had been, and no one expected a tanker owner or operator to philosophise; people expected them to deliver the goods, safely, punctually and at a reasonable price, and they did. They had become very good at it, and were not about to commit commercial suicide by suddenly withdrawing or diminishing their services. Quite the contrary. In the 15 years from 1958 to 1973, the largest of Shell's individual British tankers had grown from 38,000 to 205,000 deadweight tons, and another massive leap was about to take place: the delivery of the first of the L-class.. Between 1974 and 1977, 18 of these would join the fleet, at 315,000 dwt each, a total newbuilding of 5,670,000 dwt in just four years. Not even Sir Henri Deterding had achieved anything like that. Had someone suggested that the glory days were over? If so, self-evidently they were mistaken. And yet...

As far back as 1894, one of the critics of the oil industry, an American named Henry Demarest Lloyd, had written: 'These men...think they are the wave instead of the float, and that they have created the business which has created them.' He had been writing not of tankers or tanker men, but specifically of Standard Oil, the parent of Exxon, and the way he phrased his work showed how much he hated 'the Octopus'. Even so, nearly 80 years later, there was still something in what he said. The whole colossal post-war expansion of the industry in every aspect had been due to the low price of oil compared to other energy sources. Anyone floating on that wave would have been a fool not to have taken profit; and had prophets foretold the breaking of the wave, they would have been taken for fools themselves.

It broke in 1973. To be exact, the wave began to tumble in April, when the United States, finding its domestic production was no longer enough for demand, removed its import quotas. This accelerated an existing increase in demand, to the extent that the world's seven major oil companies (of which Shell was one of the leaders) found it hard to balance demand against supply. While the majors received unexpectedly large profits, other people began to speak of an energy shortage. Frank McFadzean (later Sir Frank), chairman of Shell Transport, was not unduly perturbed; in June, under the headline 'Problem But No Crisis', *British Fleet News* reported his AGM speech:

Our task is to prevent a crisis arising in future. Action is required to maintain the balance of supply and demand in the years ahead.

Shell's planners had begun to spell out scenarios which were very far from a simple extrapolation of past trends. Some parts of the business were able to react rapidly; others, like the VLCCs themselves, could only change direction very slowly. McFadzean advocated the most economical use of energy, especially in transport; recommended the development of hydro- carbons wherever they could be found and economically produced; and encouraged the fuller use of other energy sources, particularly coal and nuclear power. All of this

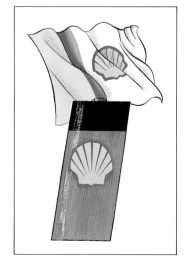

was sound common sense, even if encouraging non-oil energy resources was somewhat novel for the chief of an oil company; but it seemed far distant from working life in tankers, and readers in the STUK fleet were probably more interested to see a picture of the new house flag which was just being introduced – the one which, in 1992, is still in use.

But then, having started to tumble in

Serenia (1961-1987), 71,250dwt. Painting by L. A. Wilcox.

tanker fleet, would be inextricably tangled with OPEC. The three 'Oil Price Shocks', of 1973, 1979-80 and 1986, ensured this. In the first shock, the price of Arabian Light, the 'marker' crude oil, increased by 450%, from $2.90 a barrel to $13. In the second, it increased again, to $34, a further 260% over the new base level. In the third, it collapsed; and though it may perhaps seem strange, the effect of that collapse on STUK's fleet personnel was the worst of all.

The essential background to all this was that on 6 October 1973 (Judaism's 'Day of Atonement'), the Yom Kippur War – the fourth war between the Arab states and Israel – began with Egypt's attack against Israel. Almost simultaneously, excited by the oil companies' windfall profits in the United States, the OPEC nations demanded a 100% increase in the posted price of oil. The companies tried to negotiate, but on 16 October OPEC unilaterally set the posted price of Arabian Light at $5.11 a barrel. That in itself was a 70% increase over the previous price. Three days later, Libya embargoed oil exports to the US. The next day, Saudi Arabia followed suit. By December, oil's posted price had reached $11.65 a barrel – four times the pre-Yom Kippur War price – and, as panic took over the oil markets, spot prices of more than $22 were bid on the open market.

By that time, seven years had passed since Shell's first discovery, in 1966, of gas in the North Sea. Just as the wave hit the reef in October 1973, Shell announced that new drilling in their Brent field showed that original estimates of its recoverable oil reserves could be increased by 50%. This suggested that at peak, Brent alone would be able to supply something like 500,000 barrels a day, a quarter of the UK's existing consumption. It also made clear that the East Shetland basin, where the field lay, was likely to become one of the most productive areas anywhere in the world outside the Middle East. However, the technical difficulties and vast expense of developing the fields there meant that only one field, the Norwegian-owned Ekofisk, was actually producing oil.

Although this gave some cause for hope, even optimism, it

Mytilus *(1969-1974), 195,900dwt*

would be a long time before the North Sea fields came on stream; and in 1973, European fields had produced only 0.5% of the world's oil. Meanwhile, the new relationship between the oil-producing nations and the oil majors was swiftly seen to be irreversible. Assessing the situation, Gerrit Wagner of Royal Dutch, then the Group's Senior Managing Director, amplified McFadzean's earlier remarks, saying the base of the organization must be broadened: Shell companies must be ready to explore all new energy opportunities. McFadzean then warned against popular ideas that oil could be economically extracted from shale: instead of the dollar a barrel which some had quoted, he put its production costs at $6-7 a barrel. Both men kept faith with the market system; they were sure that, unless there was international governmental regulation, then sooner or later, price would regulate demand. However, when asked what price he thought oil might reach, McFadzean said simply, 'I think it's anybody's guess.'

Over the three days of 3-5 March 1974, while their bosses pondered the future in global terms, Shell's men in the British VLCC *Mytilus* faced a far more immediate problem: that of navigating their 207,000dwt ship through the Magellan Straits, in order to bring a cargo of Middle Eastern crude over to Chile. No one had ever taken such a huge vessel through those narrow waters before; but under the command of Captain Robert Lumsden, Commodore of the Fleet (an honorary title given to the fleet's senior Captain), they succeeded, and, a fortnight later, were equally safely followed by their sister *Mangelia*. This was the kind of experience and news which made men proud to belong to Shell, and specifically to Shell Tankers (U.K.) Ltd. They were a sure-footed breed – not complacent, but totally confident that their standards, their training and their equipment were such that a Shell tanker with a Shell crew could go anywhere and do anything; and their equipment was constantly improving. A new class of ship, the F-class product carriers, was soon to be introduced to the fleet, and would have variable pitch propellers, giving greatly improved manouevring characteristics. Reading about these in *British Fleet News*, Shell's tankermen chuckled too over a tongue-in-cheek report of 'new working rules and procedures':

Sickness: *No excuse, we will no longer accept your doctor's certificate as proof; if you're fit enough to report to a doctor, you're fit enough to report aboard.*

Leave of absence for an operation: *This practice will no longer be allowed....We believe that you will need all you have....We hired you as you are, and to have anything removed would make you less than we bargained for.*

Death (other than your own): *No excuse; there's nothing you can do for them, and we are sure someone else could take care of the arrangements...*

Death (your own): *This will be accepted as an excuse, but we would like two weeks' notice as we feel it is your duty to teach someone else your job.*

In addition, altogether too much time is spent in the toilets. In future a shift system will operate...

That was in August 1974. Exactly 12 years later, many of Shell's British tankermen looked back and thought that such conditions would be almost more acceptable than the truth.

It often seems that the closer one gets to the present, the faster time has gone; many people find that, when they look back over their most recent 20 years or so, those years seem to have passed in a flash. History seems to accelerate – perhaps because most people are reluctant to accept that their actions and reactions at any moment, and all their unreeling, unpredictable lives, are a part of history from the very moment of action. Perhaps, half a century hence, someone

else will write the story of the first 150 years of Shell's British tanker fleets. If so, then that will be the time to tell in detail the period which to us today is the most recent 20 years. That will be the time because then, these most recent 20 years will no longer be familiar: no longer the backdrop to present ways of thinking, but years which will belong to an earlier and bygone generation, and as such the customary province of historical study. Here, however, history accelerates. Henceforth, this story is of our own immediate background – the outline of history so recent that to us today, it is still tangible.

In 1965, the British merchant fleet as a whole aggregated 26.6 million dwt. Nine years later, in the summer of 1974, it had nearly doubled, and was the largest and the youngest it had ever been. A total of 2,204 vessels – 49.5 million dwt – then flew the Red Ensign; their average age was only 6½ years, with more than half of them less than five years old. Shell's fleets altogether included 419 vessels totalling 30.7 million dwt – collectively, the largest private fleet in the world, and about 12½% of world tanker tonnage. The Shell Tankers (U.K.) fleet alone was scheduled to accept 17 newbuildings before the end of 1975. These included three more of the LNG-carrying G-class (later to be re-named the B-class); four of the 32,500dwt F-class (specialized products carriers with segregated discharge systems, and, for their time and function, quite large ships); and ten of the enormous L-class, averaging around 300,000 dwt apiece. Together, the 17 ships would represent about 3,188,500 deadweight tons: the equivalent of something like 85 of Eagle's 'supertankers' from less than 20 years earlier, or some 636 vessels of the size of Marcus Samuel's original *Murex*. All had been ordered in the last heady years of the 1960s and the first year or so of the 1970s. But in the middle of the decade, would they – could they – possibly be employed?

Limatula (1974-1981), 315,695dwt

During the summer and autumn of 1974, important agreements were reached concerning the North Sea: first, the Zetland County Council (later the Shetland Islands Council) accepted an offer from four oil operators, including Shell, for the development of a pipeline terminal at Sullom Voe, with jetties specifically designed to accommodate vessels up to the size of STUK's L-class VLCCs. For their part, the operators accepted financial responsibility for the effective handling of any pollution problems. Second, readers of *British Fleet News* learned that in the Thames-side setting of Shell Centre in London, 17 oil companies agreed to operate 'the Brent system', a shared pipeline and tanker arrangement designed to serve five separate oil-fields, focused on a common terminal platform through which at least a million barrels a day would pass. But the same readers also learned that this great figure would not be reached until 1980.

Whatever else it might prove to be, the North Sea could not be an immediate scene of employment for very much tanker tonnage. Until the Middle East war of October 1973, demand for tankers had been universally buoyant; a year later, the situation could not have altered more thoroughly. 'We have always lived with change,' said Gerritt Wagner, 'but never, I think, on the scale and at the speed that we are seeing now.'

The elements of this dramatic upheaval are familiar to us all: the quadrupling of the price of crude oil; the take-over by the producing countries of a large percentage of the companies' concessions and their control of crude oil production; and the subsequent impact on the world monetary situation with all its economic consequences. Even those, and there were many, who thought that there would always be cheap and abundant energy available, now realize how wrong this was.

Nevertheless, every single ton of STUK's massive order was accepted into the fleet. There was no real alternative. The company might have fared better in the next ten years if half that tonnage had been cancelled or sold on at once, but none of it could be – it was too late to cancel, and with a worldwide rising glut of tonnage, no one would buy.

Some new and constructive uses were found for existing ships. Without ceasing to carry oil, *Opalia* became the world's first tanker to be converted into a cadet training ship, a role which she filled extremely well for nearly nine

Alinda *(1960), 18,317dwt*

years. Facing up to the scarcity of white oil cargoes, *Varicella* began carrying grain instead; and both *Drupa* and *Serenia* were converted for loading oil from the North Sea. Nevertheless, there was still (as Wagner and McFadzean together put it) 'substantial spare capacity in tankers'. Having been closed for eight years, the Suez Canal re-opened on 5 June 1975, and on 7 October, in a south-bound convoy, the 18,000dwt *Hemisinus* became STUK's first ship to pass through; but for the majority of East-West fleet movements, the re-opening made little difference – most of the ships were too big to use the Canal, and many just had no cargoes to carry.

When *Hemisinus* made that transit, tanker demand had dropped (over the two years since Egypt's attack on Israel) by an unprecedented 17.4%. Two separate blows had combined to bring this about: firstly, the drop in oil demand, after about 20 or 30 years in which demand had virtually doubled every decade; and secondly, the growth of fields in the North Sea, Mexico and Alaska, all of which sharply reduced the distance to market, compared with the Gulf. A headline in *British Fleet News* summarized the problem: 'Too Few Cargoes, Too Many Ships'. The fleet and

its costs *had* to be reduced. Eighteen ships were scrapped early; in an echo of the 1930s, others were put on slow steaming; a few were chartered out to other users; and half the huge, new and colossally expensive L-class were simply unusable. From April to October 1975 a steady procession of unemployable ships headed for lay-up in Brunei Bay: *Limatula*, *Serenia*, *Zenatia*, *Linga*, *Limnea* and *Laconica* – most having come straight from the builders. On the west coast of Scotland, in Lamlash Bay and Kames Bay respectively, *Zaphon* and *Solen* suffered the same fate, bringing the total figure in lay-up to a full 1.5 million dwt.

It was literally enough to make men weep. If they did not then, they could not avoid it in February 1976. At 1 am on the 2nd of the month, in Hamburg, the little 18,000dwt *Alinda* (formerly Eagle's *San Ernesto*) caught fire. It was not an oil fire, but an accommodation fire – the sort of thing that could happen in any home or hotel. However, that did not make it any less deadly. In the furious five-hour blaze which followed, two men (Chief Cook Lewis Magharan and Fireman/Greaser Anthony Devlin) were overcome by smoke and killed.

Thus the wretched 1970s continued, with some ups

and many downs. One of the downs was on 14 February 1976, when *Drupa* ran aground while entering the Norwegian port of Sola, suffered severe bottom damage, and lost some cargo. One of the ups was on 24 February that same year, when, in an operation generated by SIM, *Zaria* (a Dutch-flag ship) took the first delivery of oil from the North Sea Auk field, jointly owned by Shell and Exxon in equal partnership. Another was the conversion of *Solen* to be an offshore storage tanker for the African Congo wells; from her single buoy mooring in the Congo estuary, on 17-18 February, she opened Zaire's oil export trade, discharging 313,000 barrels into a Gulf Oil tanker. It was also in 1976, in the face of changing trade patterns, that STUK established a new internal division called Tanker Fleet Services. Currently managed by George Morton, STUK's commercial manager, TFS moved the company into non-Shell functions, marketing out the tanker operators' expertise not only in routine ship management but also in dealing with unusual or highly technical problems. Further positive notes occurred with the first delivery (in *Limnea*, May 1977) of crude oil to the new off-shore SBM at Amlwch in Anglesey; and in an unusual one-off employment shortly thereafter, *Limnea*'s sister *Liparus* passed a screen test and gained a starring role in the James Bond film *The Spy Who Loved Me*.

However, simultaneously, the fleet was still being slimmed down. Sometimes this was simply due to age: the 33,000dwt *Venassa* of 1959 was cut up at Ridderkerk in the Netherlands. Her middle section was rebuilt into a floating crane; her bow and stern sections were rejoined; and – by now a very peculiar-looking vessel indeed – she made her final voyage back to the UK for breaking. More often, though, departures from the fleet were because there was still not enough work. The 70,000dwt *Donacilla* of 1966 was sold when only ten years old; the 205,000dwt *Mangelia* and *Megara* of 1968 went when they were aged only eight, and their sister *Marticia* when she was only six.

Those five ships together meant that over 700,000dwt more had gone. For Shell Tankers (U.K) Ltd., there was perhaps some consolation in the thought that at any rate, they did not have the headache of trying to run the Group's two largest ships in the midst of an economic depression; that was the problem of Shell's French fleet, which though small in numbers, contained two ULCCs – not merely Very Large, but Ultra Large Crude Carriers – of 554,000dwt each. Until 1981 (when another company launched the 564,763dwt *Seawise Giant*), these two, *Bellamya* and *Batillus*, were in fact the largest ships in the world. When fully laden, there were very few ports anywhere which could handle them – indeed, when in that condition, they could not even pass through the Dover Straits. However, the answer to the problem was by then one of the Shell fleet's specialities: lightening operations, the removal by a smaller ship of part of the larger ship's cargo while at sea, so reducing the larger ship's draft. In two separate operations (10-11 September 1976), that service was provided to the gigantic *Batillus* by *Drupa* and *Naticina* in Lyme Bay.

Between them, the two smaller ships took 130,000 tons of oil from *Batillus*. Sometimes lightening was not so much a service as a rescue: in June 1977, *Laconica* lightened the disabled VLCC *Norse Queen* in Algoa Bay, off the South African coast; and ten months later in the same place, in a three-day operation (4-6 April 1978), *Litiopa* (Captain Peter Chilman) performed the largest-ever lightening. *Venoil*, the other ship (not a Shell vessel), had collided with her own sister, *Venpet*, while carrying a cargo for another oil major. Shell's expertise in lightening was unequalled, and, as it happened, *Litiopa*'s Second Officer, John Williams, had taken part in the *Norse Queen* operation. Gale force winds and seas hampered the *Venoil* operation considerably, once parting the ships' moorings. Watching them lurch and roll apart in the wind and swell, Chief Officer Colin Beath found himself thinking it was

Caprella *(1950-1959) 28,548dwt*

like 'two giant hippos taking a bath together'. In the end, though, it all went perfectly, and the almost incredible quantity of 287,000 tons of oil was safely transferred.

Despite the general gloom, there were such moments of humour and satisfaction; there had to be. One touch of humour came in the admission made by Ian MacLean, brother of the author Alistair MacLean. At the end of April 1977, after being with ships and the sea since 1935, he retired as a Director of STUK and Head of its Operations Division. Shell's German-flag fleet, Deutsche Shell Tankers AG, was about to dispose of *Caprella*, a ship formerly managed by STUK, in which MacLean had been Chief Officer in 1952. Every Shell ship, if named after a shell, had a real shell of the appropriate type displayed in a cabinet, and *Caprella* was no exception – or so everyone had always thought. Now MacLean felt the time had arrived to come clean, and he confessed that back in 1952, very soon after he had joined the ship, someone unknown had broken the display cabinet's glass and the ship's namesake

shell had been lost. Foreseeing, if he let on to the Captain, the possibility of some jeopardy to his career and the certainty of interminable paperwork, he connived a little with the Chief Engineer, Jim Stevens. A real *Caprella* is a land shell, from Venezuela. Stevens produced a box of shells from Falmouth beach; MacLean selected a couple of winkles; and the carpenter was instructed to repair the cabinet, place one of these inside, and – just in case – to make a padded box for the other, labelled 'Spare *Caprella* shell: Not to be entered in the ship's inventory'. It worked like a charm; no one ever noticed.

Without a doubt, though, the fleet's highlight in 1977 came on 28 June, on the occasion of the Queen's Jubilee Review of the Fleet at Spithead. It was a magnificent sight: 100 warships of the Royal Navy and Royal Naval Reserve; 23 more from the Royal Corps of Transport, the Royal Fleet Auxiliary Service, the Royal Maritime Auxiliary Service and the Royal Naval Auxiliary Service; 20 more foreign and Common-wealth warships; and 30 vessels other than

Ian McLean

173

warships, of which STUK's cadet training tanker *Opalia* was one. Her Captain was Simon Darroch, present in something of a dual role; he was not only Commodore of the STUK fleet, but also a Captain in the Royal Naval Reserve.

Dressed overall with bunting during the day and lights at night, *Opalia* looked superb. With her distinctive pair of red funnels – very few other Shell ships had two – her low profile, black hull and sparkling white upperworks, she stood out very proudly against the mass of grey warships; and from HMS *Ark Royal*, flagship of the Commander-in-Chief Fleet, Admiral (later Admiral of the Fleet) Sir Henry Leach KCB, came a terse signal of commendation: 'Very smart'. Simple enough, perhaps; but only one other vessel was so commended, and that was a warship.

Unfortunately, if it takes more than a swallow to make a summer, it also takes more than a glow of satisfaction to help a fleet survive. It takes good ships, good training, good sailors, good management, good trade, and a good public image too; but on 16 March 1978, the public image of the oil industry as a whole took a severe knock, when the 240,000dwt VLCC *Amoco Cadiz* had a steering failure off the coast of France and was blown onto the rocks with a full cargo – 223,000 tons of Iranian crude. On the 17th she broke her back and spilled a quarter of the cargo, covering over 100 miles of the coast. While a national disaster was declared, it became impossible to tally the amount of wildlife killed; but worse was to come, for 11 days later the forepeak broke and all the rest of the oil came pouring out in a deadly tide. Clearly this was none of Shell's fault: it was not their ship and not their crew. But it *was* their cargo, and that, in the mood of extreme public outrage in France, made them victims of hostile and sometimes violent acts.

This remains, by far, the world's worst VLCC oil spill incident; indeed, there was nothing remotely comparable until 24 March 1989, when *Exxon Valdez* ran onto Bligh Reef

Zidona (1989), 69,500dwt leaving Sydney Harbour.

in Prince William Sound, Alaska, and spilled 240,000 barrels of crude – approximately 45,000 tons, or about 20% of the quantity spilled from *Amoco Cadiz*. For Amoco, the direct commercial effects of the *Cadiz* wreck were an immediate 15% slump in retail petrol sales – a slump which endured for about three years – and law-suits which lasted even longer, eventually amounting to over $2 billion. For Shell, the commercial wound was neither so deep nor so long-lasting, but especially in France, it received harsh and widespread criticism.

Rather plaintively, the Group pointed out that a collision involving the escape of bunker oil from a large non-tanker could be just as bad as many a tanker spill. Captain Alec Dickson, Head of Marine Operational Services in SIM, added, 'The fact that on any day of the year there

may be five VLCCs arriving at Rotterdam is, unfortunately, no news at all.' Between the wrecks of *Amoco Cadiz* and *Exxon Valdez*, 11 full years passed without serious incident, and with oil pollution being such an emotive subject, it was well worth making and repeating this point: that no one outside the industry gives a second thought to all the millions of barrels of oil which are delivered by tankers punctually and in perfect safety every year. In 1978, however, this was not a point on which the public was receptive, so it was not pressed very far. Instead, as had often happened in the past, Shell took the lead again in promoting accident prevention measures, in particular calling for international agreement on uniform standards of competence for all seafarers. This was a call which all the responsible tanker companies heeded: both for conscience and commerce, none of them could easily afford to have an *Amoco Cadiz* on their hands.

Back at fleet level, further methods of coping with the depression were being discussed and carried out. The North Sea Fulmar oil field, 170 miles east of Dundee, was being developed, and the idea had arisen that a 200,000dwt VLCC could be permanently moored to the field's main platform to act as an oil storage unit. At the same time, STUK (and their Dutch counterparts) were moving into something which, for them, was a new area: the carrying of coal at sea. This tallied with remarks often repeated by Shell chiefs, to the effect that the business of Shell companies must no longer be merely oil, but energy. In October 1978, the second-hand 119,500dwt bulk carrier *Canadian Bridge* joined the fleet under her new name, *Tectus*, and was promptly put into service carrying coal.

It rapidly seemed that such moves were not a moment too soon. Following the shock of 1973, with panic driving the cost of a barrel of Arabian Light oil above $22, the price

Tribulus (1981), 125,900dwt

had eventually stabilized at around $13 a barrel. Even that was four to five times its pre-1973 level, and by 1979 the entire world economy was still reeling. Few who remember them can look back with much affection on those days: with wages chasing prices, inflation in Britain reached and stayed at an unimagined 26%. Worst hit, perhaps, were those who in middle age had never known the phrase 'index linked', and who now, as they became old, found their careful pension plans terribly inadequate for real needs. OPEC leaders had been heard to remark that they had never thought their actions might affect the lives of ordinary people in Milwaukee or Minehead – small consolation; and worse was to come, when the second oil shock arrived in 1979.

This time it was triggered by a network of separate but interlinked events – firstly, the Iranian revolution, the deposition of the Shah, the arrival of the Ayatollah

Khomeini, and the detention of 52 American hostages; then, in September 1980, the beginning of the eight-year-long war between Iraq and Iran, which at a stroke removed about 4,000,000 barrels of oil from the world's daily supply. The sequence of events prolonged the price panic: from about $13, oil rose on the spot market to $42 a barrel, and OPEC forecast that within five years, a barrel would fetch $60.

Simultaneously, the Iran-Iraq war knocked 30% off VLCC freight rates, while bunker fuel-oil prices jumped by 34%. Even with slow steaming, it now cost $2 million simply to fuel a VLCC for one round trip between Kuwait and Rotterdam – an increase of $500,000 – and oil consumption everywhere was declining. With the oil industry under pressure, the Group studied all kinds of other energy sources at that time. STUK too spread its base more widely: its Far Eastern LNG trade with the G-class ships was highly promising. At the end of 1979, the phrase 'small is beautiful' entered *British Fleet News* for the first time, with the prediction – not, by then, a very difficult one – that tankers in the 1980s would be altogether smaller than in recent years. An independent study, published in August 1980, stated firmly that coal was 'the bridge to the future'. With coal demand much influenced by oil prices, it prophesied a vast expansion in the world coal trade, proposing that over the coming 20 years, the world coal-carrying fleet would need to expand by an average of 5 million dwt annually, and that by the 1990s coal vessels would have grown to 250,000 dwt each. Today, a statistical breakdown of STUK's present tonnage shows how hard it was to get those forecasts right. Out of the fleet's current total of 4.2 million dwt, 5.4% is devoted to ore; only 6% to coal; and 10.6% to products, including among other things LPG and white and black oils. LNG comes next, with 18%; but plain ordinary crude oil still accounts for over 2.5 million dwt, a full 60% of the total tonnage.

Oil has not only remained far and away the dominant cargo, but has also retained by far the largest ships, seven of the 315,000dwt L-class of the mid-1970s. As for coal, *Tectus* was sold in 1987. Two third-hand VLOOs, or Very Large Oil/Ore carriers, joined the fleet in 1980 (*Rapana* and *Rimula*, each of 227,400dwt) but the fleet today contains only two dedicated coal-carriers, *Tribulus* and *Tricula* of 1981, each of 127,907 dwt. Put together they would barely make one unit of the huge coal fleet which, in 1980, was imagined as the 'bridge to the future'.

One reason for this goes right back to the very beginning of Shell's British tanker fleets: that old but not always reliable friend, the Suez Canal. After its re-opening in 1975, Egypt's post-Nasser government set about enlarging the waterway in an attempt to regain the high revenues it once had raised. Completed in December 1980, the operation allowed fully-laden tankers of up to 150,000 dwt to pass through. Coinciding as it did with the global fall-off in very large ships, this prompted Shell's then Marine Co-ordinator, Richard Tookey (later Chairman of STUK and President of the GCBS and, in the latter capacity, honoured with a CBE), to crystallise much of contemporary thinking into a series of published forecasts. Suggesting that the fleet had already been over-built before October 1973, he predicted the continued early scrapping of existing VLCCs. Noting, though, that big ships were still relatively cheaper than small ones (a 100,000-tonner cost 70% more per ton carried than a 250,000-tonner), he reckoned that big ships of the future would still be large, but not as large: probably 200-250,000dwt, with a maximum draft of 67 feet, which would allow them, when part laden or in ballast, to transit Suez.

This has all turned out to be substantially correct, as has Tookey's suggestion that the STUK fleet of the coming decade would be more fuel-efficient. He believed, too, that the fleet would demonstrate much greater cargo versatility than before, and was correct there as well, to the extent that 40% of the fleet's present tonnage is non-crude-carrying. He was also correct in considering that the use of diesel motor ships could markedly increase. Leaving aside the turbine-powered LNG ships (which use the boil-off gas as boiler fuel), in the STUK fleet today only the L-class and *Drupa* have steam turbines – all the rest are motor ships. Indeed, like those who foresaw coal as the future fleet's bread and butter cargo, the only predictive area in which Tookey has so far been mistaken was to say that coal firing might regain its old pre-eminence.

This is a pretty remarkable degree of accuracy. Suggestions of a substantial return to coal were not foolish: after seven

Richard Tookey CBE

Eburna (1979) 31,375dwt. On trials in Sagami Bay, Mt. Fuji in the background.

years of oil price rises, they formed a perfectly plausible scenario. In 1980, however, very few people would have guessed that within a few years more, the price of oil would tumble back again. Remembering the image of the oil industry wave which, in the 1970s, crashed against an uncharted political reef and created an overall eleven-fold increase in the cost of a barrel, the unexpected price collapse of 1986 was like a vicious and powerful undertow; in it, STUK was nearly destroyed. That, however, is the subject for the final chapter of this book; but in 1982, another completely unexpected event took place – the Falklands War.

This is a brief but honourable story. Far away in the South Atlantic, 7,000 miles from Britain, the British-owned Falkland Islands were invaded by Argentinian forces on 2 April 1982. In Britain, astonishment swiftly turned to furious indignation, and, with greater speed than anyone would have thought possible, Operation Corporate was mounted. Within a week, individually or in groups, vessels of the Royal Navy, the Royal Fleet Auxiliary and the Merchant Navy had begun the long voyage south. Those from the Merchant Navy, Ships Taken Up From Trade, sailed under the unfortunate acronym of STUFT; the department of the Ministry of Defence responsible for liaison with them was known, even less fortunately, as STUFT ONE. Its trawl for suitable and available merchant ships turned up a remarkable situation: unlike some other shipping companies, STUK had only one ship ready to hand, the 32,500dwt product tanker *Eburna*. At first, this rankled with STUK personnel; recalling the world wars, they did not like to see others making greater contributions. It was not until after the Falklands conflict was over that the reason for this inequality was perceived: namely, that for all the trading hardships of the preceding ten years, STUK's fleet was actually being very well employed – indeed, noticeably better employed than fleets which had more hulls available for government charter.

Likewise, despite all the commercial difficulties, *Eburna's* part in the Falklands War demonstrated that STUK's pride in its fleet was still a real force – alive, well, and justified. Captained by Jack Beaumont, *Eburna* was chartered on 13 April. From then until 31 July, she remained on active service – 'one of the very best ships under our control,' said STUFT ONE, 'being reliable, trouble-free and performing everything expected of her.' Terse entries in her log indicate the conditions she faced: 'Hove to in mountainous seas'; 'steaming into mountainous seas'; 'in thick fog with icebergs'; 'slow steaming in heavy weather and icebergs'; 'heavy weather, icebergs and fog'.

Eburna's function was to provide RAS, Replenishment At Sea, for the Royal Navy ships. This meant steaming at 14 knots, only 90 feet away from the ship to be supplied, and might be required at any time of day or night. At night it was made the more difficult and hazardous by an almost complete black-out of all ships. Apart from the first RAS, when the RN ship involved had a boiler failure and *Eburna* had to make an emergency break-away, all these operations were carried out with complete success; and soon, in addition to this official role, *Eburna* was given another. During her weeks with the Task Force, she was usually stationed in the middle of the Fleet, and there she was used as guide ship: her navigational equipment, and its use by her officers, proved of such a high order that the warships actually took station off

her, 'the only non-grey ship on the horizon'.

On 31 July she returned to Rosyth naval dockyard, a very proud member of the victorious Task Force. By then, the sad fatalities and terrible injuries suffered in other ships of the Force were common knowledge; but apart from one broken ankle, sustained when a wave swept over her main deck and knocked everyone off their feet, no one in *Eburna* had been injured. When they set off in mid-April, none of them knew for sure when they would return, or even *if* they would return. Of course the same applied to their counterparts in the Royal Navy, but for an RN sailor, fighting where and when ordered is part of the job; the risks are accepted. Not so for a merchant sailor; and this makes their willingness to undertake such duty all the more notable. Out of her total complement of 30, three were RFA personnel; all the rest were her normal peacetime STUK sailors, and there was not a man among them who *had* to go south.

Thinking about this willingness to undertake potentially fatal duty, an observation from the late 18th century comes to mind – Samuel Johnson's remark that 'Every man thinks meanly of himself for not having been a soldier, or not having been at sea.' Two hundred years later, Captain Jack Beaumont of Shell Tankers (U. K.) Ltd said the same sort of thing, with an additional wrinkle. Recalling that adventure of 1982, he admitted recently that when he went, he was indeed worried, yet at the same time knew that if he had not had the chance, he would have been very jealous of whoever did go. But he refused to consider that he had done any better than any of his colleagues might have done. Vehemently shaking his head at the thought, he said, 'Anyone else in STUK would have done it just as well as I did.' Asked why he was so sure, he spread his arms in a wide, simple gesture, and replied: 'Because we are Shell.'

Eburna in the Falklands – The Full Complement

Shell Tankers (U.K.) Ltd personnel:
Captain Jack Beaumont
Chief Officer Warwick Hemming
Second Officer Paul Jeffery
Third Officer Ian Reed
Radio Officer Bernard Kates
Chief Engineer John Hughes
Second Engineer James Elliott
Third Engineer Alan Price
Fourth Engineer Bruce Somers
Fifth Engineer Robert Hayes
Chief Steward Thomas Owen
Deck Cadet John Daley
Engineer Cadet Martin Dobbins
G1 CPO Rodney Francis
GP SG Gordon Fraser
GP PO Edward McMillan
GP1 EDH Frank Bartlett
GP1 EDH David Gausden
GP1 EDH Peter Hoffman
GP1 EDH Norman Pinnington
GP1 AB Bryan Marshall
GP1 AB Ian Minns
GP1 AB William Ogilby
GP CCk John Pickering
GP Stwd James Curran
GP Stwd John Kitson
GP JCR Paul Forrest

RFA Personnel:
Second Officer R. D. Craig
Radio Officer A. A. Weaver
PO J. F. H. Gould

Eburna was chartered for MoD use on 13 April 1982 and remained on charter in active service throughout the Falklands Campaign until 31 July 1982. All personnel received a memento of the campaign from the company, and all were awarded the South Atlantic Medal. _Eburna_'s complement suffered no casualties from enemy action.

At left _she is seen returning to Rosyth_.

With best wishes

Jeremy Sanders

Captain 8th Frigate Squadron.

Lima *(1977) 318,000dwt and HMS* **Nottingham** *during the Gulf War.*

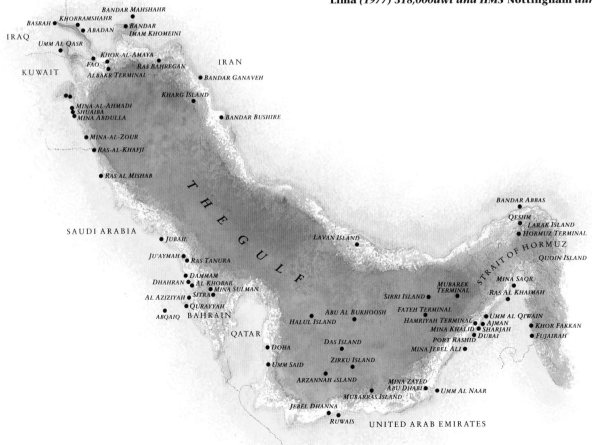

Chapter Eleven

Newbuilding
1983-1992

Isocardia *(1982-) 47,989dwt*

***Defensive preparations: In the Gulf
Captain Ernie Wilkinson follows company
instructions to sandbag* Isocardia's *bridge.***

There have been two occasions in the past 100 years when Shell's British tanker fleet nearly died. The first was in the period 1902-07, when it was still largely under the personal direction of its founder, Sir Marcus Samuel. Later on, the cause of that crisis could be seen clearly: Samuel's smoke-screen. To meet the potential challenge of a powerful group of competitors, at a time when his company was already stretched, he had bought enormous stocks of expensive kerosene on a rising market, relying on a continued rise to see him through. When, instead, the market slumped as an indirect result of famine in Russia, his business was over-committed. Urgently searching for lifelines, he entered into agreements with Guffey in America and with Henri Deterding (in the form of Asiatic Petroleum) in the Far East, but in his haste failed to ensure sound contracts with either. The lifelines were tied not with reef-knots but granny-knots; and when, on the one hand, Guffey's oilwells ran dry and, on the other hand, Deterding – just as he was allowed to – chartered cheaper vessels than Samuel's own, Samuel's fleet was essentially sunk. Its survival beyond 1907 was due solely to the amalgamation, on terms which earlier Samuel would have refused, of Royal Dutch and Shell Transport.

The second near-death of the fleet came in 1986, and its causes were basically the same: vigorous competition, and over-extension in a rising market which unexpectedly collapsed.

In the eight intervening decades, Shell companies were active in all phases of the oil industry, owning and running elements at every stage – exploration, production, transport, refining, marketing – so that, although the end product was handled at different stages by different companies within the Group, it was perfectly possible and quite usual for any given barrel of oil to be Shell-owned from well-head to petrol pump. There was nothing to stop any one of the companies from buying supplies from elsewhere, or from selling outside the Group, but they tended not to do so: long-term security of supply was usually rated more highly than short-term market opportunism.

The Group had always prided itself on its international nature, its involvement of local people in every country of operation, and the large degree of autonomy allowed to each. With its integrated structure, dividends to share-holders of Royal Dutch and Shell Transport were secured by the diversity of the Group's operations, and its financial strength allowed steady growth.

However, in the late 1950s, a long slow programme of decentralization had begun. Before the end of the 1970s, it was complete; and in 1981, the then Chairman of the Group's Committee of Managing Directors (or Senior Group Managing Director, in today's terminology), Dirk de Bruyne, said:

> We are in a different world than this industry grew up in, and the profitable survivors will be those companies which have recognized the change and are flexible enough to respond.

No longer could weaker, less profitable segments of the business be cushioned by the rest. For Shell Tankers (U.K.) Ltd, this came at a critical moment. 'One painfully obvious change in the oil tonnage sector', said Richard Tookey early in 1982, 'is the change from seemingly endless growth to seemingly endless decline...'

It was the 90th birthday year of Shell's British tanker fleet. Towards the end of the year, an oil industry analyst named Jim Glibbery wrote an assessment of the tanker world from the end of the First World War to that date. It began with a sombre note:

> The tanker market today is in a sorry state. Demand for oil is low and a chronic oversupply of tonnage, especially in the VLCC/ULCC size range, has resulted in depressed

freight rates. This in turn has accelerated the lay-up and scrapping of tonnage. Even tonnage that is actually trading is almost invariably operating at speeds well below optimum...

This was not entirely accurate: slow-steaming tankers were certainly operating at speeds well below their originally intended service speeds, but under the circumstances, that actually was the optimum, because it successfully balanced factors such as bunker consumption and employment against the alternatives of scrapping the ships or laying them up. But the meaning was clear; and curiously, this assessment labelled the period as being 'after the Lord Mayor's Show', implicitly comparing it with the years of crisis after 1902, when Marcus Samuel had been Lord Mayor of London. Its conclusion was bleak:

Short of extensive scrapping programmes and long term lay-up of tonnage, there can be little hope for buoyant conditions for some time to come.

This referred not only to the Shell fleet but to the industry as a whole, for every tanker-owning company was suffering. One of the first to take fundamental action was BP, which soon announced it was about to reduce its owned tanker fleet from 45 to 29 vessels, with the loss of 625 jobs among UK officers and ratings, and a further 560 jobs among its Indian ratings. Nevertheless, STUK's new managing director John Rendle (a former Captain in the STUK fleet, and only the second such to become MD) remained guardedly hopeful, if not optimistic, at least as far as personnel were concerned. Although at the end of 1982 he said, 'We still have a small surplus of officers in some ranks', he added: 'The situation is manageable, and should not

lead to any dramatic changes such as those which have so sadly affected the BP Fleet.'

But it was Rendle's misfortune – a double misfortune, given his sea-faring background – that within four years, he would have to preside over a similar sad drama.

There are various beaches around the world which have become graveyards for ships. The hulks that litter these places have not been wrecked by accident, but have been intentionally driven hard aground by their sailors; for these are the breakers' beaches. There is one near Karachi, in Pakistan; and there Captain Warwick Hemming took SS *Alinda*, formerly Eagle's *San Ernesto*, to her end.

Everyone who has done this agrees that it is the most unnatural experience a sailor could have. Common sense, instinct and training are all against it; the shore should be kept at a safe distance. But when a ship is ready for the breakers, suddenly the most basic rules of navigation are turned on their heads: fixing position is done not to decide how best to keep away from the land, but how best to hit it.

The previous year, Hemming had been Chief Officer in *Eburna* during the Falklands War; *Alinda* was his first command, and the last of the Eagle ships serving with STUK. On 9 April 1983, when they arrived off Karachi, there were already about 150 vessels on the beach, their sterns facing the Indian Ocean, their bows buried in the sand. Except for the small 'Beaching Party', all the staff and crew were paid off on the 11th, and the ship's new owners formally took possession. On the morning of the 12th, from a position three miles out at sea, Captain Hemming turned his ship towards the shore and rang down to the engine room an order that can be given only once in a ship's life – 'Maximum ramming speed'.

Captain John Rendle, CBE

The breakers' beaches.

She hit the beach at 16 knots, her great momentum sliding her gracefully up the sand. The shore crew swiftly made her fast, and for two hours, until high water, her engines were kept turning at Full Ahead, driving her still further up. FWE, 'Finished With Engines', is the engineers' usual note at the end of a voyage. When at last Captain Hemming rang *Alinda*'s engines off on the telegraph, his Second Engineer, Drew Dryburgh, put a terminal note in the Movement Book: FWEFE. It stood for 'Finished With Engines For Ever'.

In October 1983, for the first time in two years, the number of tankers laid up around the world fell slightly, from 23% to 22% of the global fleet. However, this still meant that 447 ships were standing idle, and by March 1984, the Malaysian authorities began to complain that with over 50 large tankers from various companies permanently anchored there, Brunei Bay was actually getting overcrowded.

Even so, there was good news too for STUK, and, amid the various causes for reflection, some things to be proud of – particularly its successes in the LNG business.

Glancing back for a moment from 1984: in Japan, the oil crises of 1973 and 1979 had brought about a concerted effort to reduce the nation's overwhelming dependence on that one fuel source. Since the first delivery (by *Gadinia*, Captain Simon Darroch) on 15 December 1972, STUK's LNG trade from Brunei to Japan had delivered well over 1,000 cargoes. The 1,000th cargo itself was delivered on 20 November 1980, again by *Gadinia*. Through a 'well-planned coincidence', Darroch, by then Commodore of the Fleet, was in command on that occasion too. In 1984 itself, backed by an already incomparable strength of experience on the Brunei-Japan run, Shell began similar deliveries from Bintulu in Malaysia to Kawasaki, carried in the five-strong MISC fleet. These ships, property of the Malaysian International Shipping Corporation and staffed partly by STUK personnel, are all called *Tenaga*, with distinguishing suffixes – *Satu*, *Dua*, *Tiga*, *Empat* and *Lima*. In Malay the

word 'Tenaga' means, roughly, force, power or strength, while 'Satu' and so on are the words for one to five.

Meanwhile, older ships, and those which were not paying their way, continued to be sold. The 315,000dwt L-class was further thinned down: *Lyria* went at the end of April 1984, *Litiopa* a year later. The 28-year-old *Acavus* arrived for scrap in Kaohsiun, Taiwan, in May 1984; *Achatina* was scrapped in Chittagong at the end of August; four months later, *Aulica* was driven at 'maximum ramming speed' up to the breakers at Gadani Beach; and at the same time as *Litiopa*, *Amastra*, the last of the British flag A-class, was taken to the Chittagong ships' graveyard.

Donax was sold to a new owner at the end of 1984; the much-loved *Opalia*, the training ship, was likewise sold in September of that year. (Sadly, in April 1985, under her new ownership, while sailing through the Gulf during the Iran-Iraq War, she was hit by an air launched missile and was abandoned ablaze.) *Halia* of 1958 – the last survivor of the H-class, in which many of today's senior Captains and Chief Engineers learned their skills – had been converted in 1969 to be a lightening ship, a role she carried out until 14 August 1985; then on 25 August, commanded by Captain Fred Croxon (who had been one of her original seamen 27 years earlier), 'the oldest and smallest of a diminishing Fleet' was taken to a breakers' beach in Spain.

However, it was not all sale and destruction, nor was any of this haphazard. During this period, the first half of the 1980s, a dozen ships joined the STUK fleet as a new strategy was implemented. The 31,000dwt *Euplecta* and *Ebalina*, both built in Chiba by the Mitsui Shipbuilding and Engineering Company, were accepted in February and May 1980 respectively, and brought the product carrying E-class to eight hulls. The third-hand *Northia* (ex-*Kronoland*, ex-*Oceanic Renown*), bought and renamed in September 1980, was refitted in Yokohama the following April to be a North Sea shuttle tanker, while *Rapana* and *Rimula* joined the fleet in 1980 performing duties very like those of the

Vietnamese boat people rescued July 1980.

original *Murex* back in 1892: as combined oil/ore carriers, they did not have to voyage in ballast, but could be profitable in both directions, east-west and west-east. Keeping pace with the growth of Shell Coal International, the dedicated coal carriers *Tribulus* and *Tricula*, built in Korea by Hyundai, were accepted in March and May 1981, and STUK's trade in coal immediately began to be profitable. The following year, 1982, brought two new 70,000dwt LPG carriers into the fleet, *Isomeria* and *Isocardia*; the ships of the E-class were joined in 1984 by the somewhat smaller and third-hand *Eulima* (ex-*Balder Apuania*, ex-*Martita*) and *Eulota* (ex-*Balder Carrara*, ex-*Liana*); and in May 1985, the 89,000dwt crude carrier *Sentis* (ex-*Atlantic Assurance*) changed her Norwegian flag for the Shell house flag.

Ever since Shell tankers had first put to sea, they had been involved from time to time in rescues of castaways. This became far more noticeable from the late 1970s, as refugees in small, often unseaworthy boats tried to escape from Vietnam, and in the middle of 1985, someone decided to tot up STUK's total of recent years. It was impressive: from the first 'boat people' (taken into *Entalina* on 28 November 1979) to the then most recent (in *Ebalina*

on 17 May 1985), company ships had rescued 523 people – men and women, old and young, and frequently children, often found just in time to save them from death by exposure, starvation or dehydration.

Thus, with slimming down, re-focusing, and the boost to morale of humanitarian acts, the August 1985 issue of *British Fleet News* carried a banner headline which was convincing and reassuring: 'The Company Is In Fine Shape'. This was the general conclusion of a long examination of the Group by the *Financial Times*, detailed in a 59-column-inch article by the newspaper's energy editor, Ian Hargreaves. As reported by *British Fleet News*, Hargreaves had written of Shell first as 'having a slightly musty image, reliable but dull', and then had gone on to describe how

> *prior to the first oil shock, Shell had made itself an aggressive fleet-footed marketer and refiner, in part by decentralisation to local management and operation control. ... Ian Hargreaves' overall verdict on the Group is that Shell's problems are by definition relatively smaller than its competitors', and in a falling oil market where the premium is upon speed of response, Shell is the company to watch.*

There was nothing untrue in the *British Fleet News* report, nor anything remotely intended to deceive; but it actually referred solely to the Group as a whole, not to every individual company within the Group. Ever since the beginning of 1975 (when Gillian Webb, in *Gastrana*, became STUK's first female trainee Radio Officer) the fleet's personnel had included women, and the great majority of personnel – male or female, seaman, cadet or captain – had long been brought up to think of themselves as Shell sailors. That was their pride and fulfilment; and the decentralization was still so comparatively recent that any sailor in the British fleet could have been forgiven for understanding the report as referring to his or her own company, Shell Tankers (U.K.) Ltd.

'The company is in fine shape....Shell is the company to watch.' They had read it in their own fleet journal, one of the channels of communication between their head office and the various far-flung ships. Perhaps they were naive, but less than a year later, by the summer of 1986, there had been very little to prepare them for the message which clattered out of their ship-board telexes on 17 July. Its gist was that, in a very short time, they would no longer be Shell sailors.

The magnitude of this shock is difficult to overstate. The seafarers were neither ignorant nor stupid, but, simply through being at sea for long periods, they were not as well informed about world events as were their colleagues on shore, and certainly were not privy to the gravity of the problems facing shore-side management. What had happened, in a nutshell, was that competition from new, non-traditional ship owners – particularly in Hong Kong and Greece – was rising, and very vigorous; and simultaneously, the price of crude oil had collapsed.

For those who followed such things in detail, there had been some warning signs that a collapse might happen. In 1982, attempting to keep its prices up, OPEC had

Sullom Voe Oil Terminal in Shetland Islands.

introduced quotas of production. In 1983, it had reduced the standard cost of a barrel of oil from $34 to $29. However, by 1985, non-OPEC production was outstripping that of OPEC, and by the end of that year some Arabian Gulf cargoes were selling for as little as $6 a barrel. Eventually the price stabilized within the broad band of $18-22; but throughout 1986, it was completely haywire, without structure or control. This was the 'third oil shock': a reversal in all the trends of the past 13 years, which was, for many of the companies involved, just as difficult to assimilate as had been the catastrophic price rises of the 1970s. Nevertheless, according to Daniel Yergin, a prominent historian of the oil industry, 'Planners at Shell in London, reading the fundamentals carefully, had geared up an "OCS", an Oil Collapse Scenario.' Yergin continued:

The company had insisted that its senior managers take it seriously even if they thought it was improbable, discuss what their responses would be, and start taking prophylactic action. Thus, when the collapse struck, in contrast to the shock observed in many other oil companies, there was an eerie calm and orderliness at Shell Centre on the south bank of the Thames. Managers there, as well as in the field, went about their jobs as though carrying out a civil defence emergency operation for which they had already practised.

If that is so, it can only be said that the OCS had not communicated itself to the sailors in the STUK fleet. For them, the events of summer 1986 came as a bolt from the blue.

In simplified terms, the position of STUK, with its existing levels of cost, had become critical. Such things had already happened to other tanker companies, and would happen to more. If STUK was to survive, a drastic internal reconstruction would have to take place. This would involve, first and foremost, making every STUK sailor redundant, and second, taking recourse to an Isle of Man company to provide STUK's future seafaring manpower.

The Isle of Man agency were prepared to consider all redundant sailors for deployment on Shell ships, and it was believed that their terms of engagement would be 'superior to most available elsewhere offshore'. But that could not disguise the fact that terms would be significantly altered. Periods at sea before leave would be longer. Leave would no longer be paid. Pensions would no longer be paid: the sailors must make their own provision for their old age. Finally, if they accepted new employment through the new offshore agency, that agency, Marine Personnel Services (IOM) Ltd, would be their employer, not Shell.

Detailing the proposed changes, the August 1986 issue of *British Fleet News* stressed that every part of Shell's marine business was similarly afflicted, including Shell International Marine and STUK's three sister fleets in Holland, Germany and France. It emphasised, too, that there was no question of seeking less stringent safety regulations offshore, and that 'contrary to popular belief, there is no company tax advantage to be gained from these arrangements'. Likewise, it pointed out that there was every intention the fleet should continue in being. The

option of 'complete withdrawal from owned fleets' – selling off not just a large part of the fleet, as BP had done, but every single ship – had been considered, but rejected because 'it was seen that there was a need to preserve the hard-earned expertise the Shell group has in the marine sector.' Think yourselves lucky, boys. As the report explained:

All this follows a period of ship rationalisation over a number of years when ships have been scrapped or sold from the Shell Group fleets. Efforts over the last six months have concentrated on continuing to reduce costs in general, but it was clear that in the UK only a radical change of organisation and registry was capable of significantly reducing personnel and administrative costs, key elements in the competitive cost structure....There is no doubt that drastic action is needed if our marine business is to survive.

The report concluded with an optimistic note from Juan Kelly. Later, as President of the GCBS, he was appointed a CBE; in 1986, having been Marine Co-ordinator since 1984, he declared himself 'convinced that we will succeed provided that we can restructure quickly enough. At best we could move into profit by the end of 1988, and at worst a few years later. It is not an easy process...'

No, indeed. It was all clear, and comparatively straightforward; but it was terribly hard for the sailors to accept. It was worse than the unexpected death of a loved one; it was as if a loved one had, without warning, demanded a divorce, or come for an embrace with a knife concealed in one hand. Utter disillusioment, a desperate sense of betrayal, a deep loss of trust – such were their feelings as they gradually understood the options available. There were really only two. No one could avoid being made redundant: that was not a matter of choice. For everyone, no matter their rank, the job of being one of Shell's British sailors had come to an end. More positively, everyone, according to rank and length of service, was given very generous financial compensation. It was after that that each individual had to make up his or her mind – either to retire, or to accept employment that was for Shell, yet not with Shell. Thirty-five per cent, including a large proportion of senior officers from deck and engine room alike, chose retirement.

After prolonged negotiation with both the National Union of Seamen and NUMAST, the officers' union, the package had been accepted. It was, in fact, the fairest that could possibly have been devised, and had not been arrived at easily. The fleet's total dissolution had been a serious possibility, against which the managing director, John Rendle, had argued long and hard. A quiet and courteous man, looking and sounding more like a country gentleman than the popular image of a hard-bitten seafarer, he had a painful sense of personal responsibility towards the sailors, his former colleagues, who were now under his command. Two factors gave him particular concern. However reasonable they could be made, the measures that were vital to the company's survival were bound to bring distress; and worse still, he could see that the long-standing trust between the fleet and shore management was in danger of breaking down completely. More than once, as discussions about the fleet's future continued, he considered resigning. On each occasion, however, he kept these thoughts private. Despite the extreme strain, a sense of duty made him stay; and in the end he knew that by staying, he had helped protect the fleet from far worse alternatives than the fate which it now faced. Years later, somewhat to his surprise, he learned that staying on had earned him more respect within the fleet than resigning would have done. He

should not have been surprised: sailors do not like a captain to abandon ship by himself.

Under Geoffrey Bryant, the Personnel Manager, every senior member of that department had a role to play in disseminating the news – writing to the ships, chairing discussion groups, explaining over and over what must happen; and someone had to handle the crux of it all. Rather than bring in an outsider to terminate existing contracts and offer new ones, Rendle believed that the sailors would prefer it to come from a member of the company. Alan Chivers, the man selected, had to interview every person affected and discuss the options with them; but there were about 1,200 men and women involved, and only two real options – retirement, or employment with Marine Personnel Services (IOM) Ltd. Every person was seen individually, but most wanted either to pour out their heart or vent their fury at length. With their great numbers, this was a practical impossibility, and the necessary brevity of the interviews left them frustrated and still more bitter.

Thinking back from his own retirement, Rendle remarked: 'It is a matter of opinion whether we would have been better using an outsider. The job had to be done quickly and required a deal of toughness.'

From the depths of their own trauma, it was hard for the sailors to realise that the situation for their colleagues on shore was scarcely better: 50% of shore staff were shed.

From every point of view, the restructuring was probably the single most shocking event in the company's first 100 years; the only other comparable period was the lead-in to the amalgamation of 1907. Only one person, the then Sir Marcus Samuel, later Viscount Bearsted, had felt the pain of that, and in a very short time even he had become reconciled: he was far too honest to be able to deny for long that, without

Juan Kelly, CBE

191

amalgamation, the name of Shell would have vanished from his ships. Without restructuring, the same would have been true in 1986; and today, in the long perspective of the history of Shell's British tanker fleets, it is clear that in general the decisions made in 1986, though abominably painful, were sound.

Six years have passed since then: the last six of the first 100, and Shell's British tanker fleet has not only achieved its centenary, but is profitable, stable and ready to embark on its second century. That in itself is by far the most important thing that needs to be said about the recent years. It is also a tribute to the good business sense shown in 1986, when the entire fleet came its closest to being FWEFE – Finished With Engines For Ever.

Even so, these recent years have not been completely uneventful; there have been both successes and tragedy. Now, therefore, as this book approaches its conclusion, a brief résumé of the period 1986-92 is appropriate.

Those sailors who chose redundancy in 1986 received generous compensation, especially the senior ones; and gradually, the 65% of sea-going personnel who had agreed to the new conditions found that even if it was no longer their employer, Shell still kept its promises. Prime amongst these was the commitment that if vacancies resulted from the restructuring, they would be filled whenever possible by the promotion of existing personnel, rather than by newcomers – which meant, for many of those who stayed, more rapid promotion than would normally have been the case.

As something of a counter-balance to this positive outcome, vacancies at middle and junior levels often had to be filled by outsiders, who brought with them different working habits, different traditions, different points of view.

At first, the former Shell sailors were

disparaging: no way could these newcomers be as good as Shell people. But they often were, and sometimes they were better: a little more efficient, a little more experienced, a little more innovative; and often a lot more clock-watching, disinclined, if their hours of duty were done, to carry on with a job until it was finished. Shell people had *never* been like that, and ex-Shell people were shocked and intrigued.

The changes of 1986 affected shore-side management almost as much as their sea going colleagues: half the office staff had to go, either through redundancy or transfer. Rod Davies, a former STUK Captain, established the Isle of Man operation and supervised its first year and a half. In Shell Centre, the traditional management separation of deck and engineering departments was done away with: instead, in a manner unique among oil companies, the two were united into Fleet Operations, and in May 1987 placed under the genial leadership of Captain John Waters, a former Eagle man.

Early in December 1986, the G-class LNG ships were sold to a new company, Brunei Shell Tankers Sendirian Berhad, in which Shell and the state of Brunei shared equally. Their livery and their names were altered; instead of shells beginning with G, they were given the Bruneian names of various fish beginning with B, and so became the B-class, with *Gari* (for instance) now *Bekulan*, the Bruneian for a tunny. They continue to be managed by STUK, are operated by the same men as before, and still, today, maintain the same regular shuttle. This appears to be one of the happiest business relationships one could wish for: Shell people describe the Bruneians as virtually ideal colleagues, scrupulous in their attention to detail, exacting in their requirements for reports, properly protective of Bruneian interests, and, with all that, still courteous, efficient, interested, and generally a pleasure to work with. Certainly there is plenty of

Under Fire

Following the principle established by Marcus Samuel, Shell's tankers are always made available for the national cause in time of war. Similarly, the Royal Navy always extends its protection to them, as to any other Red Ensign vessel, if their trade as neutrals takes them into a war zone. It was for precisely this purpose that, during the eight-year-long Iran-Iraq war, the Royal Navy established its ARMILLA patrol in the Arabian Gulf. Initially, the patrol escorted friendly merchant vessels through the narrowest and most critical area of the Gulf, the Strait of Hormuz. On 23 January 1987, however, an episode took place which showed the patrol's range might have to be extended.

After being escorted through the strait, STUK's LPG carrier *Isomeria* (Captain Gordon Scarfe) was in position 25° 42'N 55° 21'E – off the coast of Sharjah – when an Iranian frigate began to shadow her. Since, by then, her RN escort (the Type 42 destroyer HMS *Gloucester*) had returned to her patrol area, Captain Scarfe swiftly contacted his head office at Shell Centre in London for advice. A three-way telephone/satellite communications conference ensued, between the ship, Shell Centre and the Ministry of Defence's Directorate of Naval Operations and Trade (DNOT).

While *Gloucester* hurried towards *Isomeria*, members of the DNOT staff advised Scarfe through the communications link. The four RN officers involved were Captain G. W. R. Biggs, Director of Naval Operations and Trade; his deputy, Captain J. Kelly, OBE; and two desk officers, Commanders F. J. Bradshaw and J. G. Malec, OBE. The RN team displayed a calm professional certainty which impressed the Shell personnel deeply. Though they were thousands of miles from the scene, working only from Scarfe's description of events, they rapidly identified the Iranian frigate and knew just what armament she carried.

They therefore knew too how she might shape an attack. While the frigate stayed within five miles, she was shadowing; but when Scarfe reported that she had backed off to 12 miles distant, approximately 20° on his starboard quarter, then DNOT warned that an attack was probably imminent – the frigate was now in her best firing position, and Captain Scarfe and his personnel should take cover.

DNOT also advised Scarfe to look out for the flashes of the frigate's missiles as they were fired. They were Italian-made; sight-line guided; neither heat- nor radar-attracted; and the ship carried a maximum of five. If five were fired and none hit him, Scarfe and his tanker would be safe.

This knowledge was not exactly an unmixed blessing. In the tense seconds which followed, Scarfe knew that there was nothing else he could do: that the survival of *Isomeria* depended on luck alone.

Just as predicted, there were four flashes in succession, then, after a brief pause, a fifth. But luck was with him that day, for although all five missiles were close, none found the target. Instead they splashed harmlessly into the sea, and – again just as DNOT had predicted – the Iranian frigate sheered off and vanished.

As far as is possible under the circumstances, forewarned is definitely forearmed; and the staff of DNOT had shown they knew exactly what they were talking about. So, grim as it was, the experience had a very positive side too; for if they had not known it before, Shell sailors now clearly saw and gratefully recognised the cool professionalism of their counterparts in the armed fleet.

A similar reinforcing of confidence took place during the Gulf War of 1991. The Iraqi president, Saddam Hussein, had demonstrated his willingness to use weapons of mass destruction when he used poison gas on the Kurds. Naturally enough, Shell sailors were very worried by the thought that this particularly horrible form of warfare might be directed against them too. Every defensive preparation was made, under RN guidance; and *Methane Princess* found a small but useful role, when she was used as the stage for an RN training film on the subject. The resultant video was seen in every Shell ship that approached the Gulf, and its business-like straightforwardness contributed markedly to calming the crewmembers' worries.

Bebatik *loading at the Lumut terminal.*

work to do: on average, one of the seven G-class ships docks at one or other of Japan's three Brunei LNG terminals every other day throughout the year; and all have always operated with perfect safety.

John Rendle retired as MD on 1 April 1988, a few months early – his scheduled term of office did not end until the following November. In the 18 months or so that had elapsed since the restructuring began, the company's finances had remained on a knife-edge. He chose to go because, though he still felt some uneasiness about the next few years, overall he was confident that the worst was

finished; and clearly others agreed with this assessment, because just a few weeks later, in the Queen's Birthday Honours, he was awarded a CBE for his lifelong contribution to the shipping industry.

Returning from the Isle of Man, Rod Davies succeeded him, and remained in post until his own retirement at the end of August 1990. Though brief and unostentatious, his period in office was a time of consolidation, and included five major events. The first was (through the customary agency of SIM) a set of acquisitions; the second, a significant Group policy decision; the third, a serious accident; the fourth, a fatal tragedy; and the fifth, a joyous reunion.

First, the acquisitions: these were the chartering of two 69,500dwt product carriers (*Zaphon* and *Zidona*) and two more LNG carriers. These, *LNG Bonny* and *LNG Finima*, had been bought from a Swedish owner by a subsidiary of Nigeria LNG Ltd for management and operation by STUK. Strengthening still further STUK's part in one of the cleanest, most highly disciplined, stable and profitable sections of the energy transportation industry, their arrival also opened a new phase in the company's relationship with Nigeria – one which all involved confidently believe will grow as strong and solid as STUK's LNG relationships with Brunei and Malaysia.

Second, the policy decision. This followed the highly publicized grounding of *Exxon Valdez* in Alaskan waters on 24 March 1989. Although *Valdez* was an Exxon ship with an Exxon cargo, the disaster's consequences meant that every oil company, including Shell, faced literally incalculable potential risks. As far as Exxon were concerned, to say nothing of the damage to its public image, in purely monetary terms the costs of the calamity were astronomical: billions of dollars had to be paid in compensation and attempted clean-up. As far as other oil companies were concerned, the key commercial risk of trading with America was that, in the event of an oil spill, laws in some parts of the US placed unlimited liability on the ship-owners, whether or not the spill was their fault. Ian McGrath, Juan Kelly's successor as Marine Co-ordinator, explained that

A ship owner who is involved in a pollution incident in the USA even when he has behaved properly, responsibly and without negligence, may face largely uninsurable exposure to claims which far outweigh the potential reward from such trade.

Even with the strictest adherence to safety procedures, no one can ever promise that accidents at sea will not happen. Yet under this legislation, even if someone else rammed and holed a tanker, creating a cargo spill, the tanker owners would be just as legally liable as the owners of the ship which did the ramming; and the implications did not necessarily stop there, for under certain circumstances the owners of the *cargo* could also become enmeshed in an unlimited claim. To have one's cargo carried in someone else's ship was therefore no answer. Moreover, even if a holed tanker was empty of cargo, she would still be carrying bunker oil; that too could form a spill.

In pondering how best they should cope with this, Shell bore in mind that if spilled into the sea, different kinds of oil behave differently. The key distinction lay in 'black' or 'dirty' oils, as opposed to 'white' or 'clean' oils. Though black oils are nowhere strictly defined, they are generally understood to include crude petroleum, fuel-oil, heavy diesel oil and lubricating oil – the oils which, if spilled, result in a persistent harmful residue. All other oils, the refined fractions of crude, are classed as white or clean, because they disperse or evaporate quickly, without persistent harmful effect. The distinction means not only that spilled black oil does

more damage, but also that it is very much more costly to clean up a black oil spill than a white oil spill.

Oil trading, like any other business, has always been a matter of balancing risk against reward. After *Exxon Valdez*, the balance, from the oil companies' point of view, was impossibly out of kilter: the transport of a cargo of black oil offering a profit of some tens of thousands of dollars could, if spilled, entail costs of billions of dollars. This was unacceptable; so Shell took a simple but drastic policy decision.

Shipments of white oils to the US would continue as usual: the risk-reward balance for them was supportable. However, shipments of black oils would cease to all US ports but one. (The exception was the so-called LOOP, or Louisiana Offshore Oil Port. Located nearly 19 miles out at sea, in deep water, this is the only port on either the East or Gulf coasts of the US which can accept VLCCs. It also has an exceptionally good safety record.) Shell publicized this decision in June 1990, emphasizing that it was taken on purely commercial grounds, and that they had absolute confidence in the safety record of their own ships and sailors. It was quickly seen by the rest of the industry as sensible, and other major owners began to follow suit.

Shell had led the way again; but the third major event while Rod Davies was STUK's MD was a serious accident. On 5 May 1990, *Tribulus* was on passage from Seven Isles to Rotterdam with a cargo of iron ore, when, in extremely heavy weather, she lost a piece of side plating, allowing water into her No. 8 hold. Over the next two days, fortunately, her crew were able to keep her going until she reached the relative sanctuary of Bantry Bay. After temporary repairs there, she was taken to Lisbon for permanent repairs; but only a few weeks later came the fourth and worst of the major events.

Ian McGrath

Rapana, (1973) 227,411dwt. Acquired by STUK 1980.

On Monday 25 June 1990, while on passage from Borfjorden in Norway to Tranmere with a cargo of 70,000 tons of Iranian heavy crude, the oil/ore carrier *Rapana* (Captain Peter Marsland) suffered an explosion and severe fire in her pumproom. One man, Chief Engineer Ray Gill, was critically injured, and three men died – Chief Officer David Cammish, Super-intendent Alan Patience and Pumpman St Aubin Thomas.

At about 5.40 pm on 25 June, news of the incident was received in STUK by telephone direct from the vessel. The company's emergency call out procedures were promptly activated; in SIM, the 'casualty room' (not a sick bay, but an operational co-ordination centre long prepared for just such an eventuality) was manned immediately, and remained so throughout the emergency; and Captain Rod Brown from SIM joined Davies at once, in order both to assist and to learn at first hand what was happening. As Davies's designated successor, it was clear that he would probably have to oversee a good deal of the consequences.

Rapana was then off the south coast of Norway. While her crew fought the blaze, local rescue services rushed to the scene. Arrangements were made to evacuate Chief

Engineer Gill and all non-essential personnel by helicopter. In the pumproom, the fire still raged, and the nearest vessel that could help in fighting it was some hours away. Using every available means, the remaining crew continued to fight the fire; but the initial explosion had damaged the doorways, and it was impossible to batten down the top of the pumproom. It took about half an hour before partial jury closures could be rigged and the burning pumproom flooded with CO_2. Just before 7 pm, foam began to be injected as well. All this time, water was being hosed into the pumproom and onto its boundaries, to cool it inside and out, and at last it seemed all was coming under control – then a second series of explosions rocked the vessel, and the smoke poured more densely than ever from her.

Throughout the emergency, open-line communication was maintained with the SIM casualty co-ordination centre. Shell's Norwegian companies and agents offered all possible help; so did government departments in Britain and Norway. A second helicopter evacuated more personnel: the 18 who remained were all volunteers.

It was not until four hours after the first explosion that the smoke billowing out of the stricken vessel began to turn white: the

Experienced firefighting officers training Shell cadets at South Tyneside College.

Photograph Stephen Howarth

Life boat drill aboard the Bekulan

most welcome sight those 18 men had seen, for – just as their stocks of foam were beginning to run out – it was a positive indication that the critical areas were at last beginning to cool. At the same time, the Norwegian firefighters reached the ship and started pumping more foam into the seat of the fire. Boundary cooling continued without a pause, and three hours later it was confirmed that the dreadful fire was finally out.

Astonishingly, *Rapana* could still move under her own steam. Now she headed slowly towards Methil, in the Firth of Forth, escorted first by a vessel of the Norwegian Coastguard and then by a supply ship chartered in by

STUK. It was another 29 hours before she reached her destination, and it was not until September that she could be taken to Lisbon for full repairs.

It is bad enough to read of such events; it is far worse if you know the people involved and the men who were injured or killed. 'Appalling and stunning', said *Erodona*'s Captain Mike Hardy. 'It has left a mark on every one of us.' An intensive investigation began at once; and while it was under way, an official article in *Marine News* (the journal of Shell's marine sector) paid unhappy tribute:

> *If there is anything positive to be gleaned from such a tragic event, it is to say that the training of the crew plus the attention to fire drills, coupled with the bravery and determination of the volunteers who remained on board, without a doubt saved the ship from foundering.*

It is not easy to convey depth of emotion in official words. The same article concluded with thanks to the survivors and condolences to the bereft; but those who had survived and those who had been bereaved understood that these were not just platitudes. Alongside the horror are memories of the demonstrations of respect, care and even tenderness displayed by everyone in the company – from the simplest, but essential, hug of shared sorrow, to the equally necessary counselling and financial help. If it sounds sentimental, it should not: when people are hurt or killed, others respond; and though STUK is a large concern, and the Group a very large one, they are still made up of individuals. 'I personally knew two of the deceased very well', wrote Captain Hardy. 'The stark suddenness of the event and the extent of the human tragedy involved has stunned us all.' Yet life and work had to continue; and as Hardy wrote to his colleagues in the Fleet Personnel Association,

This accident also brings home to each and every one of us that we work in a dangerous environment carrying inherently dangerous material, a combination of factors that can never be underestimated.

It would be tempting fate severely to say that such terrible events will never happen again; yet despite the numerous accidents, fatal and otherwise, which have been chronicled in these pages, Shell Tankers (U.K.) Ltd actually has an almost unmatched safety record. Long may it continue so.

The fifth and final major event while Davies was MD occurred very shortly after the *Rapana* tragedy, and it was (thank goodness) a very happy one indeed. The restructuring of four years earlier had worked: the company was back in profit – a most agreeable sensation, and not only for Chris Vincent of SIM and Martin Hampstead of STUK, the men who led the Marine Sector's financial affairs. Renewed profitability meant that STUK could once more afford to be the direct employers of the fleet's sea-going personnel. In July 1990, new agreements were offered to the sailors, and were accepted with alacrity, not least because the off-shore company (now run by John McCallion, himself a former Chief Engineer) was renamed Shell

Marine Personnel (Isle of Man) Ltd. Many of the terms lost in 1986 were restored: fixed leave rates were increased; job security was enhanced; and above all, the name of Shell was restored to the sailors. In the company's official Annual Assessment, the satisfaction was stated plainly:

Success in this change was quickly obvious. Resignations diminished, recruitment of higher calibre personnel became easier even to the extent that previous employees were returning to the fold, and, most importantly, morale was boosted virtually overnight. Belonging to "Shell" was of major impact.

On 1 September 1990, command of Shell Tankers (U.K.) Ltd passed to Captain Rod Brown, a large and cheerful former sailor whose sea-going career with Shell went back to Anglo-Saxon days (the days of the Anglo-Saxon Petroleum Company, that is). Among his key objectives as MD is the fostering of the rapport and communications between ship and shore. He is also enthusiastically supportive of Shell's Cadet Scheme, not only because that is the well-spring of STUK's future health, but because the British merchant navy as a whole urgently needs new blood. He is well aware, too, of the vital importance of avoiding the temptation to over-extend the size of the fleet: 'One of my main anxieties', he said in an early interview, 'is the view some have that the fleet is doing best when it has most

ships.' Quality rather than quantity remain his watchwords, whether in terms of management or of deadweight tonnage.

He took over leadership of a company which knew it had come very close to extinction. It was also, fortunately, a company with a long and retentive collective memory, and an incalculable amount of accumulated experience and expertise. Most importantly, it had both the desire and the

Zaphon (1990) 69,500dwt.

ability to learn and to continue learning from its own past, from the past of others, and – in a world where nothing stays still – from the present as well. Because of those factors, the experience of 1986, painful as it had been, was healthy too. As Brown has put it, 'It's a fact that the decisions made then, no matter how hard, were fundamental to the healthy state of the fleet today; and the family feeling is now returning.' The company is profitable now, but all recognize that keeping it so is not merely a matter of 'steady as she goes': the market is at least as competitive as at any time in the past 100 years, and the customer is more sophisticated than ever before.

This is not the place to try and record in any detail the most recent events in the history of Shell's British tanker fleets, but two should be mentioned. Old vessels still leave, and new ones still come. *Rapana* and *Rimula* have just gone, at the end of their charter periods; and the most recent addition to the fleet is the brand-new 96,117dwt motor tanker *Siliqua,* built by the Namura Shipbuilding Company and accepted into the STUK fleet on 26 September 1991. The scheduled acceptance date had been the 27th, but it was brought forward because a typhoon was forecast; and so, as something of a symbol, the newest member of Shell's British tanker fleet joined with the classic maritime imponderables of sea and weather governing her from the start.

The final note is equally appropriate. On 21 February 1992, STUK gained a listing in Lloyd's Register of Quality Assurance. Applicants are assessed against both ISO 9002 (the manufacturing industry gauge of the International Standards Organisation) and IMO Resolution 647 – the

International Maritime Organisation's leading measurement of standards of watch-keeping, shipboard safety and pollution prevention. LRQA listing is thus a double achievement. The only other major deepsea merchant fleet in the world to have gained such a listing is Shell's Dutch fleet, and only 30% of applicants pass first time – as STUK did, reaching a new pinnacle of maritime recognition.

Now 100 years have ended, and the second century begins. Exactly 50 years ago, in the middle of wartime, a description of Shell's British tanker fleet began: 'This vast concern is the outcome of a firm founded by M. Samuel & Co. in 1892...' When Marcus Samuel and his younger brother Sam dreamed of establishing a shipping company, they would probably not have dared predict that it would become such a 'vast concern', much less that it would still be alive and well today; but it did, and it is. Similarly, no one now can foretell the shape of shipping a century hence; but if young people, and their children and grandchildren, continue to see the Merchant Navy as a fruitful career, then – with sound shore-based management in alliance with its own distinctive traditions of highly skilled and experienced sea-going leadership –' there may well still be Shell ships sailing in 2092.

Who can tell? Certainly the basis is there. The coming ten years have been carefully, but not inflexibly, charted. As ever, the Fleet's existing ships are scrupulously maintained in the best possible condition. New vessels too form an integral part of any shipping business plan, and under the present Marine Coordinator, Ian McGrath, selecting STUK's future hulls is part of SIM's task. Trading Manager Phil Owen determines coming market needs, for hull sizes and cargo requirements alike; Technical Director Sandy Tosh ensures the technical excellence of the chosen ships. Both men are former Chief Engineers from STUK, with judgement and ability based on years of practical sea-going experience.

Within STUK itself, cost-effectiveness has improved very markedly: in the period 1986-1991 inflation in Britain totalled 38%, yet in 1991 the costs of fleet and office personnel salaries were actually less in figures than in 1986. Among the sailors, back under the Shell banner and more efficient than they have ever been, morale is better than at any time since the watershed year of 1986. In all personnel, afloat and ashore, there are the highest standards of training, tradition, and trading ethics; and finally, the training ground has been maintained – the fleet is still officered entirely by British men and women.

Critics of the oil industry would probably be disappointed to encounter Shell sailors, because they are not the greedy and irresponsible tanker sailors of popular myth. Rather the contrary: they are in general more conscientious than most people about issues which affect us all, especially environmental issues. The cynical reaction might be that this is because their jobs depend upon it. That is partly true, but even if it were the whole truth, it would not make their conscientiousness any less valuable, or any less laudable. The whole truth about Shell sailors is actually very simple: they are just ordinary, decent, honest men and women, whose job it is to sail tankers safely from one port to another, loading and discharging their cargoes safely and efficiently, using, in between, all the maritime skills that 100 years of experience have imparted.

They themselves would probably stress one further thing: that they are not only sailors, they are *Shell* sailors. So to conclude, it is appropriate, in wishing them bon voyage, to quote a farewell letter from one Shell sailor to all the others. It was written by Ian MacLean, on his retirement in 1977, and in part it said:

We have had our good times and bad times. We have not always agreed, and it would have been strange if we had. But at the end of the day, we can look back and say that we have had the same common bond of interest, a love of the sea and ships – Shell ships.

Mrs Riet van Engelshoven (Siliqua's sponsor) naming the ship.

The acceptance of *28. SILIQUA* on Thursday 26 September 1991 brought the fleet's strength to 40 vessels owned or managed by STUK, and aggregating 4,193,348dwt. As this 'snapshot' shows, on that particular day (as on most others) the ships were spread world-wide, from the Far East to the Near East, the North Sea to the Caribbean.

Of the B-class LNG carriers, the 51,579dwt *1. BEKULAN* (Captain Norman Dixon) was having a routine refit in drydock in Yokohama; all the others were steadily shuttling their sub-zero cargoes from Brunei to Japan. *2. BEBATIK* (Captain Les Graham) was loading in Lumut; *3. BEKALANG* (Captain Peter Shefford) was at sea, en route from Lumut to Sodegaura; *4. BELAIS* (Captain

Ronald Firth) was likewise at sea, but en route from Sodegaura to Lumut; *5. BELANAK* (Captain John Briand) was at sea, en route from Negishi to Lumut. Those four were all of the same deadweight tonnage as *1. BEKULAN;* of the smaller two, the 41,370dwt *6. BILIS* (Captain Stuart Cutler) was discharging at Sodegaura; and her sister *7. BUBUK* (Captain Clive Turner) was at sea, en route from Sodegaura to Lumut.

The last remaining member of the D-class, the 71,917dwt *8. DRUPA* (Captain Dave Lake), was taking crude oil from Shellhaven in the Thames Estuary to Sture in Norway, and the four E's – all, give or take a deadweight ton, of 31,375dwt – were carrying white oils around the Middle East: *9. EBALINA* (Captain Richard Savage) was in

Singapore; *10. EBURNA* (Captain Karl Biscoe) was tank-cleaning off Singapore's port limits; *11. ERVILIA* (Captain Val Hope) was in Hong Kong; and *12. EUPLECTA* (Captain Richard Lawson) was bunkering off the port limits of Yokkaichi.

Both carrying LPG, the two I's – the 47,989dwt *13. ISOCARDIA* (Captain John Bateman) and the 47,594dwt *14. ISOMERIA* (Captain Ernie Wilkinson) – were respectively in the southern French port of Lavera (near Marseilles), and Saikaide in Japan.

The seven giant L-class crude oil carriers were widely scattered. The 317,996dwt *15. LAMPAS* (Captain Gordon Tigar) was at sea, en route from Fujairah in the Persian-Arabian Gulf to Cap d'Antifer, near Le Havre. *16. LATIA*

of 268,889dwt (Captain Dave Still) was at sea, en route from Ras Tanurah in the Gulf to Rotterdam, and, also proceeding from Ras Tanurah, the 317,996dwt *17. LEONIA* (Captain Tim Lant) was likewise at sea, en route for Aruba in the West Indies. *18. LEPETA* (317,996dwt, Captain Tony Searle) was bunkering off port limits of Fujairah; *19. LIMA* (318,013dwt, Captain Phil Pinches) was in the Egyptian port of Ain Sukhna, south of Suez; the 269,070dwt *20. LIMNEA* (Captain François Hugo) was tank-cleaning off the port limits of Singapore; and *21. LYRIA* (277,553dwt, Captain Roger Firth) was at sea, en route from Ju'aymah in the Gulf to Singapore.

On the same day, the two new 89,654dwt LNG

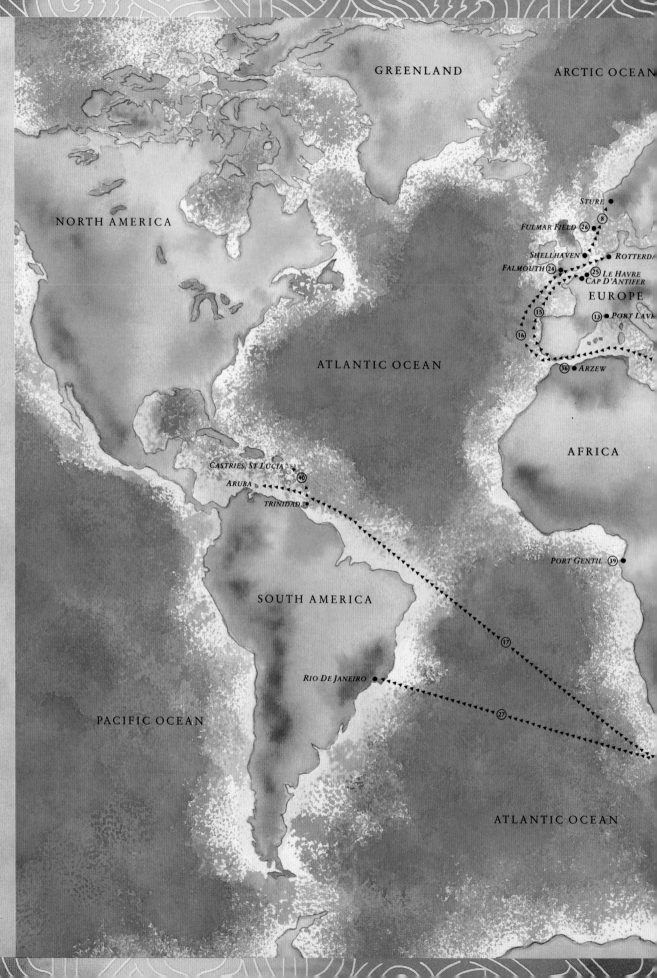

A Snapshot of the Fleet
26th SEPTEMBER 1991

IMARI
SAIKADE
OSAKA
SENBOKU
YOKKAICHI
OHGISHIMA
YOKOHAMA
NEGISHI
SODEGAURA
CHIBA

ASIA

JAPAN

HONG KONG

PORT SAID
AIN SUKHNA
KHARG ISLAND
JU'AYMAH
RAS TANURAH
AL FUJAIRAH

ARUN
SINGAPORE
LUMUT
BINTULU

MALAYSIA

INDIAN OCEAN

AUSTRALIA

NEWCASTLE

NEW ZEALAND

SOUTHERN OCEAN

ANTARCTICA

---

carriers, *22. LNG BONNY* (Captain Dave Picking) and *23. LNG FINIMA* (Captain Robin Gupta), were both at sea, voyaging respectively from Senboku in Japan to Arun in Indonesia, and from Bintulu in Malaysia to Sodegaura. With Neil Cottam as Officer-in-Charge, the 24,608dwt LPG carrier *24. METHANE PRINCESS* was laid up in Falmouth.

Of the two N-class crude oil carriers, *25. NORRISSIA* (109,999dwt, Captain Brian Cosgrove) was in Le Havre, while the 133,559dwt *26. NORTHIA* (Captain Keith Fenwick) was on the Fulmar field in the North Sea. The fleet's sole iron ore carrier, the 227,400dwt *27. RAPANA* (Captain Brian Morley), was taking a cargo from Fujairah to Rio de Janeiro; and the brand-new 96,121dwt

28. SILIQUA (Captain Dave Rayfield) was in the Japanese port of Imari, amidst the fanfare of being handed over to STUK.

Then came the five 72,083dwt LNG-carrying *TENAGA'S 29. TENAGA DUA* (Captain Tony Parkes) was at sea, en route from Chiba in Japan to Bintulu; *30. TENAGA EMPAT* (Captain Peter Boon) was in Sodegaura; *31. TENAGA LIMA* (Captain Murray Brogan) was at sea, en route from Ohgishima to Bintulu, as was *32. TENAGA SATU* (Captain Derek Wallace); and *33. TENAGA TIGA* (Captain Charlie Jarrett) was at sea, en route from Bintulu to Sodegaura.

Of the two 125,900dwt T-class coal-carriers, *34. TRIBULUS* (Captain Dave Conway) was at sea, en

route from Newcastle in Australia to Chiba in Japan, and her sister *35. TRICULA* (Captain Mike Geddes) was at Port Said, preparing to transit the Suez Canal. Moving to the Z's, the 69,500dwt product carrier *36. ZAPHON* (Captain Jerry Warman) was in the Algerian port of Arzew, and the 57,741dwt *37. ZENATIA* (Captain Malcolm Cowton), similarly laden, was at Kharg Island. Their sister, the 69,500dwt *38. ZIDONA* (Captain Jack Brown) was also at Kharg, acting as an FSU or floating storage unit, filled with white oils, while *39. BANIO*, manned by STUK personnel under Officer-in-Charge John Mercer, was likewise acting as an FSU for crude oil at Port Gentil in Gabon.

Out of alphabetical order, last in size (but in the eyes

of her Officer-in-Charge, John Fisher, certainly not least) was the tiny product carrier *40. VICENTE*, of 619dwt. On that day, Thursday 26 September 1991, she was bustling through the West Indies, at sea, en route from Trinidad to Castries in St Lucia.

So that was how the fleet lay, on a fairly typical day in the early 1990's, close to 100 years after its inception; and from the statistics some interesting figures may be drawn. The total dead weight tonnage was 4,193,348. Only the ageing *24. METHANE PRINCESS* was not actively employed – less than 0.6% of the total tonnage. To put it the other way around, more than 99.4% of the fleet's tonnage was in active employment – an impressive level of use.

Fleet List

Ships are listed in alphabetical order. The list includes all those for which records are held and which were or are owned, managed or manned by Shell's British tanker fleets. Each reference follows the same format: the name of the ship and (in brackets) her serial number, if there has been more than one of the same name; her gross registered tonnage; the date of her completion (which, for a second- or third-hand vessel, is not necessarily the date of her inclusion in the fleet); her dimensions (length overall followed by beam); and her makers. Where a name has been changed with the vessel remaining under the ownership, management or manning of Shell's British tanker fleets, only the most recent name is listed. This applies with, for example, the LNG-carrying B-class (formerly G-class) and some of the *Empire* ships.

The Fleet List has been compiled from the most authoritative sources. However, not all references are complete, and it may be that a few vessels have not been listed. Information on any oversights would be welcome and should be sent to Archives, Shell Centre, Waterloo, London, SE1 7PQ.

A

ABSIA 5,218 GRT. 400' x 52'.
(1918) Harland & Wolff Ltd,
Glasgow.

ACARDO 5,767 GRT. 412' x 53'.
(1921) Union Contruction Co.,
Oakland, California.

ACASTA 5,259 GRT. 400' x 52'.
(1918) G. Clark Ltd, Sunderland.

ACAVUS (1) 8, 010 GRT. 465' x 59'.
(1935) Workman, Clark Ltd,
Belfast.

ACAVUS (2) 12, 326 GRT. 588' x 69'.
(1958) Bremer Vulkan, Vegesack.

ACHATINA (1) 5,853 GRT. 412' x 53'.
(1921) Union Construction Co.,
Oakland, California.

ACHATINA (2) 12,326 GRT. 558' x 69'
(1958) Bremer Vulkan, Vegesack.

ADNA 5,197 GRT. 400' x 52'.
(1918) Fairfield Co. Ltd, Glasgow.

ADULA 8,040 GRT. 465' x 59'.
(1937) Blythswood S.B. Co. Ltd,
Glasgow.

AGATHA 3,369 GRT. 348' x 50'.
(1927) Harland & Wolff Ltd,
Glasgow.

AGNITA
3,552 GRT. 306' x 50'.
(1931) Hawthorn, Leslie & Co. Ltd,
Hebburn.

AKERA
5,277 GRT. 400' x 52'.
(1918) C. Connell & Co. Ltd,
Glasgow.

ALETTA
3,085 GRT. 305' x 50'.
(1927) Caledon S.B. & Eng. Co. Ltd,
Dundee.

ALEXIA 8,016 GRT. 465' x 59'.
(1935) Bremer Vulkan, Vegesack.

ALINDA 12,301 GRT. 559' x 69'.
(1959) Smiths Dock Co. Ltd,
Middlesbrough.

ALUCO 13,148 GRT. 560' x 72'.
(1959) J. L. Thompson & Sons Ltd,
Sunderland.

AMALTHUS 5,834 GRT. 412' x 53'.
(1921) Union Contruction Co.,
Oakland, California.

AMASTRA (1) 8,031 GRT. 465' x 59'.
(1935) Lithgows Ltd, Port Glasgow.

AMASTRA (2) 12,273 GRT. 559' x 69'.
(1958) Smiths Dock Co. Ltd,
Middlesbrough.

AMORIA 12,324 GRT. 560' x 69'.
(1960) Smiths Dock Co. Ltd,
Middlesbrough.

AMPULLARIA
5,857 GRT. 412' x 53'.
(1921) Union Construction Co.,
Oakland, California.

ANDARA (1) 8,009 GRT. 465' x 59'.
(1935) Harland & Wolff Ltd,
Glasgow.

ANDARA (2)
12, 280 GRT. 559' x 69'.
(1959) Hawthorn, Leslie & Co. Ltd,
Hebburn.

ANAMBA 1,835 GRT. 265' x 37'.
(1902) Hellerup Skibsv. og Msg.,
Hellerup.

ANATINA 5,236 GRT. 400' x 52'.
(1981) John Brown & Co. Ltd,
Clydebank.

ANCYLUS 8,017 GRT. 465' x 59'.
(1935) Swan Hunter & Wigham
Richardson Ltd, Wallsend.

ANOMIA 5,198 GRT. 400' x 52'.
(1918) Harland & Wolff Ltd.
Glasgow.

ANTONIA 3,313 GRT. 348' X 46'.
(1938) C. Van der Giessen,
Krimpen.

ARCA 4,839 GRT. 374' x 50'.
(1912) Palmers S.B. & Iron Co. Ltd,
Jarrow.

ARGONAUTA
5,142 GRT. 385' x 50'.
(1907) Armstrong, Whitworth &
Co. Ltd, Newcastle.

ARIANTA 13,148 GRT. 560' x 72'.
(1959) J. L. Thompson & Sons Ltd,
Sunderland.

ARINIA 8,024 GRT. 465' x 59'.
(1936) Lithgows Ltd, Port Glasgow.

ASPRELLA 12,321 GRT. 560' x 69'.
(1959) Kieler Howaldtswerke A.G.,
Kiel.

ATTAKA 310 GRT. 134' x 25'.
(1883) Lobnitz & Co., Renfrew.

AUGUST BELMONT
4,640 GRT. 372' x 50'.
(1902) C.S. Swan Hunter Ltd,
Wallsend.

AULICA 12,321 GRT. 560' x 69'.
(1960) Howaldtswerke A.G., Kiel.

AURICULA 8,257 GRT. 465' x 59'.
(1946) Hawthorn. Leslie & Co. Ltd,
Hebburn.

AURIS (1) 8,030 GRT. 465' x 59'.
(1935) Cantieri Riuniti del Adriatico,
Monfalcone.

AURIS (2) 8,269 GRT. 483' x 59'.
(1948) Hawthorn, Leslie & Co. Ltd.
Hebburn.

AXINA 12,283 GRT. 559' x 69'.
(1958) Lithgows Ltd, Port Glasgow.

B

BALEA 803 GRT. 202' x 31'.
(1945) Sir J. Laing & Sons Ltd,
Sunderland.

BANKIVIA 3,245 GRT. 306' x 47'.
(1917) Baltimore D.D. & S.B.
Corporation.

BARBATIA 3,738 GRT. 357' x 48'.
(1943) Sir J. Laing & Sons Ltd,
Sunderland.

BATISSA 3,738 GRT. 357' x 48'.
(1944) Sir J. Laing & Sons Ltd,
Sunderland.

BEBATIK 48,612 GRT. 843' x 115'.
(1972) Chantiers de L'Atlantique.

BEKALANG 48,612 GRT. 843' X 115'.
(1973) Chantiers de L' Atlantique.

BEKULAN 48,612 GRT. 843' x 115'.
(1973) Chantiers de L'Atlantique.

BELA 3,735 GRT. 343' x 48'.
(1945) Sir J. Laing & Sons Ltd,
Sunderland.

BELAIS 48,612 GRT. 843' x 115'.
(1974) Chantiers de L'Atlantique.

BELANAK 48,612 GRT. 843' x 115'.
(1975) Chantiers de L'Atlantique.

BENTON FIELD
1,220 GRT. 210' x 37'.
(1943) Barnes-Duluth S.B. Co.,
Duluth.

BERTA 2,611 GRT. 300' x 50'.
(1927) Harland & Wolff Ltd,
Belfast.

BERWINDVALE
6,114 GRT. 405' x 54'.
(1911) Sir Raylton Dixon & Co. Ltd,
Middlesbrough.

BILIS 52,708 GRT. 850' x 115'.
(1975) Constructions Navale et
Industrielles de la Mediterranée.

BITHINA 3,629 GRT. 325' x 43'.
(1893) Sir J. Laing & Sons,
Sunderland.

BOLMA 3,744 GRT. 357' x 48'.
(1945) J. L. Thompson & Sons Ltd,
Sunderland.

BORELIS 4,155 GRT. 349' x 47'.
(1901) R. Craggs & Sons,
Middlesbrough.

BORUS 3,735 GRT. 343' x 48'.
(1945) Sir J. Laing & Sons Ltd,
Sunderland.

BUBUK 52,708 GRT. 850' x 115'.
(1975) Construction Navales et
Industrielles de la Mediterranée.

BUCCINUM 5,237 GRT. 405' x 54'.
(1910) Sir Raylton Dixon & Co.
Ltd, Middlesbrough.

BULLINA
3,771 GRT. 357' x 48'.
(1945) J. L. Thompson & Sons Ltd,
Sunderland.

BULLMOUTH (1)
4,018 GRT. 347' x 45'.
(1893) W. Gray & Co. Ltd,
West Hartlepool.

BULLMOUTH (2)
7,519 GRT. 440' x 59'.
(1927) Hawthorn, Leslie & Co. Ltd,
Hebburn.

BULYSSES (1) 6,127 GRT. 410' x 52'.
(1900) Armstrong, Whitworth &
Co. Ltd, Newcastle.

BULYSSES (2) 7,540 GRT. 440' x 59'.
(1927) Hawthorn, Leslie & Co. Ltd,
Hebburn.

BURSA 3,738 GRT. 357' x 48'
(1944) Sir J. Laing & Sons Ltd,
Sunderland.

C

CAPERATA
17,995 GRT. 624' x 84'.
(1950) Bethlehem Steel Co.,
Quincy, Massachusetts.

CAPILUNA 28,434 GRT. 736' x102'.
(1960) Bethlehem Steel Co.,
Quincy, Massachusetts.

CAPISTERIA
28,435 GRT. 736' x 102'.
(1960) Bethlehem Steel Co.,
Quincy, Massachusetts.

CAPRELLA (1) 5,552 GRT. 400' x 52'.
(1918) Irvines S.B. & D.D. Co. Ltd,
West Hartlepool.

CAPRELLA (2)
8,230 GRT. 451' x 62'.
(1931) Hawthorn, Leslie & Co. Ltd,
Hebburn.

CAPRELLA (3)
17,995 GRT. 624' x 84'.
(1950) Bethlehem Steel Co.,
Quincy, Massachusetts.

CAPRINUS 17,995 GRT. 624' x 84'.
(1950) Bethlehem Steel Co.,
Quincy, Massachusetts.

CAPSA (1) 5,574 GRT. 400' x 52'.
(1919) Sir James Laing & Sons ltd,
Sunderland.

CAPSA (2) 8,229 GRT. 452' x 62'.
(1931) Hawthorn, Leslie & Co. Ltd,
Hebburn.

CAPSA (3) 17,995 GRT. 624' x 84'.
(1950) Bethlehem Steel Co.,
Quincy, Massachusetts.

CAPULONIX
28,435 GRT. 736' x 102'.
(1959) Bethlehem Steel Co.,
Quincy, Massachusetts.

CAPULUS
17, 995 GRT. 624' x 84'.
(1950) Bethlehem Steel Co.,
Quincy, Massachusetts.

CARDITA (1) 5,545 GRT. 400' x 52'.
(1919) Lithgows Ltd, Port Glasgow.

CARDITA (2) 8,237 GRT. 451' x 62'.
(1931) Swan Hunter & Wigham
Richardson Ltd, Wallsend.

CARDIUM (1) 6,127 GRT. 410' x 52'.
(1900) Armstrong, Whitworth &
Co. Ltd, Newcastle.

CARDIUM (2) 8,236 GRT. 452' x 62'.
(1931) Swan Hunter &Wigham
Richardson Ltd, Wallsend.

CARELIA 8,082 GRT. 465' x 59'.
(1938) Netherland Dock Company,
Amsterdam.

CASSIS 4,792 GRT. 380' x 52'.
(1914) Greenock & Grangemouth
Dockyard Co. Ltd, Greenock.

CASTOR 1,345 GRT. 241' x 35'.
(1904) Trondheim Mek Verksted.

CEPOLIS 5,578 GRT. 400' x 52'.
(1919) Swan Hunter & Wigham
Richardson Ltd, Wallsend.

CERION 2,588 GRT. 380' x 49'.
(1938) Smiths Dock Co. Ltd,
Middlesbrough.

CHAMA 8,077 GRT. 465' x 59'.
(1938) Rotterdam Drydock,
Rotterdam.

CHANT 65 401 GRT. 148' x 27'.
(1944) Furness S.B. Co. Ltd,
Haverton Hill.

CHIGWELL 1,824 GRT. 259' x 36'.
(1883) Bartram, Haswell & Co.,
Sunderland.

CHITON 5,540 GRT. 400' x 52'.
(1919) Lithgows Ltd, Port Glasgow.

CIRCE SHELL (1)
2,810 GRT. 296' x 45'.
(1892) Barclay, Curle & Co. Ltd,
Glasgow.

CIRCE SHELL (2)
8,207 GRT. 452' x 62'.
(1931) Howaldtswerke A.G.,
Hamburg.

CLAM (1) 3,552 GRT. 338' x 43'.
(1893) W. Gray & Co. Ltd, West
Hartlepool.

CLAM (2) 7,404 GRT. 440' x 59'.
(1927) Netherland S.B. Company,
Amsterdam.

CLAUSINA 8,053 GRT. 465' x 59'.
(1838) Rotterdam Drydock,
Rotterdam.

CLEA 8,074 GRT. 463' x 59'.
(1938) Rotterdam Drydock,
Rotterdam.

CLIONA (1) 5,563 GRT. 400' x 52'.
(1918) Sir James Laing & Sons Ltd,
Sunderland.

CLIONA (2) 8,375 GRT. 456' x 62'.
(1931) Harland & Wolff Ltd,
Glasgow.

CONCH (1) 3,555 GRT. 338' x 43'. (1892) W. Gray & Co. Ltd, West Hartlepool.

CONCH (2) 5,620 GRT. 406' x 51'. (1909) Swan Hunter & Wigham Richardson Ltd, Wallsend.

CONCH (3) 8,376 GRT. 456' x 62'. (1931) Harland & Wolff Ltd, Glasgow.

CONCHITA 2,701 GRT. 305' x 50'. (1924) W. Beardmore & Co. Ltd, Glasgow.

CONIA 5,562 GRT. 400' x 52'. (1918) Armstrong, Whitworth & Co. Ltd, Newcastle.

CONUS (1) 5,578 GRT. 400' x 52'. (1919) Palmers Co. Ltd, Jarrow.

CONUS (2) 8,132 GRT. 452' x 52'. (1931) Workman Clark Ltd, Belfast.

CORBIS (1) 5,559 GRT. 400' x 52'. (1918) Swan Hunter & Wigham Richardson Ltd, Wallsend.

CORBIS (2) 8,132 GRT. 452' x 62'. (1931) Workman, Clark Ltd, Belfast.

COWRIE (1) 4,893 GRT. 376' x 48'. (1896) Armstrong, Mitchell & Co. Ltd, Newcastle.

COWRIE (2) 8,197 GRT. 452' x 62'. (1931) Cantieri Riuniti del Adriatico, Monfalcone.

CRATHIE 498 GRT. 160' x 24'. (1883) J. Key & Sons, Kinghorn.

CRENATULA 5,563 GRT. 400' x 52'. (1918) W. Gray & Co. Ltd, West Hartlepool.

CRENELLA 5,478 GRT. 445' x 53'. (1897) Palmers S.B. & Iron Co. Ltd, Jarrow.

CRISTA 2,590 GRT. 310' x 42'. (1938) NV Werf 'Gusto' A.F. Smulders, Schiedam.

CROMWELL 1,220 GRT. 210' x 37'. (1943) Barnes-Duluth S.B. Co., Duluth.

CYMBULA 8,082 GRT. 465' x 59'. (1938) Netherland S.B. Company, Amsterdam.

CYRENA (1) 2,138 GRT. 288' x 39'. (1913) W. Gray & Co. Ltd, West Hartlepool.

CYRENS (2) 4,373 GRT. 380' x 49'. (1947) Smiths Dock Co. Ltd, Middlesbrough.

DAPHNELLA (1) 8,078 GRT. 465' x 59'. (1938) Hawthorn, Leslie & Co. Ltd, Hebburn.

DAPHNELLA (2) 39,929 GRT. 800' x 110'. (1966) J. L. Thompson & Sons Ltd, Sunderland.

DARINA (1) 8,113 GRT. 465' x 59'. (1939) Blythswood S.B. Co. Ltd, Glasgow.

DARINA (2) 39,769 GRT. 800' x 110'. (1966) Deutsche Werft A.G., Hamburg.

DARONIA 8,139 GRT. 465' x 59'. (1939) Hawthorn, Leslie & Co. Ltd, Hebburn.

DARST CREEK 1,220 GRT. 210' x 37'. (1944) Grays Iron Works Inc., Galveston.

DAVILA 8,053 GRT. 465' x 59'. (1938) Lithgows Ltd, Port Glasgow .

DELPHINULA (1) 5,238 GRT. 385' x 66'. (1908) Armstrong, Whitworth & Co. Ltd, Newcastle.

DELPHINULA (2) 8,120 GRT. 465' x 59'. (1939) Lithgows Ltd, Port Glasgow.

DESMOULEA 8,120 GRT. 465' x 59'. (1939) Lithgows Ltd, Port Glasgow.

DIALA 8, 106 GRT. 465' x 59'. (1938) Bremer Vulkan, Vegesack.

DILOMA 8,146 GRT. 465' x 59'. (1939) Cammell, Laird & Co. Ltd, Birkenhead.

DIPLODON 8,150 GRT. 465' x 59'. (1941) Hawthorn, Leslie & Co. Ltd, Hebburn.

DOLABELLA 8,142 GRT. 465' x 59'. (1939) Hawthorn, Leslie & Co. Ltd, Hebburn.

DOLIUM 1,142 GRT. 217' x 33'. (1922) J. Koster Scheeps. 'De Gideon', Groningen.

DOLPHIN SHELL 2,008 GRT. 309' x 42'. (1897) W. Hamilton & Co., Port Glasgow.

DONACILLA (1) 8,113 GRT. 465' x 59'. (1939) Blythswood S.B. Co. Ltd, Glasgow.

DONACILLA (2) 40,170 GRT. 800' x 110'. (1966) J. L. Thompson & Sons Ltd. Sunderland.

DONAX (1) 3,717 GRT. 348' x 47'. (1913) Palmers Co. Ltd, Jarrow.

DONAX (2) 8,036 GRT. 465' x 59'. (1938) Harland & Wolff Ltd, Glasgow.

DONAX (3) 42,068 GRT. 800' x 110'. (1966) Harland & Wolff Ltd, Belfast.

DONOVANIA (1) 8,149 GRT. 465' x 59'. (1941) Hawthorn, Leslie & Co. Ltd, Hebburn.

DONOVANIA (2) 39,505 GRT. 800' x 110'. (1966) Kockums Mek. Verksted, Malmo.

DORCASIA (1) 8,053 GRT. 465' x 59'. (1938) Lithgows Ltd, Port Glasgow.

DORCASIA (2) 39,505 GRT. 800' x 110'. (1967) Kockums Mek, Verksted, Malmo.

DORYSSA 8,036 GRT. 465' x 59'. (1938) Hawthorn, Leslie & Co. Ltd, Hebburn.

DOSINA (1) 5,304 GRT. 400' x 52'. (1922) Caledon S.B. & Eng. Co. Ltd, Dundee.

DOSINA (2) 8,053 GRT. 465' x 59'. (1938) Lithgows Ltd, Port Glasgow.

DROMUS 8,036 GRT. 465' x 59'. (1938) Harland & Wolff Ltd, Glasgow.

DRUPA (1) 8,102 GRT. 465' x 59'. (1939) Deutsche Werft A.G., Hamburg.

DRUPA (2) 39,796 GRT. 800' x 110'. (1966) Deutsche Werft A.G., Hamburg.

EBALINA 19,763 GRT. 556' x 85'. (1980) Mitsui S.B. & Eng. Co. Ltd, Chiba.

EBURNA (1) 4,735 GRT. 380' x 52'. (1913) Swan Hunter & Wigham Richardson Ltd, Wallsend.

EBURNA (2) 19,763 GRT. 556' x 85'. (1979) Mitsui S.B. & Eng. Co. Ltd, Chiba.

ECHUNGA 6,285 GRT. 390' x 58'. (1907) Sir Raylton Dixon & Co. Middlesbrough.

ELAX (1) 3,980 GRT. 347' x 45'. (1893) W. Gray & Co. Ltd, West Hartlepool.

ELAX (2) 7,403 GRT. 440' x 59'. (1927) Netherland S.B. Company, Amsterdam.

EL GUISR 311 GRT. 134' x 25'. (1883) Lobnitz & Co. Renfrew.

ELONA 6,192 GRT. 430' x 54'. (1936) Swan Hunter & Wigham Richardson Ltd, Wallsend.

ELPHINSTONE 1,776 GRT. 280' x 33'. (1874) Palmers Company, Jarrow.

EMPIRE BAIRN 813 GRT. 202' x 31'. (1941) Bythswood S.B. Co. Ltd, Glasgow.

EMPIRE BELGRAVE 890 GRT. 201' x 34'. (1945) A. & J. Inglis, Glasgow.

EMPIRE BOUNTY 8,128 GRT. 474' x 64'. (1944) Furness S.B. Co. Ltd, Haverton Hill.

EMPIRE BUTE 813 GRT. 202' x 31'. (1944) A. & J. Inglis, Glasgow.

EMPIRE CAMPDEN 890 GRT. 201' x 34'. (1945) A. & J. Inglis, Glasgow.

EMPIRE CHANCELLOR 9,917 GRT. 503' x 68'. (1945) Sir James Laing & Sons Ltd, Sunderland.

EMPIRE COPPICE 814 GRT. 202' x 31'. (1943) A. & J. Inglis, Glasgow.

EMPIRE CROSS 3,734 GRT. 343' x 48'. (1945) Sir J. Laing & Sons Ltd, Sunderland.

EMPIRE DAMSEL 784 GRT. 202' x 31'. (1942) Grangemouth Dockyard Co. Ltd.

EMPIRE DOMBEY 813 GRT. 202' x 31'. (1944) A. & J. Inglis, Glasgow.

EMPIRE DRURY 797 GRT. 202' x 31'. (1944) Grangemouth Dockyard Co. Ltd.

EMPIRE FAUN 846 GRT. 196' x 31'. (1943) Goole S.B. Co. Ltd.

EMPIRE FITZROY 890 GRT. 201' x 34'. (1945) A. & J. Inglis, Glasgow.

EMPIRE FLINT 8,129 GRT. 463' x 61'. (1941) Swan Hunter & Wigham Richardson Ltd, Wallsend.

EMPIRE GAWAIN 890 GRT. 202' x 31'. (1942) Grangemouth Dockyard Co. Ltd.

EMPIRE GYPSY 813 GRT. 202' x 31'. (1942) A. & J. Inglis, Glasgow.

EMPIRE HARP 861 GRT. 196' x 31'. (1942) Goole S.B. Co. Ltd.

EMPIRE INVENTOR 9,912 GRT. 503' x 68'. (1944) Sir James Laing & Sons Ltd, Sunderland.

EMPIRE JURA 813 GRT. 202' x 31'. (1944) A. & J. Inglis, Glasgow.

EMPIRE LASS 813 GRT 202' x 31'. (1946) Grangemouth Dockyard Co. Ltd.

EMPIRE LAW 8,128 GRT. 474' x 64'. (1944) Furness S.B. Co. Ltd, Haverton Hill.

EMPIRE MILNER 8,135 GRT. 474' x 64'. (1944) Furness S.B. Co. Ltd, Haverton Hill.

EMPIRE MULL 797 GRT. 202' x 31'. (1944) Grangemouth Dockyard Co. Ltd.

EMPIRE NORSEMAN 8,214 GRT. 463' x 61'. (1942) Harland & Wolff Ltd, Belfast.

EMPIRE NUGGET 9,807 GRT. 503' x 68'. (1942) Furness S.B. Co. Ltd, Haverton Hill.

EMPIRE PROTECTOR 8,148 GRT. 474' x 64'. (1944) Furness S.B. Co. Ltd, Haverton Hill.

EMPIRE SETTLER 803 GRT. 202' x 31'. (1943) Grangemouth Dockyard Co. Ltd.

EMPIRE SHETLAND 813 GRT. 202' x 31'. (1945) A. & J. Inglis, Glasgow.

EMPIRE SPENSER 8,194 GRT. 463' x 61'. (1942) Harland & Wolff Ltd, Belfast.

EMPIRE TAGANAX 10,128 GRT. 485' x 65'. (1940) Nakskov Skibs A/S, Nakskov.

EMPIRE TAVISTOCK 797 GRT. 202' x 31'. (1945) Grangemouth Dockyard Co. Ltd.

EMPIRE TEGALTA 2,299 GRT. 269' x 43'. (1944) Norderwerft.

EMPIRE TEGAYA 3,145 GRT. 343' x 45'. (1921) Deutsche Werft A.G., Hamburg.

EMPIRE TESBURY 890 GRT. 201' x 32'. (1946) Bartram & Sons Ltd, Sunderland.

EMPIRE TESDALE 890 GRT. 201' x 32'. (1946) Swan Hunter & Wigham Richardson Ltd.

EMPIRE TESELLA 805 GRT. 201' x 32'. (1946) Harland & Wolff Ltd, Govan.

EMPIRE TIGOON 674 GRT. 186' x 30'. (1942) N.V. Wilton Fijenoord, Schiedam.

EMPIRE TROTWOOD 797 GRT. 202' x 31'. (1944) Grangemouth Dockyard Co. Ltd.

ENSIS 6,207 GRT. 432' x 54'. (1937) Rotterdam Drydock, Rotterdam.

ENTALINA 19,656 GRT. 556' x 85'. (1978) Saint John S.B. & D.D. Co. Ltd, St. John.

ERINNA 19,656 GRT. 556' x 85'. (1977) Saint John S.B. & D.D. Co. Ltd, St. John.

ERODONA (1) 8,040 GRT. 432' x 54'. (1937) C. Van der Giessen & Sons, Krimpen.

ERODONA (2) 9,656 GRT. 556' x 85'. (1978) Saint John S.B. & D.D. Co. Ltd, St. John.

ERVILIA 19,763 GRT. 556' x 85'. (1979) Mitsui S.B. & Eng. Co. Ltd, Chiba.

ESTURIA 2,143 GRT. 275' x 39'. (1910) Armstrong, Whitworth & Co. Ltd, Newcastle.

ETREMA 19,656 GRT. 556' x 85'. (1978) Saint John S.B. & D.D. Co. Ltd, St. John.

EULIMA (1) 6,207 GRT. 432' x 54'. (1937) N.V. Wilton Fijenoord, Schiedam.

EULIMA (2) 17,955 GRT. 560' x 85'. (1982) Nuovi Cantieri Apuania spA, Carrara, Italy.

EULOTA 17,995 GRT. 560' x 85'. (1983) Nuovi Cantieri Apuania SpA, Carrara, Italy.

EUPLECTA 19,763 GRT. 556' x 85'. (1980) Mitsui S.B. & Eng. Co. Ltd, Chiba.

EUPLECTELA 3,918 GRT. 340' x 44'. (1894) Armstrong, Mitchell & Co. Ltd, Newcastle.

FAUNUS 3,800 GRT. 344' x 46'. (1914) Completed by Caledon S.B. Co. Ltd, Dundee.

FELANIA 3,882 GRT. 344' x 46'. (1914) Netherland S.B. Company, Amsterdam.

FELIPES (1) 891 GRT. 193' x 34'. (1946) A. & J. Inglis Ltd, Glasgow.

FELIPES (2) 3,052 GRT. 331' x 46'. (1950) John Crown & Sons Ltd, Sunderland.

FELIPES (3) 19,274 GRT. 560' x 85'. (1975) Haugesund Mek. Verksted.

FICUS (1) 5,779 GRT. 503' x 68'. (1942) Furness S.B. Co. Ltd, Haverton Hill.

FICUS (2) 19,274 GRT. 560' x 85'. (1976) Haugesund Mek. Verksted.

FIONA SHELL 2,443 GRT. 284' x 42'. (1892) Workman, Clark & Co. Ltd, Belfast.

FISCHERIA 891 GRT. 193' x 34'. (1946) A. & J. Inglis Ltd, Glasgow.

FLAMMULINA (1) 8,203 GRT. 465' x 59'. (1943) Harland & Wolff Ltd, Belfast.

FLAMMULINA (2) 19,274 GRT. 560' x 85'. (1976) Haugesund Mek. Verksted.

FLEETWOOD 655 GRT. 183' x 28'. (1867) R. Steele, Greenock.

FORMOSA 1,651 GRT. 256' x 38'. (1883) Russel & Co., Port Glasgow.

FORNEBO 4,401 GRT. 360' x 52'. (1906) Sir Raylton Dixon & Co. Ltd, Middlesbrough.

FORRERIA 933 GRT. 193' x 34'. (1946) Short Bros, Sunderland.

FORSAKALIA 947 GRT. 193' x 34'. (1947) Sir J. Laing & Sons Ltd. Sunderland.

FOSSARINA (1) 947 GRT 193' x 34' (1947) Sir J. Laing & Sons Ltd. Sunderland.

FOSSARINA (2) 980 GRT 193' x 34' (1945) Harland & Wolff Ltd., Belfast.

FOSSARUS 2,370 GRT. 301' x 44'
(1945) Grangemouth Dockyard
Co. Ltd.

FOSSULARCA 2,370 GRT. 301 x 44'
(1945) Grangemouth Dockyard
Co. Ltd.

FRAGUM (1) 980 GRT. 201' x 34'
(1946) Swan Hunter & Wigham
Richardson Ltd, Wallsend.

FRAGUM (2) 2,926 GRT. 320' x 46'
(1952) Smiths Dock Co. Ltd.,
Middlesborough

FRENULINA 891 GRT. 201' x 34'.
(1945) A. & J. Inglis, Glasgow.

FUH WO 802 GRT. 30' x 26'.
(1902) Boyd & Co., Shanghai.

FULGUR 979 GRT. 201' x 34'.
(1945) Harland & Wolff, Glasgow.

FUSINUS (1) 891 GRT. 201' x 32'.
(1946) A. & J. Inglis Ltd, Glasgow.

FUSINUS (2) 975 GRT. 193' x 34'.
(1946) Bartram & Sons Ltd,
Sunderland.

FUSUS (1) 891 GRT. 201' x 32'.
(1946) A. & J. Inglis Ltd, Glasgow.

FUSUS (2) 19,274 GRT. 560' x 85'.
(1975) Haugesund Mek. Verksted.

G

GADINIA (1)
5,924 GRT. 401' x 62'.
(1950) Smiths Dock Co. Ltd,
Middlesbrough.

GALEOMMA
5,437 GRT. 401' x 62'.
(1946) J. L. Thomspon & Sons Ltd,
Sunderland.

GANESELLA
5,557 GRT. 401' x 62'.
(1946) J. L. Thompson Ltd,
Sunderland.

GANGES 1,903 GRT. 267' x 33'.
(1868) London & Glasgow
Company, Glasgow.

GAPER SHELL 1,363 GRT.
(1891) C. Hill & Sons, Bristol.

GARI (1) 5,437 GRT. 401' x 62'.
(1947) Smiths Dock Co. Ltd,
Middlesbrough.

GASTRANA (1)
5,437 GRT. 401' x 62'.
(1949) Smiths Dock Co. Ltd,
Middlesbrough.

GEMMA 5,439 GRT. 401' x 62'.
(1949) Smiths Dock Co. Ltd,
Middlesbrough.

GENA 5,436 GRT. 401' x 62'.
(1947) Smiths Dock Co. Ltd,
Middlesbrough.

GENEFFE 363 GRT. 134' x 25'.
(1884) Lobnitz & Co., Renfrew.

GEOMITRA (1)
5,437 GRT. 401' x 62'.
(1946) Smiths Dock Co. Ltd,
Middlesbrough.

GLESSULA 5,775 GRT. 401' x 62'.
(1949) Smiths Dock Co. Ltd,
Middlesbrough.

GOLD SHELL 8,208 GRT. 452' x 62'.
(1931) Bremer Vulkan, Vegesack.

GOLDEN MEADOW
1,220 GRT. 210' x 37'.
(1943) Lancaster Iron Works Inc.,
Perryville.

GOLDMOUTH (1)
7,446 GRT. 471' x 56'.
(1903) Swan Hunter & Wigham
Richardson Ltd, Wallsend.

GOLDMOUTH (2)
7,208 GRT. 440' x 59'.
(1927) Rotterdam Drydock,
Rotterdam.

GOMPHINA 5,437 GRT. 401' x 62'.
(1948) J. L. Thompson & Sons Ltd,
Sunderland.

GOULDIA (1) 5,437 GRT. 401' x 62'.
(1946) Smiths Dock Co. Ltd,
Middlesbrough.

H

HADRA 12,669 GRT. 555' x 69'.
(1954) Smiths Dock Co. Ltd,
Middlesbrough.

HADRIANIA
12,160 GRT. 555' x 69'.
(1954) Smiths Dock Co. Ltd,
Middlesbrough.

HALIA 12,183 GRT. 555' x 69'.
(1958) Hawthorn, Leslie & Co. Ltd,
Hebburn.

HALIOTIS 1,659 GRT. 242' x 40'.
(1898) Armstrong, Whitworth &
Co. Ltd, Newcastle.

HAMINEA 12,191 GRT. 555' x 69'.
(1955) Smiths Dock Co. Ltd,
Middlesbrough.

HAMINELLA 12,189 GRT. 555' x 69'.
(1957) Smiths Dock Co. Ltd,
Middlesbrough.

HANETIA 12,189 GRT. 555' x 69'.
(1954) Smiths Dock Co. Ltd,
Middlesbrough.

HARPA (1) 3,007 GRT. 305' x 50'.
(1931) Hawthorn, Leslie & Co. Ltd,
Middlesbrough.

HARPA (2) 12,202 GRT. 555' x 69'.
(1953) Harland & Wolff Ltd,
Belfast.

HARPULA 12,258 GRT. 555' x 69'.
(1955) Harland & Wolff Ltd,
Belfast.

HARVELLA
12,224 GRT. 555' x69'.
Harland & Wolff Ltd, Belfast.

HASTINGS 1,220 GRT. 210' x 37'.
(1944) Todd Galveston D.D. Inc.,
Galveston.

HASTULA
12,180 GRT. 555' x 69'.
(1956) Smiths Dock Co. Ltd,
Middlesbrough.

HATASIA 12,161 GRT. 555' x 69'.
(1956) J. L. Thompson & Sons Ltd,
Sunderland.

HAUSTELLUM
12,122 GRT. 555' x 69'.
(1954) Hawthorn, Leslie & Co. Ltd,
Hebburn.

HAUSTRUM 12,090 GRT. 555' x 69'.
(1954) Hawthorn, Leslie & Co. Ltd,
Hebburn.

HAVRE 2,073 GRT. 228' x 39'.
(1905) W. Gray & Co. Ltd,
Hartlepool.

HELICON (1) 1,753 GRT. 250' x 42'.
(1918) Sunderland S.B. Co. Ltd.

HELICON (2) 12,091 GRT. 555' x 69'.
(1954) Swan Hunter & Wigham
Richardson Ltd, Wallsend.

HELDIA 12,149 GRT. 555' x 69'.
(1955) Swan Hunter & Wigham
Richardson Ltd, Wallsend.

HELICINA 12,167 GRT. 583' x 70'.
(1946) Swan Hunter & Wigham
Richardson Ltd, Wallsend.

HELISOMA 12,149 GRT. 555' x 69'.
(1956) Swan Hunter & Wigham
Richardson Ltd, Wallsend.

HELIX (1) 3,007 GRT. 305' x 50'.
(1931) Hawthorn, Leslie & Co. Ltd,
Hebburn.

HELIX (2) 12,089 GRT. 555' x 69'.
(1953) Swan Hunter & Wigham
Richardson Ltd, Wallsend.

HEMICARDIUM
12,215 GRT. 555' x 60'.
(1953) Cammel, Laird & Co. Ltd,
Birkenhead.

HEMIDONAX (1)
12,185 GRT. 555' x 69'.
(1953) Cammel, Laird & Co. Ltd,
Birkenhead.

HEMIDONAX (2)
12, 215 GRT. 556' x 69'.
(1953) Cammel, Laird & Co. Ltd,
Birkenhead.

HEMIFUSUS
12,182 GRT. 555' x 69'.
(1954) Cammel, Laird & Co. Ltd,
Birkenhead.

HEMIGLYPTA 12,180 GRT. 555' x 69'.
(1955) Cammel, Laird & Co. Ltd,
Birkenhead.

HEMIMACTRA
12,215 GRT. 555' x 69'.
(1956) Cammel, Laird & Co. Ltd,
Birkenhead.

HEMIPLECTA
12,192 GRT. 555' x 60'.
(1955) Cammel, Laird & Co. Ltd,
Birkenhead.

HEMISINUS 12,207 GRT. 555' x 69'.
(1957) Cammel, Laird & Co. Ltd,
Birkenhead.

HEMITROCHUS
12,265 GRT. 559' x 69'.
(1959) Cammel, Laird & Co. Ltd,
Birkenhead.

HERMES 3,768 GRT. 349' x 46'.
(1914) Palmers Co. Ltd, Jarrow.

HEYSER 1,220 GRT. 210' x 37'.
(1944) Grays Iron Works Inc.,
Galveston.

HIMA 12,257 GRT. 555' x 69'.
(1957) Odense Stallskibs A/S,
Odense.

HINDSIA 12,212 GRT. 555' x 69'.
(1955) Vickers-Armstrong (S.B.)
Ltd, Barrow.

HINEA 12,211 GRT. 555' x 69'.
(1956) Vickers-Armstrong (S.B.)
Ltd, Barrow.

HINNITES
12,186 GRT. 555' x 69'.
(1956) Vickers-Armstrong (S.B.)
Ltd, Barrow.

HOLOSPIRA
12,180 GRT. 555' x 69'.
(1956) Smiths Dock Co. Ltd,
Middlesbrough.

HORN SHELL (1)
2,413 GRT. 284' x 42'.
(1892) Workman, Clark & Co. Ltd,
Belfast.

HORN SHELL (2)
8, 272 GRT. 456' x 62'.
(1931) Deutsche Werft A.G.,
Hamburg.

HOROMYA
12,183 GRT. 555' x 69'.
(1956) Hawthorn, Leslie & Co. Ltd,
Hebburn.   •

HUMILARIA 11,955 GRT. 555' x 69'.
(1959) Cammel, Laird & Co. Ltd,
Birkenhead.

HYALA 12,164 GRT. 555' x 69'.
(1955) Lithgows Ltd, Port Glasgow.

HYALINA 12,287 GRT. 583' x 70'.
(1948) Swan Hunter & Wigham
Richardson Ltd, Wallsend.

HYDATINA 12,161 GRT. 555' x 69'.
(1956) Lithgows Ltd, Port Glasgow.

HYGROMIA 12,161 GRT. 555' x 69'.
(1956) Lithgows Ltd, Port Glasgow.

HYRIA 12,132 GRT. 555' x 69'.
(1954) Lithgows Ltd, Port Glasgow.

I

ISOCARDIA 39,932 GRT. 688' x 103'.
(1982) Harland & Wolff Ltd,
Belfast.

ISOMERIA
39,932 GRT. 688' x 103'.
(1982) Harland & Wolff Ltd,
Belfast.

J

JUBILEE 152 GRT. 123' x 20'.
(1887) Samuda Brothers, London.

K

KATELYSIA 6,430 GRT. 420' x 54'.
(1914) Palmers S.B. & Iron Co. Ltd,
Jarrow.

KELLETIA 7,522 GRT. 450' x 61'.
(1929) Swan Hunter & Wigham
Richardson Ltd, Wallsend.

KELLIA 5,666 GRT. 410' x 53'.
(1929) Swan Hunter & Wigham
Richardson Ltd, Wallsend.

KELLIELLA 6,236 GRT. 420' x 54'.
(1913) Swan Hunter &Wigham
Richardson Ltd, Wallsend.

KENNERLEYA 8,028 GRT. 463' x 61'.
(1941) Furness S.B. Co. Ltd,
Haverton Hill.

KHODOUNG 1,460 GRT. 235' x 34'.
(1900) Armstrong, Whitworth &
Co. Ltd, Newcastle.

KLEINELLA (1) 861 GRT. 196' x 31'.
(1943) A. & J. Inglis Ltd, Glasgow.

KLEINELLA (2) 5,621 GRT. 406' x 53'.
(1913) Reiherst Schiffs., Hamburg.
KLUANG 303 GRT. (1951)
Camper Nicholson

KUPHUS 6,433 GRT. 420' x 54'.
(1913) Palmers S.B. & Iron Co. Ltd,
Jarrow.

L

LABIOSA (1)
6,473 GRT. 430' x 54'.
(1948) Hawthorn, Leslie & Co. Ltd,
Hebburn.

LABIOSA (2)
138,460 GRT. 1085' x 170'.
(1975) Chants de L'Atlantique,
St. Nazaire.

LACONICA
159,648 GRT. 1102' x 182'.
(1975) Mitsui S.B. & Eng. Co. Ltd,
Ichibara.

LACUNA 5,882 GRT. 393' x 51'.
(1916) J. Readhead & Sons Ltd,
South Shields.

LAMPANIA 6,438 GRT. 430' x 54'.
(1947) Hawthorn, Leslie & Co. Ltd,
Hebburn.

LAMPAS (1) 5,631 GRT. 370' x 51'.
(1916) Craig, Taylor & Co. Ltd,
Stockton.

LAMPAS (2)
161,632 GRT. 1102' x 181'.
(1975) Harland & Wolff Ltd,
Belfast.

LANDAK 200 GRT.

LANG 200 GRT.

LANISTES
159,936 GRT. 1085' x 170'.
(1975) Mitsui S.B. & Eng. Co. Ltd,
Ichibara.

LATIA (1) 6,442 GRT. 430' x 54'.
(1946) Hawthorn, Leslie & Co. Ltd,
Hebburn.

LATIA (2) 138,456 GRT. 1085' x 170'.
(1974) Chants de L'Atlantique, St.
Nazaire.

LATIRUS (1) 6,476 GRT. 430' x 54'.
(1949) Smiths Dock Co. Ltd,
Middlesbrough.

LATIRUS (2)
138,456 GRT. 1085' x 170'.
(1974) Chants de L'Atlantique, St.
Nazaire.

LEMBULUS (1)
6,503 GRT. 430' x 54'.
(1948) Swan Hunter & Wigham
Richardson Ltd, Wallsend.

LEMBULUS (2)
130,586 GRT. 1080' x 169'.
(1974) Verolme Dok & Schps,
Rozenburg, Rotterdam.

LEONIA
161,626 GRT. 1102' x 181'.
(1976) Harland & Wolff Ltd,
Belfast.

LEPETA
161,632 GRT. 1102' x 181'.
(1976) Harland & Wolff Ltd,
Belfast.

LEPTON 6,446 GRT. 430' x 54'.
(1947) Harland & Wolff Ltd,
Belfast.

LIMA 161,632 GRT. 1102' x 181'.
(1977) Harland & Wolff Ltd,
Belfast.

LIMATULA (1)
6,476 GRT. 430' x 54'.
(1950) Smiths Dock Co. Ltd,
Middlesbrough.

LIMATULA (2)
160,423 GRT. 1107' x 185'.
(1974) Odense Staalskib A/S,
Odense.

LIMAX 3,365 GRT. 313' x 65'.
(1914) Cammel, Laird & Co. Ltd,
Birkenhead.

LIMICANA 5,861 GRT. 380' x 50'.
(1917) Richardson, Duck & Co.
Ltd, Stockton.

LIMNEA (1)
5,698 GRT. 412' x 53'.
(1921) North of Ireland S.B. Co.
Ltd, Londonderry.

LIMNEA (2)
160,420 GRT. 1107' x 185'.
(1975) Odense Staalskibs A/S,
Odense.

LIMOPSIS 160,423 GRT. 1107' x 185'.
(1976) Ofrndr Staalskibs A/S,
Lindo.

LINGA (1) 6,452 GRT. 430' x 54'.
(1946) Harland & Wolff Ltd,
Belfast.

LINGA (2) 160,420 GRT. 1107' x 185'.
(1975) Odense Staalskibs A/S,
Odense.

LINGULA 6,445 GRT. 430' x 54'.
(1947) Harland & Wolff Ltd,
Belfast.

LIPARUS (1) 6,473 GRT. 430' x 54'.
(1948) Harland & Wolff Ltd,
Glasgow.

LIPARUS (2)
160,420 GRT. 1085' x 170'.
(1975) Odense Staalskibs A/S
Odense.

LITIOPA (1) 5,311 GRT. 400' x 52'.
(1917) Bartram & Sons Ltd,
Sunderland.

LITIOPA (2)
159,633 GRT. 1085' x 170'.
(1977) Mitsui S.B. & Eng. Co. Ltd ,
Ichibara.

LNG BONNY
85,616 GRT. 942' x 138'.
(1981) Kockums Shipyard, Malmo,
Sweden.

LNG FINIMA
85,616 GRT. 942' x 138'.
(1983) Kockums Shipyard, Malmo,
Sweden.

LOMA NOVIA 1,220 GRT 210' x 37'.
(1943) Barnes-Duluth S.B. Co.,
Duluth.

LOTORIUM (1)
6,490 GRT. 430' x 54'.
(1947) Harland & Wolff Ltd,
Belfast.

LOTORIUM (2)
138,037 GRT. 1085' x 170'.
(1975) Harland & Wolff Ltd,
Belfast.

LOVELLIA 28,435 GRT. 736' x 102'.
(1959) Bethlehem Steel Co.,
Quincy.

LULING 1,200 GRT. 210' x 37'.
(1943) Frays Iron Works,
Galveston.

LOTONG 215 GRT. 118' x 23'.
(1921) W. S. Bailey & Co.,
Hong Kong.

LYRIA (1) 6,220 GRT. 430' x 54'.
(1946) Harland & Wolff Ltd,
Belfast.

LYRIA (2) 160,420 GRT. 1107' x 185'.
(1976) Odense Staalskibs A/S,
Lindo.

MACTRA (1) 6,193 GRT. 430' x 54'.
(1936) Swan Hunter & Wigham
Richardson Ltd, Wallsend.

MACTRA (2)
104,772 GRT. 1067' x 155'.
(1969) Howaldswerke-Deutsche
Werft, Kiel.

MAJA 8,181 GRT. 452' x 62'.
(1969) C. Van der Giessen & Zonen
Schp, Krimpen.

MANGELIA
105,138 GRT. 1067' x 155'. (1968)
Kawasaki Dockyard Co.Ltd, Kobe.

MANNINGTON
1,220 GRT. 210' x 37'.
(1943) Barnes-Duluth S.B. Co.,
Duluth.

MARINULA (1)
7,449 GRT. 440' x 54'.
(1916) Vickers Ltd, Barrow.

MARINULA (2)
98,876 GRT. 1077' x 144'.
(1968) Odense Staalskibs A/S,
Lindo.

MARISA 105,495 GRT. 1066' x 155'.
(1968) Hitachi Zosen, Sakai.

MARSELLA 2,698 GRT. 305' x 50'.
(1924) Rotterdam Drydock,
Rotterdam.

MARTICIA 104,561 GRT. 1067' x 155'.
(1970) Netherland S.B. Company,
Amsterdam.

MEDORA 105,252 GRT. 1067' x 155'.
(1968) Mitsubishi Heavy
Industries, Nagasaki.

MEGARA 7,931 GRT. 423' x 59'.
(1929) Ateliers & Chant de la
Seine, Rouen.

MEGARA (2)
105,245 GRT. 1066' x 155'.
(1968) Mitsubishi Heavy Industries
Ltd, Nagasaki.

MELANIA (1) 5,824 GRT. 412' x 53'.
(1914) Craig, Taylor & Co. Ltd,
Stockton.

MELANIA (2)
104,561 GRT. 1067' x 155'.
(1969) Netherland S.B. Company,
Amsterdam.

MELO 105,138 GRT. 1067' x 155'.
(1969) Kawasaki Heavy Industries,
Sakaide.

MELONA 5,948 GRT. 418' x 55'.
(1917) Earles Co. Ltd, Hull.

META 105,521 GRT. 1067' x 155'.
(1968) Mitsubishi Zosen, Sakai.

METHANE PRINCESS
21,867 GRT. 621' x 81'.
(1964) Vickers Armstrong (S.B.)
Ltd, Barrow.

METHANE PROGRESS
21,875 GRT. 621' x 81'.
(1964) Harland & Wolff Ltd,
Belfast.

MIN 540 GRT. 190' x 30'.
(1900) Mordey, Carney Ltd,
Southampton.

MIRALDA 8,013 GRT. 465' x 59'.
(1936) Netherland S.B. Company,
Amsterdam.

MITRA (1) 5,592 GRT. 406' x 51'.
(1912) Swan Hunter & Wigham
Richardson Ltd, Wallsend.

MITRA (2) 98,876 GRT. 1077' x 144'.
(1969) Odense Staalskibs, Lindo.

MUREX (1) 3,564 GRT. 338' x 43'.
(1892) W. Gray & Co. Ltd,
West Hartlepool.

MUREX (2) 5,830 GRT. 412' x 53'.
(1922) H.M. Dockyard,
Portsmouth.

MUREX (3)
104,772 GRT. 1067' x 155'.
(1968) Howaldswerke-Deutsche
Werft, Kiel.

MYR SHELL 2,511 GRT. 300' x 43'.
(1902) A. McMillan & Sons Ltd,
Dumbarton.

MYSELLA 104,561 GRT. 1067' x 155'.
(1970) Netherland S.B. Company,
Amsterdam.

MYSIA 105,248 GRT. 1066' x 155'.
(1969) Mitsubishi Heavy
Industries, Nagasaki.

MYTILUS (1) 5,716 GRT. 412' x 53'.
(1916) Swan Hunter & Wigham
Richardson Ltd, Wallsend.

MYTILUS (2)
105,521 GRT. 1066' x 155'.
(1969) Hitachi Zosen, Sakai.

NACELLA 8,196 GRT. 465' x 59'.
(1943) Swan Hunter & Wigham
Richardson Ltd, Wallsend.

NANINIA
8,166 GRT. 465' x 59'.
(1943) Swan Hunter & Wigham
Richardson Ltd, Wallsend.

NARANIO 8,126 GRT. 465' x 59'.
(1943) Blythswood S.B. Co. Ltd,
Glasgow.

NARICA 8,213 GRT. 465' x 59'.
(1943) Harland & Wolff Ltd,
Belfast.

NASSA (1) 5,825 GRT. 412' x53'.
(1922) H.M. Dockyard,
Portsmouth.

NASSA (2) 8,134 GRT. 465' x 59'.
(1942) Blythswood S.B. Co. Ltd,
Glasgow.

NASSARIUS 8,246 GRT. 465' x 59'.
(1944) Harland & Wolff Ltd,
Belfast.

NATICA 5,579 GRT. 406' x 51'.
(1912) Swan Hunter & Wigham
Richardson Ltd, Wallsend.

NATICINA (1)
8,179 GRT. 465' x 59'.
(1943) Hawthorn, Leslie & Co. Ltd,
Hebburn.

NATICINA (2)
60,703 GRT. 870' x 138'.
(1967) Odense Staalskibs A/S,
Lindo.

NAVICELLA 8,255 GRT. 465' x 59'.
(1944) Hawthorn, Leslie & Co. Ltd,
Hebburn.

NAYADIS 8,224 GRT. 465' x 59'.
(1944) Harland & Wolff Ltd,
Belfast.

NEAERA 8,254 GRT. 465' x 59'.
(1946) Hawthorn, Leslie & Co. Ltd,
Hebburn.

NEOCARDIA 8,211 GRT. 465' x 59'.
(1943) Blythswood S.B. Co. Ltd,
Glasgow.

NEOTHAUMA 8,229 GRT. 465' x 59'.
(1946) Blythswood S.B. Co. Ltd,
Glasgow.

NEOTHYRIS 8,243 GRT. 465' x 59'.
(1946) Harland & Wolff Ltd,
Belfast.

NERITE (1) 4,893 GRT. 376' x 48'.
(1895) Armstrong, Mitchell & Co.
Ltd, Newcastle.

NERITE (2) 2,042 GRT. 258' x 46'.
(1904) Armstrong, Whitworth &
Co. Ltd, Newcastle.

NERITINA 8,228 GRT. 465' x 59'.
(1943) Harland & Wolff Ltd,
Belfast.

NERITOPSIS 4,762 GRT. 465' x 59'.
(1946) Harland & Wolff Ltd,
Belfast.

NEVERITA 8,265 GRT. 465' x 59'.
(1944) Swan Hunter & Wigham
Richardson Ltd, Wallsend.

NEWCOMBIA
8,292 GRT. 465' x 59'.
(1945) Harland & Wolff Ltd,
Belfast.

NICANIA
8,179 GRT. 465' x 59'.
(1942) Hawthorn, Leslie & Co. Ltd,
Hebburn.

NINELLA 8,134 GRT. 465' x 59'.
(1943) Blythswood S.B. Co. Ltd,
Glasgow.

NINTY SIX
10,277 GRT. 506' x 68'.
(1945) Alabama D.D. & S.B. Co.,
Mobile, Alabama.

NISO 8,273 GRT. 465' x 59'.
(1944) Harland & Wolff Ltd,
Belfast.

NORD 1,843 GRT. 269' x 42'.
(1900) Grangemouth & Greenock
Dockyard Co. Ltd

NORRISIA (1) 8,246 GRT. 465' x 59'.
(1944) Harland & Wolff Ltd,
Belfast.

NORRISIA (2)
65,179 GRT. 865' x 134'.
(1980) Uddevallavarvet, Uddevalla.

NORTHIA (1) 8,211 GRT. 465' X 59'.
(1944) Blythswood S.B. Co. Ltd,
Glasgow.

NORTHIA (2) 68,246 GRT. 919' x
135'.(1971) Brostroms Rederi A/B,
Sweden.

NUCULA 4,614 GRT. 370' x 48'.
(1906) Armstrong, Whitworth &
Co. Ltd, Newcastle.

NUCULANA
8,179 GRT. 465' x 59'.
(1942) Hawthorn, Leslie & Co. Ltd,
Hebburn.

NUTTALIA 8,241 GRT. 465' x 59'.
(1945) Blythswood S.B. Co. Ltd,
Glasgow.

OBOE SHELL 733 GRT. (1958)
Portuagal.

OLIVA 5,694 GRT. 412' x 53'.
(1916) Swan Hunter & Wigham
Richardson Ltd, Wallsend.

OPALIA (1)
6,195 GRT. 430' x 54'.
(1938) Netherland Dock Company,
Amsterdam.

OPALIA (2)
32,122 GRT. 748' x 102'.
(1963) Cammel, Laird & Co. Ltd.
Birkenhead.

ORMER 1,357 GRT. 234' x 34'.
(1915) Howaldtswerke, Kiel.

ORTHIS 1,144 GRT. 210' x 34'.
(1918) W. Gray & Co. Ltd,
West Hartlepool.

ORTINA SHELL
2,603 GRT. 309' x 42'.
(1891) Richardson, Duck & Co.
Stockton.

OSCILLA 32,129 GRT. 748' x 102'.
(1963) Cammel, Laird & Co. Ltd,
Birkenhead.

OTINA (1) 6,217 GRT. 430' x 54'.
(1938) Odense Staalskibs, Odense.

OTINA (2) 32,221 GRT. 748' x 102'.
(1962) Cammell, Laird & Co. Ltd,
Birkenhead.

OUADY 364 GRT. 134' x 25'.
(1884) Lobnitz & Co., Renfrew.

OVATELLA 6,316 GRT. 431' x 54'.
(1939) Odense Staalskibs, Odense.

PALLIUM
13,007 GRT. 560' x 72'.
(1959) Deutsche Werft A.G.,
Hamburg.

PALUDINA (1)
5,881 GRT. 412' x 53'.
(1921) Hong Kong & Whampoa
Dockyard Co. Ltd, Hong Kong.

PALUDINA (2) 6,414 GRT. 446' x 54'.
(1949) Swan Hunter & Wigham
Richardson Ltd, Wallsend.

PALUDINA (3)
15,385 GRT. 574' x 75'.
(1968) Verolme Dok & Schpsb.
Rozenburg, Rotterdam.

PARTULA 13,007 GRT. 560' x72'.
(1959) Deutsche Werft A.G.,
Hamburg.

PATELLA (1) 5,617 GRT. 406' x 51'.
(1909) Swan Hunter & Wigham
Richardson Ltd, Wallsend.

PATELLA (2) 7,468 GRT. 440' x 59'.
(1927) Palmers Co. Ltd, Jarrow.

PATELLA (3) 8,277 GRT. 465' x 59'.
(1946) Harland & Wolff Ltd,
Belfast.

PATRO 28,410 GRT. 736' x 102'.
(1959) Bethlehem Steel Co.,
Quincy, Massachusetts.

PAULA 2,770 GRT. 305' x 50'.
(1927) Harland & Wolff Ltd,
Glasgow.

PECTAN (1) 4,778 GRT. 375' x 48'.
(1895) Armstrong, Mitchell & Co.
Ltd, Newcastle.

PECTAN (2) 7,291 GRT. 481' x 55'.
(1902) W. Gray & Co. Ltd,
West Hartlepool.

PECTEN 7,725 GRT. 440' x 59'.
(1927) Palmers Co. Ltd, Jarrow.

PELLICULA 6,254 GRT. 430' x 54'.
(1936) Cammel Laird & Co. Ltd,
Birkenhead.

PELUSE 344 GRT. 134' x 25'.
(1884) Lobnitz & Co., Renfrew.

PERLAK 1,899 GRT. 242' x 42'.
(1926) Fijenoord Maats,
Rotterdam.

PETRIANA 1,854 GRT. 260' x 34'.
(1879) Andrew Leslie & Co.,
Hebburn.

PETRICOLA 5,880 GRT. 412' x 53'.
(1922) Hong Kong & Whampoa
Dockyard Co. Ltd, Hong Kong.

PETRONELLA 2,770 GRT. 305' x 50'.
(1927) Harland & Wolff Ltd,
Glasgow.

PHILIS 359 GRT. 140' x 24'.
(1936) E. J. Smit & Son,
Westerbroek.

PHOLAS 5,743 GRT. 306' x 52'.
(1908) Sir Raylton Dixon & Co.,
Middlesbrough.

PHORUS 4,120 GRT. 360' x 47'.
(1900) Sir James Laing & Sons Ltd,
Sunderland.

PHYSA 3,899 GRT. 361' x 46'.
(1904) William Pickersgill & Sons,
Sunderland.

PINNA (1) 4,100 GRT. 420' x 52'.
(1901) Armstrong, Whitworth &
Co. Ltd, Newcastle.

PINNA (2) 6,121 GRT. 400' x 52'.
(1910) J. C. Tecklenborg A.G.,
Wesermunde.

PLACUNA 4,968 GRT. 370' x 51'.
(1913) Short Brothers, Sunderland.

PLAGIOLA 11,007 GRT. 525' x 66'.
(1954) Deitscje Werft A.G.,
Hamburg.

PLANORBIS 5,876 GRT. 412' x 53'.
(1922) Hong Kong & Whampoa
Dockyard Co. Ltd, Hong Kong.

PLATIDIA 11,007 GRT. 525' x 66'.
(1955) Deutsche Werft A.G.,
Hamburg.

PLEIODON 5,878 GRT. 412' x 53'.
(1922) Hong Kong & Whampoa
Dockyard Co. Ltd, Hong Kong.

POMELLA (1) 6,766 GRT. 457' x 57'.
(1937) Cammel, Laird & Co. Ltd,
Birkenhead.

POMELLA (2) 15,815 GRT. 574' x 74'.
(1967) Verolme Dok & Schpsb,
Rozenburg, Rotterdam.

PRESIDENT GOMEZ
5,344 GRT. 353' x 52'.
(1922) J. Koster Scheeps 'De
Gideon', Groningen.

PRESIDENT SERGENT
1,133 GRT. 217' x 33'.
(1923) Atels. & Chants de France,
Dunkirk.

PRYGONA 7,550 GRT. 446' x 52'.
(1900) Barclay, Curle & Co. Ltd,
Glasgow.

PURPURA 4,409 GRT. 349' x 50'.
(1904) Ropner & Son, Stockton.

PYRULA
8,455 GRT. 500' x 60'.
(1894) Harland & Wolff Ltd,
Belfast.

RADIX 6,698 GRT. 412' x 55'.
(1919) W. Doxford & Sons Ltd,
Sunderland.

RAMSES 356 GRT. 134' x 25'.
(1884) Lobnitz & Co., Renfrew.

RANELLA 5,590 GRT. 406' x 51'.
(1912) Swan Hunter & Wigham
Richardson Ltd, Wallsend.

RAPANA (1) 8,017 GRT. 465' x 59'.
(1935) N.V. Wilton Fijenoord,
Schiedam.

RAPANA (2)
117,289 GRT. 1092' x 150'.
(1973) A/B Gotaverken Arendal,
Gothenburg.

RIMULA (1) 577 GRT. 169' x 26'.
(1920) Echevarrieta Y Larrinage,
Cadiz.

RIMULA (2)
121,165 GRT. 1092' x 150'.
(1974) A/B Gotaverken Arendal,
Gothenburg.

RITA 3,188 GRT. 343' x 56'.
(1935) Netherland S.B. Company,
Amsterdam.

ROBERT DICKINSON
2,100 GRT. 278' x 35'.
(1881) Andrew Leslie & Co.
Hebburn.

ROCK LIGHT
3,287 GRT. 312' x 40'.
(1889) Oswald, Mordaunt & Co.,
Southampton.

ROMANY 3,983 GRT. 350' x 47'.
(1902) Armstrong, Whitworth &
Co. Ltd, Newcastle.

ROSA 3,255 GRT. 343' x 56'.
(1935) Netherland S.B. Company,
Amsterdam.

ROYAL 375 GRT. 175' x 25'.
(1924) Chants. & Atels. de la
Gironde, Harfleur.

 S

SABINE RICKMERS
1,026 GRT. 200' x 30'.
(1894) Rickmers Act. Ges,
Geestemunde.

SAID 344 GRT. 134' x 25'.
(1884) Lobnitz & Co., Renfrew,

SAIDJA 6,671 GRT. (1939)
Rotterdam

SALT CREEK 1,220 GRT. 210' x 37'.
(1943) Barnes-Duluth S.B. Co.,
Duluth.

SAN CAMILO 2,450 GRT. 305' x 51'.
(1927) J. L. Thompson & Sons Ltd,
Sunderland.

SAN PATRICIO
10,711 GRT. 525' x 67'.
(1955) Furness S.B. Co. Ltd,
Haverton Hill.

SAN VERONICA 4,787 GRT. 465' x 59'.
(1942) Harland & Wolff Ltd,
Belfast.

SAXET 1,220 GRT. 210' x 37'.
(1943) Todd Galveston D.D. Inc.,
Galveston.

SAXICAVA 5,693 GRT. 412' x 53'.
(1922) Swan Hunter & Wigham
Richardson Ltd, Wallsend.

SCALARIA 5,683 GRT. 412' x 53'.
(1921) Swan Hunter & Wigham
Richardson Ltd, Wallsend.

SCALA SHELL 3,283 GRT. 330' x 47'.
(1902) A. McMillan & Sons Ltd,
Dumbarton.

SCAPHA 654 GRT. 190' x 36'.
(1906) Edwards & Co. Ltd.

SENTIS 50,272 GRT. 800' x 130'.
(1985) Kawasaki H. I., Sakaide.

SEPIA 6,214 GRT. 430' x 54'.
(1936) Swan Hunter & Wigham
Richardson Ltd, Wallsend.

SERENIA 42,082 GRT. 817' x 112'.
(1961) Vickers-Armstrong Ltd,
Newcastle.

SERAPEUM 368 GRT. 134' x 25'.
(1884) Lobnitz & Co., Renfrew.

SEVEN SISTERS
1,220 GRT. 210' x 37'.
(1943) Grays Iron Works Inc.,
Galveston.

SHELL MEX 1 927 GRT. 190' x 32'.
(1915) G. Pot, Bolnes.

SHELL MEX 2 349 GRT. 163' x 28'.
(1915) N.B. Scheep W., Dordrecht.

SHELL MEX 8
349 GRT. 136' x 24'.
(1928) Charles Hill & Sons Ltd,
Bristol.

SHELL QUEST
4,015 GRT. 384' x 51'.
(1930) D. & W. Henderson Ltd,
Port Glasgow.

SIAM 1,557 GRT. 258' x 36'.
(1890) J. Priestman & Co.,
Sunderland.

SILIQUA 54,962 GRT. 794 ' x 138'.
(1991) Imari Shipyard, Japan.

SILVERLIP (1) 7,492 GRT. 470' x 55'.
(1903) Armstrong, Whitworth &
Co. Ltd, Newcastle.

SILVERLIP (2) 9,718 GRT. 530' x 66'.
(1914) Armstrong, Whitworth &
Co. Ltd, Newcastle.

SIMNIA 6,197 GRT. 430' x 54'.
(1936) Harland & Wolff Ltd,
Glasgow.

SITALA 6,218 GRT. 430' x 54'.
(1937) Harland & Wolff Ltd,
Glasgow.

SOLARIUM 6,239 GRT. 430' x 54'.
(1936) Cantieri Riuniti del
Adriatico, Monfalcone.

SOLEN (1) 5,693 GRT. 412' x 53'.
(1922) Swan Hunter & Wigham
Richardson Ltd, Wallsend.

SOLEN (2) 42,162 GRT. 817' x 112'.
(1961) Swan Hunter & Wigham
Richardson Ltd, Wallsend.

SPINDLETOP 1,220 GRT. 210' x 37'.
(1943) Lancaster Ironworks Inc.,
Perryville.

SPIRILA 5,695 GRT. 412 ' x 53'.
(1922) Swan Hunter & Wigham
Richardson Ltd, Wallsend.

SPONDILUS (1) 4,129 GRT. 347' x 45'.
(1893) J. Laing, Sunderland.

SPONDILUS (2) 7,291 GRT. 471' x 55'.
(1903) W.Gray & Co. Ltd,
West Hartlepool.

SPONDILUS (3) 7,402 GRT. 440' x 59'.
(1927) Wilton Fijenoord,
Schiedam.

STANDELLA 6,197 GRT. 430' x 54'.
(1936) Harland & Wolff Ltd,
Glasgow.

STROMBUS 6,163 GRT. 410' x 52'.
(1900) Armstrong, Whitworth &
Co. Ltd, Newcastle.

SUEZ 365 GRT. 134' x 25'.
(1884) Lobnitz & Co., Renfrew.

SULPHUR BLUFF
1,220 GRT. 210' x 37'.
(1944) Grays Iron Works Inc.,
Galveston.

SULTAN VAN KOETEI
1,862 GRT. 241' x 41'.
(1904) Nederland Scheeps. Maats,
Amsterdam.

 T

TAGELUS
10,678 GRT. 506' x 68'.
(1945) Alabama D.D. & S.B. Co.
Ltd, Mobile, Alabama.

TANEA 3,060 GRT. 332' x 46'.
(1950) J. Crown & Sons Ltd,
Sunderland.

TARENTUM 1,220 GRT. 210' x 37'.
(1943) Barnes-Duluth S.B. Co.,
Duluth.

TARON 8,054 GRT. 465' x 59'.
(1936) Deutsche Werft A.G.,
Hamburg.

TECTARIUS 10,678 GRT. 506' x 68'.
(1944) Alabama D.D. & S.B. Co.,
Mobile, Alabama.

TECTUS (1)
10,689 GRT. 506' x 68'.
(1945) Alabama D.D. & S.B. Co.,
Mobile, Alabama.

TECTUS (2)
65,135 GRT. 858' x 133'.
(1974) Harland & Wolff Ltd,
Belfast.

TELENA (1)
4,778 GRT. 375' x 48'.
(1895) W. Gray & Co. Ltd,
West Hartlepool.

TELENA (2)
7,406 GRT. 440' x 59'.
(1927) New Waterway S.B.
Company, Schiedam.

TENAGA DUA
68,085 GRT. 922' x 138'.
(1981) Soc. Metallurgique &
Navale Dunkirk, Normandy.

TENAGA EMPAT
68,085 GRT. 922' x 138'.
(1981) Cons. Nav. & Ind. de la
Mediterranee, La Seyne.

TENAGA LIMA
68,085 GRT. 922' x 138'.
(1981) Cons. Nav. & Ind. de la
Mediterranee, La Seyne.

TENAGA SATU
68,085 GRT. 922' x 138'.
(1982) Soc. Metallurgique &
Navale Dunkirk, Normandy.

TENAGA TIGA
68,085 GRT. 922' x 138'.
(1981) Soc. Metallurgique &
Navale Dunkirk, Normandy.

TENAGODUS 10,661 GRT. 506' x 68'.
(1944) Alabama D.D. & S.B. Co.,
Mobile, Alabama.

THALAMUS 10,701 GRT. 506' x 68'.
(1945) Kaiser Inc., Portland,
Oregon.

THALLEPUS 10,693 GRT. 506' x 68'.
(1945) Kaiser Inc., Portland,
Oregon.

THAUMASTUS
10,686 GRT. 506' x 68'.
(1945) Kaiser Inc., Portland,
Oregon.

THELICONUS 10,691 GRT. 506' x 68'.
(1944) Alabama D.D. & S.B. Co.,
Mobile, Alabama.

THELIDOMUS
10,643 GRT. 506' x 68'.
(1944) Kaiser Inc., Portland,
Oregon.

THEOBALDIUS
10,662 GRT. 506' x 68'.
(1945) Kaiser Inc., Portland,
Oregon.

THEODOXUS
10,696 GRT. 506' x 68'.
(1945) Kaiser Inc., Portland,
Oregon.

THIARA
10,364 GRT. 505' x 64'.
(1939) Swan Hunter & Wigham
Richardson Ltd, Wallsend.

TIMSAH 349 GRT. 134' x 25'.
(1884) Lobnitz & Co., Renfrew.

TITUSVILLE 1,220 GRT. 210' x 37'.
(1943) Barnes-Duluth S.B. Co.,
Duluth.

TOMOCYCLUS
10,706 GRT. 506' x 68'.
(1944) Kaiser Inc., Portland,
Oregon.

TOMOGERUS
10,689 GRT. 506' x 68'.
(1944) Kaiser Inc., Portland,
Oregon.

TONKAWA 1,220 GRT. 210' x 37'.
(1943) Barnes-Duluth S.B. Co.,
Duluth.

TORINIA
10,364 GRT. 505' x 64'.
(1939) Swan Hunter & Wigham
Richardson Ltd, Wallsend.

TORNUS
8,054 GRT. 465' x 59'.
(1936) Bremer Vulkan, Vegesack.

TOUSSOUM
362 GRT. 134' x 25'.
(1884) Lobnitz & Co., Renfrew.

TRESUS
10,669 GRT. 506' x 68'.
(1944) Kaiser Inc., Portland,
Oregon.

TRIBULUS (1)
10,699 GRT. 506' x 68'.
(1945) Kaiser Inc., Portland,
Oregon.

TRIBULUS (2)
69,230 GRT. 867' x 134'.
(1981) Hyundai Heavy Industries,
Ulsan.

TRICULA (1)
6,221 GRT. 430' x 54'.
(1936) Howaldtsweke A.G., Kiel.

TRICULA (2)
69,230 GRT. 867' x 134'.
(1981) Hyundai Heavy Industries,
Ulsan.

TRIGONIA
1,167 GRT. 242 ' x 40'.
(1898) Armstrong, Whitworth &
Co. Ltd, Newcastle

TRIGONOSEMUS
10,693 GRT. 506' x 68'.
(1944) Kaiser Inc., Portland,
Oregon.

TRIVIA 4,781 GRT. 376' x 51'.
(1918) Russel & Co., Port Glasgow.

TROCAS (1)
4,129 GRT. 347' x 45'.
(1893) J. Laing, Sunderland.

TROCAS (2) 7,406 GRT. 440' x 59'.
(1927) Rotterdam Drydock,
Rotterdam.

TROCHISCUS
10,668 GRT. 506' x 68'.(1944)
Kaiser Inc., Portland, Oregon.

TROCHURUS
10,692 GRT. 506' x 68'.
(1945) Kaiser Inc., Portland,
Oregon.

TROPHON 3,847 GRT. 350' x 46'.
(1901) C. S. Swan & Hunter,
Wallsend.

TURBINELLUS
10,641 GRT. 506' x 68'.
(1944) Kaiser Inc., Portland,
Oregon.

TURBO (1) 4,134 GRT. 347' x 45'.
(1892) J. Laing, Sunderland.

TURBO (2) 4,782 GRT. 374' x 50'.
(1912) Sir James Laing & Sons Ltd,
Sunderland.

TURRITELLA
5,528 GRT. 422' x 55'.
(1906) Flensburger Schiffs. Ges.,
Flensburg.

 U

UNDA 1,404 GRT. 240' x 35'.
(1903) J. Priestman & Co.,
Sunderland.

UNIO 1,773 GRT. 250' x 36'.
(1902) Armstrong, Whitworth &
Co. Ltd, Newcastle.

V

VALVATA 21,180 GRT. 661' x 84'.
(1960) Furness S.B. Co. Ltd,
Haverton Hill.

VARICELLA 21,843 GRT. 665' x 85'.
(1959) Swan Hunter & Wigham
Richardson Ltd, Wallsend.

VELLETIA
18,661 GRT. 619' x 80'.
(1952) Swan Hunter & Wigham
Richardson Ltd, Wallsend.

VELUTINA
18,666 GRT. 619' x 80'.
(1950) Swan Hunter & Wigham
Richardson Ltd, Wallsend.

VENASSA (1)
21,321 GRT. 560' x 69'.
(1959) Kieler Howaldtswerke A.G.,
Kiel.

VENASSA (2)
20,952 GRT. 670' x 90'.
(1982) Mitsubishi H. I., Nagasaki.

VERCONELLA
20,894 GRT. 660' x 84'.
(1958) Cammel, Laird & Co. Ltd,
Birkenhead.

VERENA 18,612 GRT. 619' x 80'.
(1950) Harland & Wolff Ltd,
Belfast.

VERMETUS
21,179 GRT. 661' x 87'.
(1959) Furness S.B. Co. Ltd,
Haverton Hill.

VERTAGUS
20,893 GRT. 660' x 84'.
(1959) Cammel, Laird & Co. Ltd,
Birkenhead.

VEXILLA
20,798 GRT. 659' x 84'.
(1955) Cammel, Laird & Co. Ltd,
Birkenhead.

VIBEX 20,787 GRT. 659' x 84'.
(1955) Harland & Wolff Ltd,
Belfast.

VICENTE
532 GRT. 171 ' x 33'.
(1989) Hardinxveld-Giessendam,
Holland.

VITRINA 20,802 GRT. 660' x 84'.
(1957) Harland & Wolff Ltd,
Belfast.

VITTA 20,889 GRT. 659' x 84'.
(1957) Vickers-Armstrong Ltd,
Barrow.

VOLA 20,736 GRT. 659' x 84'.
(1956) Hawthorn, Leslie & Co. Ltd,
Hebburn.

VOLSELLA (1)
1,979 GRT. 281' x 40'.
(1906) W. Gray & Co. Ltd,
Hartlepool.

VOLSELLA (2)
18,605 GRT. 619' x 80'.
(1950) Cammell, Laird & Co. Ltd,
Birkenhead.

VOLUTA
24,406 GRT. 665' x 90'.
(1962) Furness S.B. Co. Ltd,
Haverton Hill.

VOLUTE 4,006 GRT. 347' x 45'.
(1893) W. Gray & Co. Ltd,
West Hartlepool.

VOLVATELLA
20,801 GRT. 659' x 84'.
(1956) Hawthorn, Leslie & Co. Ltd,
Hebburn.

VOLVULA
20,732 GRT. 659' x 84'.
(1956) Swan Hunter & Wigham
Richardson Ltd, Wallsend.

W

WALNUT BEND
1,220 GRT. 210' x 37'.
(1943) Barnes-Duluth S.B. Co.,
Duluth.

Z

ZAPHON
24,802 GRT. 700' x 89'.
(1957) Swan Hunter & Wigham
Richardson Ltd, Wallsend.

ZENATIA (1)
24,790 GRT. 700' x 89'.
(1957) Cammell, Laird & Co. Ltd,
Birkenhead.

ZENATIA (2)
37,685 GRT. 750' x 105'.
(1981) Mitsui S.B. & Eng. Co. Ltd,
Tamano.

ZIDONA
43,398 GRT. 751' x 108'.
(1989) B. & W. Skibsvaerft A/S,
Copenhagen.

Index

Books by Stephen Howarth

The Koh-i-Noor Diamond: The History and the Legend

The Knights Templar

Morning Glory:
A History of the Imperial Japanese Navy, 1895-1945

August '39: The Last Four Weeks of Peace in Europe

To Shining Sea:
A History of the United States Navy, 1775-1991

Men of War: Great Naval Leaders of World War Two
(Editor)

With David Howarth:

The Story of P&O:
The Peninsular and Oriental Steam
Navigation Company, 1837-1987

Nelson: The Immortal Memory